THE
APOSTOLIC FATHERS
A New Translation and Commentary

THE APOSTOLIC FATHERS

A New Translation and Commentary

edited by Robert M. Grant

University of Chicago

THE
APOSTOLIC FATHERS

A New Translation and Commentary

Volume 3

Barnabas and the Didache

by

Robert A. Kraft

THOMAS NELSON & SONS

Toronto   NEW YORK   *London*

to CAROL
CINDY, SCOTT, TODD,
and RANDY

PREFACE

In October of 1962, as I was beginning my second year of teaching at the University of Manchester, England, a letter arrived from Professor R. M. Grant asking if I would be interested in preparing this volume. The subject matter gave no cause for hesitation—for several years I had been engaged in research on the Epistle of Barnabas in connection with my Harvard Ph.D. dissertation (1961), and during the previous year at Manchester I had conducted a seminar on the Didache. What did concern me not a little, however, was the thought of attempting to perform this task adequately within the suggested limits of about 150 pages—especially since my previous study had dealt with only one aspect of Barnabas and had run to twice that size!

Some of the anticipated difficulty has been alleviated by the fact that, through the kindness of the editor and publisher, this volume has been allowed to exceed the originally suggested length. The tactical problem of how to include what seemed to me to be of basic importance for understanding this literature, in a way that would be both readable and useful for further reference, however, could not be overcome simply by adding a few pages. To best utilize the space, therefore, I have attempted to eliminate repetitious explanatory prose by means of a rather elaborate (I hope not cryptic) system of cross-referencing. On some occasions I have also resorted to the often frustrating (for the reader) practice of simply listing, without comment, actual and possible (sometimes rather remote, I confess) parallel passages from other ancient literature. Ideally, the supposed parallels should be quoted and commented upon, but in view of the space limitations it seemed best to err on the side of quasi-completeness rather than to omit the material entirely. In this way it is hoped that the book will prove worthwhile to a variety of readers as an introduction to Barnabas and the Didache, and as a pointer

vii

to further avenues of investigation: not only to the relatively uninitiated layman and college student, but also to those more intimately involved in things pertaining to the history of religion. An attempt has been made to provide the necessary assistance to those who require it in the Aids to the Reader section.

My debt to other students of Christian Origins and related subjects is far greater than the bibliography and notes suggest, although I have tried to indicate the more important sources and reference works there. In a variety of ways, apart from published writings, numerous other people have influenced the materials contained herein, not the least of whom were my teachers and fellow students at Harvard. With reference to the actual work of preparing the material for the press, I have found the publisher's staff, and especially Mrs. Bernice C. Rich (Production Editor), to be most gracious and patient and helpful, despite the many tedious hours that they have had to spend over what must have been a rather difficult project. Finally, to Mrs. Max Rifkin, who salvaged time from her duties as secretary to the Department of Religious Thought at the University of Pennsylvania to type the manuscript, and to Miss Antonia Tripolitis (University of Pennsylvania) and Dr. Hans Dieter Betz (School of Theology at Claremont), who proofread the material at various stages, my gratitude is due.

Robert A. Kraft

University of Pennsylvania
July 1965

CONTENTS

Translation and Commentary

Indexes

AIDS TO THE READER

General Abbreviations and Notations

In the attempt to include in this relatively slim volume as much relevant information as possible, it has seemed advisable to use a system of symbols, abbreviations, and notations which is, for the most part, self-explanatory. On some of the specific methods used in the translation and commentary, the "Remarks on Procedure" (see below) also should be consulted.

b.	preceding reference to a Rabbinic text indicates Babylonian Talmud
frg.	fragment
Gk.	Greek language
mg.	written in the margin
MS(S)	manuscript(s)
par. (parr.)	and parallel passage (or passages), particularly with reference to the Synoptic Gospels
Ps-	pseudo; the alleged, but not the probable, author
Syr.	Syriac language
var.	textual variant
§	indicates chapter and section of the Introduction
* (2:7*)	following a reference to Barnabas or the Didache, to indicate that an explicit quotation is in view;
* (S*)	following a manuscript symbol, to indicate the *original* text of the manuscript in a passage which has subsequently been altered
/	links alternative ideas (either/or, king/ruler)
(?)	indicates that the claim is probable, but significant doubt also exists

Modern Literature: Selected Significant Works

Only a few of the most significant books, along with the most frequently mentioned periodicals, are listed here. For additional literature, the reader is referred to Volume I of this series and to the standard Patrologies of J. Quasten (3 vols., Westminster [Md.], 1950–1960) and B. Altaner (translated by H. Graef,

Freiburg, 1960). Normally, when one of the following works is mentioned in this volume, it will be by the name of the author alone.

AUDET, J.-P.   *La Didachè: Instructions des apôtres.* Études Bibliques. Paris, 1958. English language review in *JTS* 12 (1961), 329–333.

BOUSSET, W.   *Jüdisch-christlicher Schulbetrieb in Alexandria und Rom: literarische Untersuchungen zu Philo und Clemens von Alexandria, Justin und Irenaeus.* Göttingen, 1915.

GOODSPEED, E. J.   "Appendix" to *The Apostolic Fathers.* New York, 1950.

GRANT, R. M.   *The Apostolic Fathers: An Introduction.* New York, 1964.

HEER, J. M.   *Die Versio latina des Barnabasbriefes und ihr Verhältnis zur altlateinischen Bibel.* Freiburg, 1908.

JBL   *Journal of Biblical Literature* (Philadelphia).

JTS   *Journal of Theological Studies* (Oxford).

KNOPF, R.   *Die Lehre der zwölf Apostel . . . . Lietzmann's Handbuch zum NT*, Ergänzungs-band, 1. Tübingen, 1920.

KOESTER, H.   *Synoptische Überlieferung bei den Apostolischen Vätern.* TU 65. Berlin, 1957.

MUILENBURG, J.   *The Literary Relations of the Epistle of Barnabas and the Teaching of the Twelve Apostles.* Marburg, 1929.

PRIGENT, P.   *Les testimonia dans le christianisme primitif: l'Épître de Barnabé I–XVI et ses sources.* Études Bibliques. Paris, 1961. English language review in *JTS* 13 (1962), 401–408.

ROBINSON, J. A.   *Barnabas, Hermas, and the Didache.* London, 1920.

TU   Texte und Untersuchungen (series of texts and studies). Leipzig and Berlin.

VOKES, F. E.   *The Riddle of the Didache: Fact or Fiction, Heresy or Catholicism?* London, 1938.

WINDISCH, H.   *Der Barnabasbrief. Lietzmann's Handbuch zum NT*, Ergänzungs-band, 3. Tübingen, 1920.

ZNW   *Zeitschrift für die neutestamentliche Wissenschaft* (Berlin).

Ancient Literature: Method of Citation, Translations

(1) For the convenience of the English reader, the chapter and verse divisions for *biblical references* are based on the Revised Standard Version, even where the sources refer to the Greek Old Testament (Septuagint), which sometimes employs a different chapter and verse division from that of the RSV and the Hebrew. Standard abbreviations for biblical books are used.

(2) *Apocryphal, Pseudepigraphical, and Hellenistic Jewish literature.* Translations of the Old Testament Apocrypha and Pseudepigrapha are available in the collection edited by R. H. Charles (2 vols., Oxford, 1913; reprinted 1963). As with biblical references, the Old Testament Apocrypha are cited according to the Revised Standard Version chapter and verse divisions. For Philo and Josephus, the most convenient recent translations are found in the Loeb Library editions (Cambridge, Mass.). The titles of Philo's works normally are abbreviated on the basis of the Latin titles listed in Loeb. Other abbreviations are as follows:

Ps-Aristeas	The Epistle of Aristeas to Philocrates
2 Baruch	The Syriac Apocalypse of Baruch
1 Enoch	The Ethiopic Book of Enoch
2 Enoch	The Slavonic Book of the Secrets of Enoch
4 Ezra	The Latin Apocalypse of Ezra (= 2 Esdras in RSV)
Macc.	The books called "Maccabees" (1, 2, 3, 4)
Pss. Sol.	The Psalms of Solomon
Orac. Sib.	The Sibylline Oracles
Sirach	Ecclesiasticus, or the Wisdom of Jesus the Son of Sirach
Testaments (T. Dan)	The Testaments of the Twelve Patriarchs (the Testament of Dan, etc.)
Wisd. Sol.	The Wisdom of Solomon

(3) *Qumran literature* is cited by the usual English title in shortened form—Manual (of Discipline), Hymns, etc.—according to the column and line of the original text. Unfortunately, few English translations include the exact column and line notation. The most convenient translations probably are by T. H. Gaster, *The Dead Sea Scriptures* (2nd ed., New York, 1964) and G. Vermes, *The Dead Sea Scrolls in English* (Baltimore, 1962).

(4) *Rabbinic Jewish texts* are cited from various sources, primary and secondary. For the Mishna, see H. Danby's translation (Oxford, 1933). The complete Babylonian (b.) Talmud is available in the Soncino translation (London, 1935–1952) edited

by I. Epstein. The tractate *Pirke Abot* (wisdom/sayings of the Fathers) is separately available in several editions.

(5) *Early Christian and Patristic literature.* For translations of the Apostolic Fathers, see the bibliography in Volume I of this series. Most of the other Christian writings are available in one of the following: *The Apocryphal New Testament* (Gospels, Acts, etc.), edited by M. R. James (Oxford, 1924; corrected and supplemented, 1953); *The Ante-Nicene Fathers,* edited by A. Roberts, J. Donaldson, A. Menzies, and A. C. Coxe (10 vols., Buffalo, 1884–1886); *A Select Library of Nicene and Post-Nicene Fathers of the Christian Church,* edited by P. Schaff and H. Wace (28 vols., Buffalo, 1886–1900). The following abbreviations frequently occur:

ApCo	The Apostolic Constitutions (see §7:5).
Cl.A.	Clement of Alexandria (see §3:4). Because the older texts (including the translation noted above) use a different system of numbering passages from the best recent Greek editions, references to Clement's writings will include both sets of numbers; thus *Stromateis* (*Str.*) 5:(10):63:1 indicates 5:10 in the older system = 5:63:1 in the new.
1 Clem.	The epistle to the Corinthians, traditionally attributed to Clement of Rome.
2 Clem.	The homily/sermon which tradition (wrongly) attributed to Clement of Rome and which circulated as a "second" epistle to the Corinthians.
Ps-Clem.	The so-called *Homilies* (*Hom.*) and *Recognitions* (*Rec.*) that tradition (wrongly) attributed to Clement of Rome.
G. Hebrews	Gospel According to the Hebrews.
G. Peter	Gospel of Peter.
G. Thomas	The Coptic Gospel of Thomas, edited and translated by A. Guillaumont, *et al.* (New York, 1959).
Hermas	The Shepherd of Hermas. Although the latest and best Greek edition has renumbered the passages by discarding the older divisions of Visions (Vis.), Mandates (Mand.), and Similitudes (Sim.), these divisions have been retained below.
Eusebius, *H.E.*	The *Ecclesiastical History* of Eusebius.

Hippolytus,   The *Apostolic Traditions* of Hippolytus, which
   Ap.Trad.   circulated in various textual forms and ver-
                     sions (see §2:5:2, §7:6). For translations, see
                     G. Dix (London, 1937), and B. S. Easton
                     (Cambridge, 1934). The Ethiopic, Arabic,
                     and Sahidic versions were translated by G.
                     Horner, *The Statutes of the Apostles...*
                     (London, 1904).
Ign.   Ignatius of Antioch.
Irenaeus   Both the *Adversus Haereses* (*Adv. haer.*) and
                     the relatively recently recovered *Demonstra-
                     tion of the Apostolic Preaching* (*Ap. preach.*)
                     are cited. For a translation of the latter, see
                     J. A. Robinson (London, 1920).
Odes Sol.   For translations of the Odes of Solomon, see
                     J. H. Bernard (London, 1912); J. R. Harris
                     and A. Mingana (Manchester, 2d ed., 1916–
                     1920).

For the abbreviations employed in discussions of the text of
Barnabas and Didache, see §2:5, §3, and §7.

Glossary

Semitic/Hellenistic Judaism refer primarily to the difference in
   language between ancient Hebrew or Aramaic-speaking (and
   -writing) Judaism, and Greek-speaking Judaism—whether in
   Palestine or elsewhere.
Midrashic/targumic/halakic/haggadic refer to various Jewish
   approaches to types of religious material and its interpretation.
   In general, *midrashic* exegesis involves a running commentary
   on a given text in which phrases of the text are quoted piece
   by piece throughout the commentary; *targumic* paraphrase is
   an interpretative reworking of a passage (usually narrative)
   into a relatively new form, without recourse to actual quotation; *halakic* material deals with problems of (religious) law
   and legal interpretation; *haggadic* refers to that which is not
   halakic, such as historical narrative, future hopes, and so on.
Eschatological/apocalyptic both relate to what the particular
   author considers to be "the last times/events." *Apocalyptic*
   designates a way of looking at the final eschatological events
   in which concrete symbolism (warfare, signs in the heavens,
   plagues, etc.) is employed and which usually is said to have
   been revealed from above (by visions, angelic intermediaries,

trips to heaven, etc.). *Eschatological* is the more general term for things pertaining to the "last times" and the "other world."

Cultic/liturgical refer to conduct in worship. *Cultic* usually is applied to religious practices which give the appearance of concentrating on external ritual, such as circumcision, sacrifice, and so forth, carried out by a priesthood at a particular holy shrine. *Liturgical* also refers to religious practices, but to those which seem to involve a greater degree of personal participation (and mysticism?), such as public prayer, chanting, and so on.

Catechesis/parenesis/exhortation are all used in connection with religious instruction. *Catechesis* signifies the formal instruction of people (catechumens) in preparation for their becoming full members of the religious community; *parenesis* refers to formal instruction and exhortation (usually ethical) of those associated with the community (whether full members or not); *exhortation* is the most general term and can mean simply encouragement or strong (ethical) prompting.

Remarks on Procedure

1. *Text and Notes.* The translation of Barnabas and the Didache is based on my own "eclectic" Greek text. The notes to the translation are intended to provide a sampling of the more interesting and/or significant problems relating to the text itself, and occasionally to comment on a translation problem. On a few occasions the information contained in the textual notes to Barnabas may vary from the standard critical Greek editions (Gebhardt-Harnack, Funk) with respect to manuscript **H** (§3:1; see, e.g., to Barn. 3:2*, 4*; 4:4^mg.). This is because Barnabas **H** has only recently become available in microfilm, which now makes it possible to correct the small percentage of misreadings that found their way into critical texts of the Western world (although Bryennios tried to correct most of them in the modern Greek introduction to his 1883 edition of the Didache). For the most part, I have not listed variants which are peculiar to a single witness in opposition to the consensus of other witnesses (especially with such common variants as "us"/"you," "Lord"/"God," etc.) unless they are especially noteworthy. For information about the textual witnesses referred to in the notes, see §3 (Barnabas), §7 (Didache), and §2:5 (separate Two Ways source).

2. *Translation.* In the translation I have attempted both to preserve the "flavor" of the text and to communicate its message

without resorting to free paraphrase. That is, where the Greek text tends to be abrupt or flowery or argumentative, I have tried to retain that impression in the English; where the Greek preserves somewhat archaic (e.g., Septuagintal) idiom, I have not attempted to erase this impression completely (e.g., "behold," "blessed are . . ."—on the other hand, there is no reason for using the Old English pronouns "thee" or "thou" in such contexts, since Greek has no equivalent "double standard"). The main problems have arisen with respect to anthropologic idioms such as "to love more than *my own soul*," where idiomatic English would say ". . . more than *myself*"; or in similar references to people as "spirits" (see §5:2:20). I must confess that I have not been entirely consistent in such passages, depending on whether an appreciation of the passage and its "flavor" seemed to require an awareness of the (archaic) Semitic-Greek idiom or not. Nor, incidentally, have I considered it necessary at all costs to render the same Greek wording in the same way throughout. Understanding often can be enhanced by comparing alternate legitimate translations. Thus, for example, the "Introduction" may include brief passages which vary slightly from the "Translation," or a Two Ways passage in Barnabas may be exactly equivalent to the Didache (a fact indicated by the use of *italics*), but the translation may vary somewhat. Occasionally, for the sake of capturing the intention of the text, it has been necessary to supply words which are implied but not actually stated in the Greek. Usually these are included in parentheses.

3. *Cross References, Quotations.* Although there is a danger that the translation may look somewhat "cluttered," it seemed that the most economical way to relate "Introduction" to "Translation and Commentary" was to include cross references in brackets in the translation itself—for example, ". . . spirit [§5:2: 20]." The same procedure is used for noting closely related passages in the same document and in the Jewish and Christian Scriptures, or for indicating the probable sources of quotations. This means that the "Commentary" can, in general, bypass matters that have already been discussed in the "Introduction," and concentrate on such things as the background of each particular passage and problems of detail. Because of the abundance of "quotations" introduced by formulas in Barnabas, it seemed advisable to use indentation rather than quotation marks to set them off from their surroundings. Similarly, "poetic" and related contexts (i.e., with balanced structure) have been reproduced in such a way as to call attention to the structure.

4. *Verse Division.* Although the normally accepted verse divisions are sometimes awkwardly placed (e.g., Barn. 4:6, 9; 9:4), this seemed to be neither the time nor the place to set things right. Thus I have often introduced supplementary letters to distinguish between various thought-units of a verse (e.g., 4:1b; 5:2e, etc.), which also makes possible greater precision in commentary and cross reference.

INTRODUCTION

General Orientation

§1. Barnabas and the Didache as "Evolved Literature"

1. *"Evolved Literature" and the Role of Author-Editor.*
Both the so-called Epistle of Barnabas and the Teaching (in
Greek, *Didaché*) of the (Twelve) Apostles, are examples of
what may be called "evolved literature," in contradistinction
to writings which have a single author in the modern sense
of the word.[1] That is to say, both Barnabas and the Didache,
as we now have them, show clear evidence of being products
of a developing process. Some individual, it is true, has put
them into the form(s) preserved for us. But he is at best an
"author-editor," who reproduces and reworks older materials.
Thus we sometimes are able to uncover in such evolved literature various layers of composition (see below, §2, §4, §8).
The latest stage *may* provide some information about the
final author-editor, his thought and situation, but equally
important for a real appreciation of such literature are the
vestiges which remain from earlier stages of its history.

Usually no clear-cut method by which this final author-
editor has selected his sources and compiled his treatise can
be discovered. Sometimes older materials are simply juxtaposed with little or no attempt at harmonizing whatever
minor disagreements may exist between them. In one way or
another they are supposed to be relevant for his purpose—
he may have decided that they should be included, or his

---

[1] Numerous ancient writings, and not only those in the Judeo-Christian
tradition, can be included in this general category—e.g., the Historical Books
of the Old Testament, the Synoptic Gospels and Revelation in the New
Testament, the Jewish Talmud and Midrashim, etc. The same principle is
evident in our own times on an even more impersonal plane in various reference works (dictionaries, encyclopedias, handbooks) which continually
are being streamlined and re-edited.

1

background tradition may have decided it for him. Sometimes an older source consciously or unconsciously is turned to a new end; again, it is not always easy to determine at what stage of the evolution the reinterpretation was introduced. Finally, there are times when the evolved literature appears to embody further elaboration of the attitudes of its sources. In such cases the viewpoint of the final author-editor is seen to be closely related to, or derived from, that of certain of his traditional materials.

Thus the end product of this process, or better, the stage which has been preserved for us to examine (for still further elaboration and editing often occurs, as is clear from the history of the Didache; see §7, §8:5), is as much the product of its sources as it is the work of any individual. It provides an avenue into a living, many-sided tradition—it is a "school" or "community" product, if you wish. What the author-editor has received, he transmits. He may add certain of his own insights and emphases; he may apply the materials to new situations and embody them in new contexts; he may apply his own judgment as to what is or is not relevant. But he does not usually rise above his tradition to appear as a clearly defined personality who has produced a piece of original literature in accord with our usual ideas of authorship. He has not consistently digested his materials so that they become a part of him; he has not integrated them by means of a perspective which may be called, in a special way, his own. Rather, his tradition speaks through him. *It* is of prime importance. He is its *vehicle,* but the focus remains on the traditional material, not on the author-editor.

2. *Barnabas and the Didache as Representatives of School and Community.* Within this general category of "literature," however, various types are distinguishable. For example, the two writings with which we are concerned, Barnabas and the Didache, differ greatly between themselves as to the precise kind of evolved literature which they respectively represent. Barnabas, on the one hand, takes the *form* of an epistle. Thus it contains several personal touches mixed in

with its wealth of traditional instruction.[2] The author-editor, Pseudo-Barnabas, is attempting to deal with what he considers to be a significant need among a community known to him. Thus the elements of personality, time, and space are relatively prominent in the framework into which Pseudo-Barnabas has chosen to incorporate his traditions (§4:3). The Didache, on the other hand, is in the form of a fairly impersonal community manual. We do not even catch a glimpse of the individual responsible for the publication of the manual. Its instructions are presented as timeless "apostolic" teachings to successive generations in the community. Even the eschatological section in chapter 16 shares this flavor of impersonal timelessness.

As far as the respective *contents* of Barnabas and the Didache are concerned, another important difference is apparent. The Didache transmits community instructions for proper conduct and worship. It is a "community" product. Barnabas, however, is concerned with correct understanding of how to interpret the past (present and future), as well as how to live in the present. Thus Barnabas transmits instructions which, in origin, may more helpfully be called "school" interests (exegetical traditions, commentary, etc.) than "community" materials in a strict sense (liturgical conduct, church order, etc.). Nevertheless, in their different ways, both writings are interested in catechesis, in instruction, in exhortation, and thus find their use and preservation in the community.

---

2 Sometimes, however, even these apparently personal touches may simply be the reflection of accepted literary conventions; cf., e.g., Barn. 4:9a with Ign. Eph. 8:1; 18:1 (similar to the English idiom "I am your humble servant"); or Barn. 1:5; 17:1; 21:9 with Irenaeus, *Ap. Preach.* 1 (the emphasis on a "brief" communication of "necessary" things, as the writer "is able").

§2. The Two Ways Tradition Common to Barnabas and the Didache

1. *Background of the Two Ways Approach.* The most obvious piece of common ground between Barnabas and the Didache is the "Two Ways" tradition of ethical exhortation (Barn. 18–21; Did. 1:1–6:2). It has long been debated whether, for this material, (1) Barnabas has used the Didache, (2) the Didache used Barnabas, or (3) both independently used a common source.[3] The present tendency, which is shared by this writer, is to prefer the last alternative (see §2:4)—especially in the light of the Qumran *Manual of Discipline* 3:18 ff., which shows that a similar Two Ways device was also in vogue in a predominantly Semitic-speaking Jewish community in pre-Christian times.

But there is no reason to think that the form of the Two Ways tradition shared by Barnabas and the Didache had direct and immediate ties with Semitic Judaism. Rather, it seems to have flourished in the Greek schools of Hellenistic Judaism for decades, if not centuries, before early Christian writers came to adopt it. Its ultimate origins are obscure and its family tree in terms of Greek and Semitic (and even Egyptian) developments cannot be reconstructed with any assurance. In its Jewish form(s), probably Deuteronomy 30:15–19 and Psalm 1 played a central role along with passages such as Jeremiah 21:8; Proverbs 2:13; 4:18 f., and so

---

[3] The originality of the Didache has been defended by a minority of commentators, such as O. Bardenhewer, F. X. Funk, and R. D. Hitchcock-F. Brown. Those who have argued for Barnabean priority include F. C. Burkitt, R. H. Connolly, J. Muilenburg, and J. A. Robinson. Among advocates of a "common source" hypothesis are J.-P. Audet, J. M. Creed, E. J. Goodspeed, A. von Harnack (later view), K. Kohler, R. Knopf, B. H. Streeter, and C. Taylor. For a recent treatment of the Two Ways material and the New Testament, see E. Kamlah, *Die Form der katalogischen Paränese im NT* (*Wissenschaftliche Untersuchungen zum NT* 7, Tübingen, 1964); on related Hellenistic material see also H. D. Betz, *Lucian von Samosata und das NT* ... (*TU* 76, Berlin, 1961), 205 n.2.

forth. In any event, the theme is ancient and is by no means exclusively Jewish or Judeo-Christian in popularity (see, e.g., the "Choice of Heracles" in Xenophon, *Memorabilia* 2:1:21 ff.). Thus it is impossible to say precisely how, when, or where the Two Ways theme took the form which became known to Barnabas and the Didache. The least that can be said is that it seems to have been a separate written tractate, in Greek, which came into early Christianity by way of Hellenistic Judaism and its practices (a "proselyte catechism"?).

2. *Pervasiveness of the Two Ways in Barnabas.* A close examination of Barnabas reveals that the influence of the Two Ways motif is not limited to chapters 18–20. This is one of the themes that pervades the entire epistle (§5:4–5), and it comes to expression most clearly in the references to the "way of righteousness" (1:4; 5:4; cf. 11:7*; 12:4*) or "of light" (18:1; 19:1, 12) in contrast to the "way of wickedness" (4:10; cf. 10:10*; 11:7*), "of darkness" (5:4; 18:1; cf. 20:1) and "of death" (19:2c; 20:1b)—cf. also "the error" which now ensnares some men (2:9; 4:1; 12:10; 14:5; 16:1). But it can scarcely be explained simply as an original contribution of the final author-editor himself. This becomes clear from a closer examination of the characteristic emphases shared by Pseudo-Barnabas and his school tradition—emphases which *presuppose* the Two Ways scheme, presented in an *eschatological setting*, for their very existence (see §5:1–5)—as well as from the growing awareness of the antiquity of this approach (§2:1). To be more specific, the obviously traditional ethical interpretations offered in Barnabas 10 (cf. 19:2c, 6b), which *in form* resemble Didache 3:1–6, but which do not seem to have come from the common Two Ways source, help illustrate the degree to which Pseudo-Barnabas' school tradition was oriented toward such material. And when the author-editor abruptly appends the Two Ways material of chapters 18–20 to his treatise, he as much as says he is reproducing extant catechetical material—"another *gnosis* and *didache*" (18:1; cf. the conclusion at 21:1, "as many ordi-

nances as have been written"). Far from being a creation of Pseudo-Barnabas, the Two Ways tradition which he transmits has played a formative role (along with "gnostic" exegesis [§5:1] and eschatology [§5:3]) in the particular type of Christianity to which he subscribes.

3. *The Two Ways in the Didache.* By way of contrast, the Two Ways theme in the Didache is almost exclusively limited to Didache 1:1–6:2. Its absence from Didache 6:3–15:4 is perhaps explicable in view of the subject matter (liturgical-cultic, ecclesiastical). It is possible that some connection once existed between the apocalyptic appendix to the Didache (ch. 16) and a Two Ways tradition presented in a vivid eschatological setting, as in Barnabas. But this is part of a larger problem that requires special treatment (see §2:7). For the present, it suffices to note that some material present in the Two Ways (Did. 4:2; Barn. 19:10b) is echoed both in Didache 16:2a and in Barnabas 4:10b, and probably in Hermas, Similitudes 9:26:3b—

Didache 4 (see Barn. 19)	*Didache 16* (cf. 14:1)	*Barnabas 4*	*Hermas*
		Do not retire to yourselves and live alone	[some believers criticized for]
and daily	and frequently be gathered	... but gather together in harmony	... not fellowshiping
seek out the faces of the saints	seeking the things necessary to your souls	seeking what is of common benefit	with the servants of God, but
that you might find rest in their words.	[cf. Barn. 17:1 var.; Ign. Eph. 13:1; 2 Clem. 17:3].	[cf. 19:8a; 21:2b; Heb. 10:25].	living alone they destroy their souls.

Furthermore, Didache 16:2b is almost verbally identical to Barnabas 4:9b—

Didache: For the whole time of your faith will not profit you unless in the last time you are perfect.

Barnabas: For the whole time of our life and faith will profit us nothing unless now, in the lawless time and in the scandals to come . . . we resist.

—and Barnabas 4:9b–14 clearly incorporates Two Ways imagery.

Whatever the solution to this complex situation, Didache 1–6 shows no real interest in eschatology. This is especially striking by comparison to Barnabas 18–20, which shares with the rest of the epistle an atmosphere charged with present eschatological drama (see §2:2; §5:3). Contrast, for example, Barnabas 18 with Didache 1:1, or Barnabas 19:10a with Didache 4:1a. In the Didache eschatology either is subsumed under liturgy (8:2*; 9:4; 10:5–6) or forms an appendix (ch. 16) in which the reader is admonished to be ready when the last times finally do arrive, and he is made aware of certain *future* preludes to the consummation. Barnabas and the Didache are in two different worlds at this point. Their common ground is almost entirely limited to the Two Ways *ethic.*

4. *Source of the Two Ways Material in Barnabas and the Didache.* Thus we are faced with the knotty problem of trying to suggest how this situation could have come about. The evidence is almost completely against the hypothesis that Barnabas took its Two Ways material from the Didache. By comparison with Barnabas 18–19, the first part of the Two Ways tradition in Didache 1–4 is both more systematically arranged and is significantly longer. There can be little doubt that Didache 1:3b–2:1 is a late, Christian addition to the basic tradition (see §8:2); similarly, Didache 3:1–6 contains a separate, carefully structured tradition of prohibitions (see also §8:4). Neither of these sections has left any clear imprint on Barnabas (the variant to Barn. 19:11a almost certainly is secondary). Furthermore, the or-

ganization of such passages as Didache 1:2; 2:2–3 (cf. 5:1); 4:1–11, stands in marked contrast to the haphazard (at least by our standards) presentation of the same material in Barnabas. On the other hand, there is one relatively extensive passage in which Barnabas and the Didache follow exactly the same sequence and have almost exactly the same wording (Barn. 20:2 = Did. 5:2). It is not at all tempting to believe that Barnabas systematically eliminated these two blocks of Didache material (including those vices in Did. 5:1 which are also mentioned in Did. 3:1–6), and then scrambled the remaining items *except* for Didache 5:2.

In order to accept the hypothesis that the Didache took the Two Ways material from Barnabas, however, one must be willing to attribute the Didachist with the following editorial functions: He first purged the entire tradition of characteristically Barnabean emphases such as eschatology (§2:2–3), "darkness" (and "light"?) in ethical symbolism (Barn. 5:4; 10:10; 14:5 ff.; 18:1; 20:1, etc.), "gnosis" (§5: 1–2), glory/glorification (Barn. 2:10*; 8:2; 11:9; 19:2 f., etc.), theology of the word (§5:8)—as well as several seemingly "Jewish" ideas (e.g., Barn. 19:2a, 9b; 20:2d, 2h) and even one of the "ten commandments" (Barn. 19:4e—but note textual problem). He then reorganized and extensively expanded the first part of the material, while retaining the last part (Barn. 20) with very little alteration.

Surely the difficulty, if not impossibility, of either of these alternatives is reason enough to invoke the aid of a hypothetical common source. In short, both Barnabas 18–20 and Didache 1–5 provide strong indications that the Two Ways ethic which they share had already been through a significant amount of development in the respective background traditions from which these two documents come *before* it was finally incorporated into the present forms of Barnabas and the Didache. The basic "common source" probably was not *directly* used by either Pseudo-Barnabas or the Didachist (almost certainly not by the latter; see §2:5)—it is "common" to *their traditions* but seems to lie at some distance in the shadowy background.

5. *The Separate Circulation of the Two Ways Material.* In addition to the various direct witnesses to the present forms of Barnabas (§3) and the Didache (§7), early Christian literature attests the separate circulation of a form of the Two Ways ethic that is closely related to Didache 1:1–6:1 but *without* the material in 1:3b–2:1. Indeed, Goodspeed has argued that this separate Two Ways tradition actually represents the source common to Barnabas and the Didache. But to put the case in just that way is to oversimplify the relationship (see §8:5). The differences between this independent Two Ways tract and the Didache are slight in comparison to its differences from Barnabas—for example, it includes the twofold command of love (Did. 1:2; contrast Barn. 19:2) along with most of the Didache 3:1–6 "supplement," and it lacks most of Barnabas' eschatological preoccupation (although it is more "mythological" than the Didache at the outset, mentioning two "angels"). Thus it would seem to represent the immediate source upon which the final author-editor of the Didache drew for his Two Ways material. But as we have seen, Barnabas 18–20 must have been derived from an earlier form of this ever-growing tradition (lacking Did. 3:1–6, and less ordered), a form which already was united with eschatological emphases in the school tradition on which Pseudo-Barnabas depends. Thus of the three Christian forms of this Two Ways tradition, Barnabas 18–20 represents the most primitive offshoot from the ancient common stock, while the following witnesses attest a later stage which came to be incorporated directly into the Didache.

(1) **Dctr** = the Latin "Doctrina." It is known from two manuscripts, the oldest of which (ninth-tenth centuries) is incomplete and parallels only Didache 1:1–3a plus 2:2–6a, while the other (eleventh century) contains the complete **Dctr**—paralleling (in general) Didache 1:1–3a plus 2:2–6:1.

The points of unique agreement between **Dctr** and Barnabas against the Didache are almost completely limited to the opening words of the Two Ways, where **Dctr**-Barn. use the imagery of light/darkness and refer to corresponding angelic powers. There are also some faint similarities between the closing words of **Dctr** and Barnabas 21 (cf. Barn. 4:9b = Did. 16:2b).

(2) **CO** = the "Apostolic Church Order" (or "Ordinances"), also known as the "Ecclesiastical Canons of the (Holy) Apostles" (see also §7:6). This form of the church manual tradition probably dates from the early fourth century and circulated widely in the East (Egypt-Syria). The shortest form is contained in four Greek manuscripts dating from the tenth to the fifteenth centuries, and has sometimes been called (among other titles) the "Judgments of Peter." It contains, roughly, the material of Didache 1:1–3a plus 2:2–4:13, with some adaptations and additions, and a few smatterings of peculiarly Barnabean wording (see §3:7). The general order follows the Didache, but the teaching is sectioned off and put into the mouths of various apostles— for example, Peter gives Didache 2:2–7, Andrew gives 3:1–2, and so on. In one Greek manuscript from the twelfth century, as well as in the Latin, Syriac, Sahidic, Ethiopic, and Arabic versions, this reworked Two Ways tradition forms the first part of a much longer manual which continues with regulations governing church offices, and so forth (clearly related to the *Apostolic Tradition* of Hippolytus; see §7:6). The textual problems between these various forms of the Apostolic Church Order are often very complex. Most witnesses also include brief verbal parallels to Didache 10:3b and 13:1/2 (?) in the expansion which follows the admonitions of Didache 4:2, but this material is not extensive enough to encourage the belief that our full Didache was used for the Two Ways of **CO**. Rather, **CO** seems to have added excerpts from at least Barnabas and possibly the Didache to the **Dctr**-like form of the Two Ways on which it is based.

(3) **Shenuti** = the Arabic (but not Coptic) form of the *Life of Shenuti,* from the seventh century (?). This hagiography opens with parallels to the **Dctr-CO** form of the Two Ways. Didache 1:3b–2:1 is not represented and the negative approach of 5:1–2 is severely abridged (cf. **CO**, where it is lacking). The personal catechetical approach is heightened through the frequent insertion of "my son," and there is a great deal of expansion and adaptation of the basic Two Ways material.

(4) **Syntagma** = the *Syntagma Didascalias* ("Summary of Doctrine") attributed (wrongly?) to Athanasius. The **Syntagma** dates from the fourth century, and contains some teachings which obviously depend on the Two Ways, but which constitute only a small portion of the rules for Christian (especially monastic) life enjoined therein. It is impossible to say with complete assurance that the **Syntagma** rests solely on the **Dctr-CO** form rather than on the larger Didache. A passage on giving *may* be related to Didache 1:4d–e, but is not necessarily so—otherwise the Didache 1:3b–2:1 material is lacking. Similarly, the practices of fasting and giving reflected in Didache 8:1 and 13:3 are taught in the **Syntagma,** but this cannot be pressed as a proof of *literary* dependence.

(5) **Fides** = "The Faith and Teaching of those in Nicaea." This fourth-century Greek manual especially for clerics and monastics unites a form of Athanasius' "Confession of Faith" with a slightly variant form of the **Syntagma.** At one or two points, the **Fides** includes Two Ways phraseology not paralleled in the **Syntagma,** but usually the two documents present the same material in the same order and almost identical wording.

6. *General Characteristics of the Two Ways Teaching.* A closer examination of these materials permits some general observations about the common Two Ways source. If one is permitted to make a very subjective judgment on the basis of the relatively stable (but limited) context in Barnabas 20:2 = Didache 5:2, the order of items in the source would

seem to have been more "haphazard" than "systematic." This tends to support the suspicion that the Doctrina-Didache form of especially the Way of Life has been extensively reworked with respect to sequence. In terms of content, it is not clear whether, or to what extent, eschatology appeared in the source; what has remained as common to Barnabas and Doctrina-Didache is almost exclusively ethical—duties toward God (Barn. 19:2a, d, f = Did. 1:2a; 4:12b, 13a), neighbor (Barn. 19:3d, 6a, 8a = Did. 2:6b, 2c; 4:8), children (Barn. 19:5c, d = Did. 2:2b; 4:9), rulers and slaves (Barn. 19:7b, c = Did. 4:11, 10); vice lists (Barn. 19:4a; 20:1 = Did. 2:2 f.; 5:1); etc. In style, there is a marked tendency to parallelistic couplets which are strongly reminiscent of Jewish Wisdom Literature, such as Proverbs and Sirach (cf. also Testaments of the Twelve Patriarchs)—we find the linking of two ideas that are roughly synonymous (e.g., Barn. 19:2d–e, 5c = Did. 4:12a–b, 2:2b; cf. Did. 3:9a), or sometimes antithetical (e.g., Barn. 19:8a = Did. 4:8; cf. Barn. 19:3a, Did. 3:9b), or in which the second part builds on the first to supplement and strengthen the teaching (e.g., Barn. 19:7a, 8b = Did. 2:4; see also Did. 4:14). There are also straightforward prohibitions and positive admonitions, as well as occasional teachings with properly "theological" overtones (e.g., Barn. 19:6c, 7c–8a = Did. 3:9c; 4:8, 10; cf. Did. 4:1b). Finally, it should be noted that at several places Barnabas uses a stylistic device of grouping *three* items together (not always related in context)—for example, 19:2a, 4a, 4d, 6b. The fact that the number three plays a special role in the Barnabean tradition (see §5:5:3), however, causes some hesitation in claiming this as a stylistic tendency of the "original" Two Ways source.

7. *Didache 16, the Eschatology of Barnabas, and the Two Ways.* There remains the problem of how Didache 16 is related (*a*) to Barnabas, and (*b*) to the Two Ways. We have already noted that Didache 16:2 and Barnabas 4:10b, 9b use the same admonitions (§2:3). There are, in fact, several

other apparent parallels between Didache 16 and Barnabas (esp. 4:9b–14):

> The admonition to watchfulness (Did. 16:1) is a frequent theme in Barnabas (see esp. 4:9b; §5:4);
>
> Both documents refer to the Christian quest for salvation as "your/our life" (Did. 16:1a; Barn. 2:10b, 4:9b);
>
> Both can describe salvation as "perfection" (Did. 16:2b; cf. §9:5; Barn. 6:19; cf. Barn. 4:11b; §5:4);
>
> Both warn of lawlessness and error/deceit "in the last days" (Did. 16:3–4; Barn. 4:1, 3a; see §5:3);
>
> Both recognize that some men, including the "sheep" (Did. 16:3; Barn. 16:5*), will fall away from salvation in the time of crisis (Did. 16:5; Barn. 4:3, 9b, 13–14);
>
> At least Barnabas (7:9) and perhaps Didache (16:5b) picture the victorious Jesus as one who previously had been cursed;
>
> Possibly the "sign spread out in heaven" (Did. 16:6) is related to the "type" of the cross described in Barnabas 12:2–4;
>
> Both speak of the world/unbelievers "seeing" the Lord when he comes (Did. 16:8a; Barn. 7:9, cf. 5:10);
>
> Finally, the role of the "world-deceiver" who "resembles a son of God" and who conquers earth with "signs and wonders" (Did. 16:4) sharply contrasts with Barnabas' picture of Jesus, "God's Son" (see §5:7), who is rejected despite "signs and wonders" (Barn. 5:8 f.; see 4:14a); similarly, Christians should also act as "God's sons" (Barn. 4:9b), and should "endure" (Did. 16:5b) as Jesus "endured" (Barn. 5:1–12; 14:4).

It is obvious that some of these items reflect apocalyptic commonplaces current in early Christianity (see also Koester on Did. 16); nevertheless, this material is extensive enough to at least suggest the possibility that the undeniable relationship that exists between Didache 16:2 and Barnabas 4:10b, 9b may be only part of a larger problem concerning Didache 16 and Barnabas 4 in general.

(1) One possibility to be tested, then, is that the whole of
Didache 16 is somehow related to Barnabas. But in that
event, it is unlikely that the Didache has directly used Barnabas,[4] since that would necessitate a systematic reorganiza-
tion and expansion of the "borrowed" material along more
strictly apocalyptic lines (like Mark 13, etc.), plus the systematic elimination of many Barnabean peculiarities (the
immediacy of the crisis, emphasis on judgment, etc.). Might
Barnabas have used the Didache, then? Again, this is unlikely since numerous allusions in Didache 16 which would
have been congenial to Barnabas are not, in fact, adopted—
for example, "world-deceiver" (16:4) or even "deceiver"
(see §5:3), the "fiery trial" (16:5; cf. Barn. 15:5), or the
coming of the Lord "on the clouds" (16:8, cf. Barn. 7:9;
15:5). And where minor parallels between Barnabas and the
Didache do exist, they usually are more characteristic of the
former, which indicates that Barnabas' *tradition* spoke in
such a way, and thus that (mechanical) "borrowing" from
the Didache is precluded. In short, if we begin with the possibility of a large-scale relationship, the best solution is to
postulate a common apocalyptic source which roughly followed the Didache 16 pattern (call to vigilance, last days in
general, "world-deceiver" and final crisis, signs and arrival of
the Lord, judgment). Pseudo-Barnabas knew such apocalyptic material—and much more—but he has admittedly re-
frained from dealing with "things future" as such (17:2).
But he cannot hide the widespread influence that the apocalyptic has had on his tradition, and this background is especially obvious in chapter 4.

(2) An alternative approach would be to reject the suggested minor parallels between Didache 16 and Barnabas as
superficial and coincidental, and to concentrate on the clear
relationship between Didache 16:2 and Barnabas 4:10b, 9b
(for the texts, see §2:3). From a close analysis of the wording, it is impossible to determine whether one has borrowed

---

[4] Despite B. C. Butler, *JTS* 11 (1960), 265–283.

from the other, or which form is more "original"—for example, the general thought-world of Barnabas is reflected in such concepts as "faith" = "life" (i.e., the salvation quest; see 2:2, 10b; §5:4), "lawless time" (15:5; 18:2), "scandals to come" (4:3a); but the Didache also elsewhere contains this idea of "faith" (10:2; 16:5) and of "perfection" (1:4b; 6:2; 10:5). Thus Barnabas might have originated the material and the Didache adapted it, or vice versa, or both adapted a common source. There is some additional evidence to support the last alternative. As we have noted (§2:3), Didache 16:2a = Barnabas 4:10b may be a variant form of Two Ways material known from Didache 4:2. This possibility is greatly strengthened by the Hermas parallel (§2:3), since Hermas also knew the Two Ways tradition (see to Did. 1:1). Furthermore, 1 Clement 34:7—35:6 preserves ideas similar to Didache 16:2 = Barnabas 4:10b, 9b in a Two Ways setting:

> Therefore we should come together in harmony with one mind.... Therefore let us strive to be found among the number of those who endure, that we may receive a share of the promised gifts. But how? ... If we seek out the things which are pleasing ... to him, if we bring to perfection the things necessary ... and we follow in the Way of Truth ... [a vice list follows].

Not only does Barnabas 4:9b–14 also employ Two Ways imagery, but the idea of the "lawless time" is used in Barnabas' introduction to the Two Ways (18:2b). Didache 16 also may contain some faint echoes of such a setting—does "life" = Way of Life in 16:1a?; note also the contrast between love and hate in 16:3, and especially the contrast between the "signs of the truth" (16:6) and "the one who leads the world into error" (16:4). There is a good possibility, then, that Didache 16:2b = Barnabas 4:9b derive from the original conclusion to the common Two Ways source (cf. the **Dctr** conclusion), and partly fill the gap left by the present divergent endings in Didache 6 and Barnabas 21.

(3) It would also be possible to solve the problem at hand

by synthesizing various aspects of the two preceding hypotheses: for example, at one time the common Two Ways source circulated in connection with an apocalyptic appendix similar to Didache 16; [5] or, at one time the admonition of Didache 16:2b = Barnabas 4:9b formed part of the Two Ways conclusion, but it later came to be incorporated into an apocalyptic tradition which circulated separately and was used by the Didache and Barnabas.

Admittedly such hypotheses are extremely complicated and highly speculative. But the situation itself is so complex that any simpler "solution" (the Didache made direct use of Barnabas, or vice versa) actually creates more problems than it solves. Thus, until some fresh evidence is uncovered which can illuminate these matters, some sort of "common source" theory must be invoked with reference to Didache 16 = Barnabas 4, as well as for the Two Ways material shared by Didache 1–5 and Barnabas 18–20.

---

[5] Such a combining of ethical catechism with apocalyptic ideas can be illustrated from many Judeo-Christian sources—see esp., the Testaments. Indeed, K. Baltzer, *Das Bundesformular* (1960), has argued that such a combination is expected in the kind of literature represented by the Didache (and Barnabas).

THE EPISTLE OF BARNABAS

§3. Sources for the Text of Barnabas

There exist numerous Greek manuscripts containing the epistle in whole or in part. For text-critical purposes, however, they can be reduced to three important witnesses—**H, S,** and **G** (see below). The frequent and often lengthy quotations in Clement of Alexandria (**Cl.A.**) constitute a (partial) fourth Greek witness, and the textual evidence provided by the ancient Latin version **L,** although often difficult to assess, cannot be ignored. There is some additional relevant material, as we shall see, but its contribution is negligible.

(1) **H** (Codex Hierosolymitanus) is the manuscript discovered by P. Bryennios in 1873. It dates from the year 1056 and is most famous for containing the Didache (see §7:1). Because it was discovered in Constantinople, some earlier editors refer to it as "C." In addition to Barnabas and the Didache, **H** includes Chrysostom's "Synopsis of the Old Testament," 1–2 Clement, the Epistles of Ignatius ("long" recension), and two shorter, hitherto unknown documents. Its text of Barnabas is most closely related to the first hand of **S** and to **Cl.A.**

(2) **S** designates the Codex Sinaiticus (often called "Aleph"), which C. Tischendorf discovered in 1859. This manuscript dates from the late fourth or early fifth century, and contains biblical books (OT-NT) plus Barnabas (right after Revelation) and the Shepherd of Hermas. The original text of **S** (**S***) and its contemporary corrections (**S¹**) are closely related to **H.** But several later corrections (seventh

17

century?) have also been made from a text which is very similar to family **G**. We will refer to these as **S**^{2}. It is sometimes difficult to distinguish **S**^{1} from **S**^{2}.

(3) **G** is a convenient designation for the family of nine Greek manuscripts in which Barnabas 5:7 ff. is welded on to Polycarp, Philippians 9:2 without any indication, thus forming a hybrid document which is half Polycarp, half Barnabas. The oldest of these manuscripts dates from the eleventh century, and they are all obviously derived from a common mutilated ancestor which is at least that old. That the type of text preserved in **G** is often even older may be seen by its frequent support from the corrections in **S**^{2}. Sometimes **G** and **L** show a tendency to agree against **H** and **S***.

(4) **Cl.A.** indicates Clement of Alexandria, who explicitly quotes the epistle seven times and uses similar materials without acknowledgment elsewhere (see §6:1, 7).

(5) **L** is the ancient Latin version which may have been made as early as the third (or late second?) century, but which is now preserved only in a single corrupt ninth-century manuscript in Leningrad (Codex Corbeiensis). The extant text of **L** contains only Barnabas 1–17, and that in a much shorter form than the Greek. It is not always clear whether the translator (plus later corruption in the Latin tradition) is responsible for abridging his Greek *Vorlage,* or whether he knew a shorter Greek form of Barnabas (which did not include the Two Ways!).[1] The text presupposed by **L** sometimes supports **G** against **H** and **S***.

(6) **Syr** signifies fragments of Barnabas 19:1 f., 8; 20:1 in Syriac translation published by A. Baumstark in *Oriens Christianus* 2 (1912), 235–240.

(7) **CO** indicates the allusions to Barnabas 1:1; 19:2a, 9b; and 21:2–4 (in some MSS), which are embedded in the predominantly Didache type Two Ways tradition in the Greek

---

[1] So E. J. Goodspeed, *The Apostolic Fathers* (New York, 1950), 286. See also §4:4.

Apostolic Church Orders and its Sahidic-Arabic-Ethiopic versions (§2:5:2).

(8) The Two Ways tradition itself, in its various forms (§2:5; §7) is also important for determining the text of Barnabas 18–20.

§4. Barnabas as a "School" Product

1. *Explicit Quotations* (see the Indexes). Even the most cursory encounter with Barnabas 1–17 should make one thing clear: Pseudo-Barnabas repeatedly *claims* to be quoting from older materials, almost all of which may be traced directly or indirectly back to Jewish religious literature. There are nearly one hundred formulas of quotation, most of which are general and vague ("scripture says," "it is written," "the prophet says," "the Lord/God says/said," "it/he says"), but some of which refer to the supposed book or human speaker or author by name (Jacob, Moses, David, Isaiah, Daniel, Enoch). Rarely, an attempt is made to identify a citation with even more precision, as 10:2 ("in Deuteronomy"—but where?), 15:1 ("in the ten words" or "Decalogue"—but see the passage!), 15:3 ("at the beginning of creation"—Gen. 2:2).

Approximately one fourth of Barnabas' explicit quotations derive (directly or indirectly) from the Septuagint of Isaiah. Phrases and verses from the Psalms are also frequent and usually betray some relation to known Septuagint text forms. Pentateuchal material is often cited, but seldom shows widespread verbal agreement with extant texts. Septuagint Proverbs is used once (5:4a), and Jeremiah provides a few passages (in basically LXX garb). Reminiscences of Zechariah, Ezekiel, Daniel, and Jewish apocalyptic literature (Enoch [see 4:3], 4 Ezra [see 12:1], 2 Baruch [see 11:9 f.]) also lie behind a few citations, and at one place—and only one (4:14)—a phrase which we now find in our canonical Matthew is formally quoted ("as it is written"). Otherwise there is no clear evidence that Pseudo-Barnabas knew any part of our present New Testament *in written form*.[2] Nor is there any clear allusion to the Old Testament "historical" books outside of the Pentateuch.

2. *Blocks of Traditional Material.* But it is not simply a matter of introducing individual proof-texts that we encounter in the epistle. Time and again two or more quotations (sometimes with related commentary—e.g., 2:4–3:6; 11:6–11; chs. 15–16) are found to be linked by means of common words or ideas which recur in each quotation (e.g., 4:4–5; 6:3–4; 9:1–3; 11:2–5; 12:10–11; 14:7–9), and the awkwardness with which these smaller units sometimes are incorporated into the present form of the epistle points to the wholesale use by Pseudo-Barnabas of available blocks of tradition. The variety of these traditional materials [3]—*halakic* (chs. 7–8) and *haggadic* (e.g., 4:7 f.; 14:2 f.; 12:2–7) midrash, Hellenistic-Jewish propaganda (e.g., 2:4–3:6; ch. 10), moralized Greek natural history (10:6–8), various "proof-text" excerpts and blocks (e.g., 9:1–3), typology/allegory traditions (e.g., 6:8–19; 11:6–11; chs. 12–13), apocalyptic sources (e.g., 4:3–5; 5:12[?]; 6:13 f.; 11:9 f.[?]; 12:1, 9; 15:4; 16:3, 5–6), and so forth—and the ways in which these sources are arranged in the epistle (often mechanically by topics, or sometimes simply juxtaposed) strongly suggest that the final author-editor has worked from a "school" background which is closely related to Hellenistic Judaism.

3. *"Pseudo-Barnabas" as a Teacher.* In fact, the claims of Pseudo-Barnabas point in the same direction. Although he does not wish to address his readers in the formal capacity of "Teacher" (1:8; 4:6b, 9a), he is acting as a transmitter of what he has received (1:5; see 4:9a; 21:9) and he expects them to receive his teachings (9:9; 17:1 f.; 18:1; 21:2, 7). Although he is capable of teaching them more difficult mat-

---

[2] On the problem of Barnabas' relation to the Gospel tradition, see also Koester.

[3] See the recent work of Prigent on the "testimonia" used in Barnabas; cf. also Windisch.

ters (17:2), he has attempted to write briefly and simply (1:5; 4:9; 6:5) about the "things which are able to save us" (4:1; see 17:1 var.). Apparently he is motivated not only by his personal relationship with the recipients (1:3–8; 4:6; 6:5) but by the hope that he may claim them as *his* students when the day of judgment comes (see 1:5; 21:7 ff.; cf. 2 Cor. 1:14; Phil. 2:16; 2 Clem. 19:1). They are his "sons and daughters" (1:1; cf. 19:5d), his "children" of love and joy and peace (7:1; 9:7; 15:4; 21:9; cf. 9:3c), and his "brethren" (2:10; 3:6; 4:14; 5:5; 6:10; 6:15), whom he loves more than his own self (1:4; 4:6; see 6:5; 19:5b). He hopes that they too will become "good lawgivers" and "faithful advisers" (21:4), meditating on his teachings, which are the Lord's teachings (21:7 f.; see 1:4).

4. *"Pseudo-Barnabas" as an Author-Editor.* The final product of this well-intentioned but hasty reiteration of school traditions has often provoked adverse comment from modern commentators. But Pseudo-Barnabas' lack of care and/or talent in organizing and editing his materials proves a boon to us in that many of the "seams" between these tradition blocks remain obvious and thus permit us partially to reconstruct the background from which at least one early Christian teacher operated. The main seam is, of course, between chapters 17 and 18. In fact, it has sometimes been suggested that the epistle once circulated in a short form (chs. 1–17, as in L—see §3:5), which later was expanded (by the same author-editor?) to include the Two Ways material. In any event, Barnabas 2–16 itself often reads like a crude attempt at writing an erudite research paper (but without footnotes). The author-editor shows a wide range of acquaintance with diverse methods and materials which he considers worth-while. But it is a superficial acquaintance. He has not always made the school materials his own. Thus his work often lacks real coherence and suffers from the overzealous attempt to apply to his own purposes various sources and arguments which sometimes originally served other ends. He is not a brilliant "Teacher" by any standards; but

he draws upon what must have been a respectable educational heritage (see §6:7–11). His aim is not to present a well-ordered flow of argument, but to emphasize, by means of repetition and juxtaposition, the things that are important for salvation, for that is his theme (see §5:4).

§5. The Type of Christianity Represented in Barnabas

Despite the fact that Barnabas incorporates various tradition blocks, and that Pseudo-Barnabas often fails to impose any systematic organization on his adopted school materials, there are certain basic themes that run throughout the epistle and which, when isolated and closely examined, can provide a fairly clear portrait of the thought world from which it came. We should not expect Barnabas to present an entirely consistent theology. For the most part, Pseudo-Barnabas does not seem to be interested in speculative "theology"—he is more concerned with practical matters, with exhortation and parenesis, with correctly understanding the Lord's commandments and living thereby. But behind his catechesis a rather sophisticated thought structure is assumed—mainly derived by Pseudo-Barnabas from his school tradition, to be sure—which revolves around a special understanding of God's action in human history, and a vivid consciousness of living in the last times. It is impossible to appreciate the epistle without having these themes of "gnosis" and eschatology clearly in view.

1. *Exegetical and Ethical Gnosis.* The express purpose of the epistle (or at least of chs. 1–17) is to pass along to the readers some of the special insights which the author has himself received—insights that will supplement their already present faith (1:5), and will assist them in their quest for ultimate salvation (§5:4). This special insight is called "gnosis" (among other things, see below), and is a gift which God bestows on (all of ?) his children, enabling them to interpret the course of the history of salvation—past, present, and future (1:7; 5:3). Although Pseudo-Barnabas concen-

trates on providing insight into what has happened (especially the history of Israel and the work of Jesus; §5:6–7),
he claims also to be able to interpret present and future
events (17:2), and he sometimes does so (e.g., 4:3–5; 15:
3–7). Not every man has this gnosis, but only those whose
"ears and hearts" have been circumcised (9:1; 10:12), that
is, those who have (obediently) "heard" the Lord's voice
(8:7–9:4). Thus gnosis and action are closely connected—he
who "hears" the Lord's voice understands what is being
commanded, and he who rightly understands is better able
to obey the Lord's commands. The cultic, literalistic Jews
did not "hear" (8:7), thus they could not understand (10:
12a; see §5:6). Nevertheless, certain individuals in Jewish
history were blessed with gnosis—Abraham (9:7 f.), Jacob
(13:5), Moses (10:1–11; 4:8 = 14:3, etc.), David (10:10;
12:10), the "prophets" (1:7; 2:4; 5:6, etc.). It is because
Pseudo-Barnabas has witnessed for himself that his readers
have already received from the Lord a generous "implantation of the pneumatic gift" (1:2 f.; see 9:9) that he feels
justified in helping to bring their gnosis to perfection (1:5;
cf. 13:7b).

There is nothing strange or illegitimate about referring to
this attitude as "gnostic." In fact, Pseudo-Barnabas probably
would not have hesitated to use the word of himself, just as
his admirer, Clement of Alexandria, later does (§6:1, 7). It
is true that this is not the "Gnosticism" which developed
among certain second-century groups and which came to be
condemned by the developing "orthodox" church for its dif-
ferentiation between the hidden God of Jesus and the in-
ferior creator God of the Jews, its obsession for cosmological-
theological speculation (often at the expense of ethical-social
responsibility), and so forth.[4] Nevertheless, the importance
of gnosis for Barnabas and its tradition must not be mini-
mized. As the appended list of terminology which deals

---

[4] See Robert M. Grant, *The Apostolic Fathers, An Introduction* (New
York, 1964), 98 ff.

directly or indirectly with this matter of special insight in Barnabas shows, it is basic to the world of thought with which we are concerned (see §6:7). But gnosis for Barnabas is not an end in itself. The term is used technically to refer to two closely related ideas: "exegetical gnosis," which enables the recipient better to understand salvation-history (see 6:9; 9:8; 13:7), and "ethical gnosis," which is the correct understanding of the Lord's requirements for conduct (see 18:1; 19:1; 21:5). Sometimes these two aspects of gnosis become so intertwined as to be indistinguishable (see 1:5; 5:4; 10:10 [2:3 ?]). The main thrust of the epistle remains parenetic (moral exhortation and instruction) even where its approach is most gnostic. This also is a characteristic of Barnabas' tradition, as we shall see (§6:7–11).

2. *Gnostic-Parenetic Terminology.* The main terms in Barnabas relating to special (exegetical) insight into God's actions and requirements are:

(1) *aisthanesthai:* to "perceive/understand" the *real* meaning of a text—2:9; 6:18; 11:8; 13:3.

(2) *akouein (akoē):* to "hear" ("hearing") or "hearken," in the sense (*a*) of paying close attention to what is spoken/ revealed and thus understanding (obeying) it—7:3; 8:7; 9: 1–3* (10:12); 13:2 (cf. 12:8); or (*b*) of receiving the "word" (§5:8) of salvation—9:4a; 11:11b (cf. 19:4).

(3) *blepein:* to "perceive" with gnostic insight—10:11e; 13:6 (cf. 1:7; 3:6a; 4:14; 9:7).

(4) *gignōskein:* to "have (special) knowledge" (*gnōsis*) —7:1; 12:3; 14:7; 16:2c (see also 9:1*; 11:4*; 19:11; 20:2).

(5) *gnōrizein:* to "make known" the meaning of events in salvation-history—1:7 = 5:3.

(6) *gnōsis:* "knowledge" of what God requires from man (18:1; 19:1; 21:5), or of what is meant by a text/act in salvation-history (6:9[?]; 9:8; 13:7[?]), or something of each (1:5; 2:3; 5:4; 10:10).

(7) (*hupo-/epi-*) *deiknunai:* to "exemplify," "provide example of," "point out" to the diligent listener/observer some-

thing that otherwise might be obscure—1:8; 5:6 f.; 5:9; 6:13; 7:5; 12:6; 13:3.

(8) *dēloun:* to "make clear"—9:8; 17:1.

(9) *dōrea:* the "gift" of pneumatic-gnostic insight—1:2; 9:9.

(10) *eidenai* (*ide*): to "see/know" gnostically (cf. 9:9!), especially the meaning of "types" (§5:2:24)—6:14; 7:10; 8:1; 12:10 f.; 13:5*(?); 15:7 f.; also to "inquire" by gnostic means —13:1; 14:1 (var.); (see *zētein*, §5:2:13).

(11) *epistēmē:* "knowledge"—associated with *sophia, sunesis,* and *gnōsis* in 2:3; 21:5 (see also the verb in 4:11*; 6:10b*).

(12) *heuriskein: to* "discover" by gnostic perception—9:5; 16:7.

(13) *zētein:* to "seek after" information through gnostic exegesis—2:9; 11:1; 14:1 (var.); 16:6 (see *eidenai,* §5:2:10); also used of the ethical quest (§5:4).

(14) *legein:* to "say," in the sense of to really mean— 10:11; 11:8, 11; 15:5, etc.

(15) *manthanein:* to "learn," used primarily (cf. also 9:9; 21:1a) as an exhortation to pay attention to the gnostic exegesis—5:5; 6:9; 9:7 f.; 14:4; 16:2; 16:7 f.

(16) (*ana*)*marukasthai:* to "ruminate" or "chew" on the Lord's word and thus discover its *real* meaning—10:11c (cf. Irenaeus, cited in Eusebius, *H.E.* 5:20:7).

(17) *meletan:* to "meditate," "concentrate," "study"—10: 11c; 21:7 (see 4:11; 11:5*; 19:10).

(18) *noein* (*nous*): to "understand" ("understanding")— 4:14; 6:10*; 7:1; 8:2; 10:12; 17:2.

(19) *parabolē:* a "parable," which requires gnostic understanding to serve its *real* purpose—6:10*; 17:2 (cf. *tupos,* §5:2:24).

(20) *pneuma:* "spirit," often used in the sense of man's God-related component, his gnosis-receiving faculty, thus the phrase "in the spirit" to indicate gnostic comprehension —9:7; 10:2 = 10:9; 13:5b (cf. 14:2*; 19:2b); or his salvation-related faculty—11:11a. The physical body is a "vehicle of

the spirit" (7:3c; 11:9b[?]; cf. 21:8), and the recipients of
Barnabas are referred to as highly favored (by God) "spirits"
(1:2, 5; cf. 21:9). Similarly, they are exhorted to "be pneumatics"—4:11 (cf. 16:10). God has provided them with this
"pneumatic gift" (1:2), which probably means he has especially prepared their spirits for gnostic insight (cf. 6:14;
19:7c), or has even given them a special measure of spirit
(see 1:3). Otherwise "the Lord's Spirit" refers to the divine
agent for providing prophetic gnosis—6:14(?); (9:2 var.);
12:2; 14:2*(?); 14:9*; cf. 19:7c(?); see §5:10.

(21) *prosechein:* to "pay attention" to what is taught—
7:4, 6, 7, 9; 15:4; also used in an ethical sense, to "walk circumspectly"—2:1; 4:6b, 9b. Both senses may be present in
4:14; 16:8.

(22) *sophizein* (*sophia*): to "make wise" ("wisdom")—
5:3 (cf. 9:4, in a bad sense); 2:3 = 21:5; 6:10; 16:9.

(23) *sunienai* (*sunesis*): to "understand" ("understanding"), roughly synonymous with *noein* (see 10:12)—2:3 =
21:5; 4:6a; 4:8 = 14:3; 10:1b(?); 10:12; 12:10 (see 4:11*).
For the negative use (the opposite of *gnōsis*), see 2:9; 5:3.

(24) *tupos:* a "type" is a person, situation, or event in salvation-history which carries symbolic meaning that can be
gnostically discovered—7:3, 7, 10, 11; 8:1; 12:2, 5, 6, 10; 13:5
(cf. *parabolē,* §5:2:19).

(25) *phaneroun* (*phaneros/-oteron*): to "make clear" to
the perceptive listener—2:4; 7:3, 7; 12:8, 10(?); 13:4; 16:5.
Also, to "make clear before" something happens (to "pre-
dict," *prophaneroun*)—3:6; 6:7; 7:1; 11:1. The same verb is
used of Jesus' being "made manifest"—5:6, 9; 6:7, 9, 14; 12:
10(?); 14:5(?); 15:9.

(26) *charis:* "grace," in the special sense of gnostic insight
—1:2; 5:6; 9:8(?).[5]

Conspicuous for their absence from this list are the terms
allegoria ("allegory"), *musterion* ("mystery"), *sumbolon*

---

[5] See T. F. Torrance, *The Doctrine of Grace in the Apostolic Fathers*
(Edinburgh, 1948), 108 ff.

("symbol"), and their cognates.[6] Nevertheless the evidence is more than adequate to show how completely the thought of Barnabas is ruled by this "gnostic" approach, which claims to understand salvation-history (§5:6) in the way it was pneumatically-gnostically intended to be understood (cf. 10: 12a)—and to live in accord with this gnosis, which is a gift from God but which to some extent can also be taught.

3. *Eschatalogical Atmosphere.* The other pervasive underlying theme which cannot be ignored, if Barnabas is to be understood, is the epistle's eschatology. The entire atmosphere in which Pseudo-Barnabas (and many of his traditions) exists is charged with a view of "the last times" which borders on the apocalyptic and which makes the task of parenesis all the more important and urgent. These are "the last days," the climax of evils which will usher in the "age to come" (2:1; 4:1, 3, 9; 16:5 f.). The Christian must walk in this present wicked world, but he must walk carefully (see §5:2:21) and perform his righteous tasks with deliberate haste (19:1b; 21:7b; cf. 1:5; 4:9a) as he continually looks forward to the imminent holy age (8:6; 10:11d; 21:1, 3). The Lord is about to judge (4:12; 5:7; 7:2; 15:5; cf. 10:5; 12:9*) and the Christian must be prepared for this "day of recompense" (11:8; 19:10 f.; 20:2c; 21:6; see §5:4, 7). Two alternative courses of action are now open, righteousness and lawlessness (see §2:2). "Each man will receive payment in accord with his deeds—if he was good, his righteousness precedes him; if he was wicked, the reward of wickedness goes before him" (4:12).

The roots of this moral struggle and of this contrast of the "ages" in the Barnabas tradition lie in its gripping mythological presentation of the spirit world.[7] The Christian's adversary is Satan (18:1), the "Black One" (4:10a; 20:1), the

---

[6] On technical exegetical terminology in the ancient Greek world at large, see Robert M. Grant, *The Letter and the Spirit* (London, 1957), 120–142.

[7] See, in general, F. X. Gokey, *The Terminology for the Devil and Evil Spirits in the Apostolic Fathers,* Catholic University of America: Patristic Studies 93 (Washington, D.C., 1961).

"Wicked One" (2:10b; 21:3), the "Lawless One" (15:5 var.),
the "Wicked Archon (Ruler)" (4:13), who is in control of
this "present lawless time" (2:1; 4:1; 18:2). He is able to
"shove us away from the kingdom" (4:13) and "hurl us from
our life" (2:10b) if he can ensnare us in "the error of the
present time" (4:1; 5:4). The "angels of Satan" control the
"way of darkness" (18:1), and it was partly because of deceitful "enlightenment" by a wicked angel that Israel failed
to find her potential place in salvation-history (9:4b; see
§5:6). But if (with the help of the "angels of God" [18:1])
Christians can endure to the end, in righteousness, salvation
will be the reward. "He who does these things will be glorified in the kingdom of God; he who chooses those things
will perish with his works" (21:1; see §5:4).

Apparently, at least for the traditional material used in
chapters 7–8, the present time of struggle is thought of as
the "kingdom" of Jesus in which there are "evil and foul
days" (8:6) characterized by Jesus' own suffering (8:5) and
continued in the subsequent suffering of those who desire to
appropriate the kingdom (= the church? [7:11]) for themselves. But "at the end of days" Jesus will be victorious over
the forces of evil (12:9*) and will "come to his inheritance"
(4:3b; cf. 12:10 f.). Pseudo-Barnabas does not elaborate in
what sense Jesus has already, in his death and resurrection,
defeated the adversary (see 10:5; 14:5), although he is definite that salvation is impossible apart from those events
(§5:7). In any case, the final victory, accompanied by judgment and re-creation of the universe, is yet future and ushers
in the true "sabbath rest" for the Creator and his righteous
people (15:5–7). This "sabbath rest" is also pictured as the
"beginning of another world"—of an "eighth day" (i.e., a new
first day [15:8]). It is not clear whether Pseudo-Barnabas
intends to refer to this final state of the righteous as the
"kingdom of God" (21:1; cf. 4:13), in contrast to a temporary
"kingdom" of Jesus which gains the victory (cf. above and
1 Cor. 15:25–28), but such an interpretation is at least possible. Nor is it entirely clear whether Pseudo-Barnabas ex-

pects a literal "millennium" of rest after the final victory and
before the "eighth day"—15:5 ff. is ambiguous, if not con-
fused, on the relationship between the "true sabbath" and
the "eighth day." [8]

In any event, it is clear that the entire epistle—including
the Two Ways section (§2:2–3)—is eschatologically oriented.
It would be quite misleading to see its "eschatology" *only* in
such concrete apocalyptic imagery as the political situation
in the last days (4:3–5), the triumphal return of the Lord
(4:3; 15:5), the resurrection and judgment (5:7; 11:8[?];
15:5; 21:1c, etc.), the "sabbath rest" and the "new world"
(15:5, 8). Just as the Barnabas tradition lives in a "gnostic"
thought-world, it breathes an eschatological atmosphere.
These factors give the epistle its life.

4. *The Quest for Salvation.* For Pseudo-Barnabas, the mo-
tivation for writing and the goal of this gnosis in an eschatological setting is ultimate salvation, for which he (1:3) and
they strive (21:9). There is no idea here of the Christian
already having attained (4:13)—he is not "declared righteous" once and for all through faith, but rather, he must
carry out a sustained quest for salvation during these evil
times (2:1; 4:1; 21:6, 8). Nor can salvation be gained by
escaping from the wicked world into a solitary, individual
existence; it must be sought in social situations and through
the community which is God's true Temple (4:10 f.; 19:10
[contrast Did. 4:2!]; 21:2). Righteousness depends on correctly understanding and consistently obeying God's righteous ordinances: "agonize to keep his commandments" in
order to be able to rejoice at the judgment (4:11 f.), "never
relax" (4:13), "flee vanity" (4:10) and press on to attain
salvation (see 17:1 var.; 21:9). "For the whole time of our
life and faith will be of no value to us unless we resist now,
in the lawless time" (4:9b; see Did. 16:2). Salvation results
from victory over the present wicked world (§5:3), and is

---

[8] See further, J. Daniélou, *Vigiliae Christianae* 2 (1948), 1–16; A. Her-
mans, *Ephemerides Theologicae Lovanienses* 35 (1959), 849–876.

the ultimate (eschatological) attainment of perfect righteousness (4:10; 6:18 f.; 15:6 f.)—the Christian's reward for
works of righteousness (4:12; 5:4; 19:1, 10; 21:1; cf. 1:6).
It is something for which the Christian hopes (1:3; see 12:3),
something he desires (16:10). For the most part, salvation
has to do with *future* deliverance (8:6; 21:9, etc.), although
there may also be some *present* implications by way of an-
ticipation (5:10; 12:7*; 19:10; cf. 10:5?). The danger of failure is ever present (2:10b; 3:6; 4:1–2, 6b, 13 f.; 5:4, etc.).

5. *The Terminology of the Salvation Quest.* Certain key
phrases and words are emphasized in Barnabas in connection
with salvation and bear out the above analysis. For example:

(1) "Hope" is often used in preference to "faith." The
Christian is "to hope" in God/Jesus/him/the name/the cross
(19:7c; 6:9; 11:11; 8:5; 12:2; 16:8; 11:8), which apparently
means the same as "to believe" in God/him (16:7; see 6:3*).
These two ideas are frequently juxtaposed in the epistle
(1:6; 4:8; 6:3; 11:8; 12:7*) [9]—in fact, L often renders the
Greek "to hope" by *credere*, "to believe."

(2) "Righteousness" and its cognates ("to be made righteous," the "righteous" person or action) have an overwhelm-
ingly ethical/moral flavor in such connections as "Way of
Righteousness" (1:4; 5:4; see §2:2), "works done in righteousness" (1:6b), "reward of righteousness" (20:2 = Did. 5:2),
the "basis and result of judgment" (? 1:6a; cf. 19:11; 20:2).
Even a potentially ambiguous reference such as 3:4* must
be interpreted ethically in the light of 4:12. It would be interesting to know in greater detail what Pseudo-Barnabas
understood by Gen. 15:6 (cited in 13:7*)—Abraham's belief
was a righteous act? Both times when Pseudo-Barnabas employs the verb in connection with salvation, it has future
reference—*not* that "we have already been made righteous"

---

[9] This is not uncommon in other early Christian literature; e.g., Heb. 11:1;
Justin, *Dial.* 72:1 (in an unidentified "Ezra" quotation known also to Lactantius, *Epitome* 48 = *Div. Inst.* 4:18:22).

(4:10), but we *will be* "then" (15:7, cf. 6:18b f.). Nevertheless, the adjective can be applied to men now, both in a
favorable way (10:11; 19:6; see 6:7*; 11:7*), and echoing
the less than favorable Synoptic use (self-righteous? 5:9).
The overtones remain ethical in these passages. But the mem-
ber of this family of words which bears the heaviest technical use in Barnabas is *dikaiōmata*—the "righteous ordinances"
of the Lord. In its first occurrence (1:2), the term is quite
ambiguous—it could refer to God's "saving acts" toward the
recipients (see 4:11; 16:9; 21:5), or perhaps to the "rules of
action" which he has given them. Some later passages clearly
require the ethical (as opposed to cultic) meaning of "rules,"
by which the believer fulfills God's righteous demands (10:
2*, 11; 21:1). Observance of these rules *is* the basis for salvation in these perilous times (2:1), and a man must diligently seek out the real meaning of the righteous ordinances
by means of God-given gnosis (10:2; 21:5; see §5:1–2), discover the wisdom displayed therein (16:9), and pattern his
conduct thereon (21:1).

(3) Closely related to the *dikaiōmata* are the *dogmata*—
"dogmas," "doctrines," or "dictates." Whenever this word appears in Barnabas, it is associated with the number "three":
the positive Christian characteristics of hope-righteousness-
love (1:6); the gnostic meaning of Abraham's 318 servants
(9:7); the *gnostically* understood ethical-social prohibitions
revealed to Moses and David (10:1, 9–10). In this last context, they are explicitly identified with the *dikaiōmata* (10:
2*).

(4) Another related idea is conveyed by *entolē*, "commandment." Again, it is in 10:2 that this term is brought into
closest contact with *dikaiōmata* and *dogmata*. Just as Moses
understood the *real* meaning of his legislation (10:11), we
also, who have true gnosis, can speak forth God's true "commandments" (10:12) which we ourselves strive to keep (4:11;
cf. 2:1), not forsaking (19:2 = Did. 4:13) but fulfilling them
(21:8). God dwells in us through both "the commands of the
teaching (*didachē*)" and "the wisdom of the ordinances

(*dikaiōmata*)" (16:9). Elsewhere, *entolē* also is used of particular precepts (6:1[?]; 7:3; 9:5; 10:11b).

(5) "Love of neighbor" seems to be a formal obligation in Pseudo-Barnabas' mind. Not only is it one among other admonitions in the Two Ways (19:5b = Did. 2:7b)—note that it is not actually placed at the head of the list in Barnabas (19:2) as it was in the Didache tradition (Did. 1:2)—but it seems to spur the author-editor's efforts in behalf of his readers (1:4; 4:6; cf. 4:9; 6:5). Love should also characterize the reciprocal relationship between God and man (1:1; 4:1; 6:10*; 19:2) as well as attitudes within the community (1:4b; 1:6; 9:7; 19:9; 21:9). Love and joy sometimes are linked directly (1:6; cf. 4:11) or indirectly (cf. 7:1 with 9:7 = 21:9); similarly love and faith (1:4; 11:8) or love and peace (21:9).

(6) Finally, there is a sense in which the quest for salvation can be described by the typically Jewish phrase "fear of the Lord." The best illustration is 4:11, where concentration on the fear of God (cf. 11:5*) is closely associated with exhortations to be pneumatic (see §5:2:20), and to keep his commandments (cf. 10:11).[10] The Two Ways clearly uses the phrase ethically (19:5 = Did. 4:9; 20:1d, 2e), and ethical overtones may not be absent from other occurrences of "fear" in Barnabas (1:7b; 2:2; 10:10c; 11:11; 19:7), although it could not be said that the connection is obvious.

In short, salvation in Barnabas is primarily a *future* reward which will be granted to the person who meets the divine requirements of righteousness at the coming judgment. As we shall see, the quest for salvation is made possible by the work of Jesus (§5:7), but the subsequent responsibility of the believer lies in well-disciplined ethical-moral (not cultic-ritualistic) conduct during these crucial eschatological times. It is here that the overriding parenetic tone of Barnabas finds its explanation.

---

[10] See also Hermas, Mand. 7:1—"Fear the Lord and guard his commandments."

6. *Salvation-History.* To understand more precisely the
role of Jesus in this quest for salvation, and the relationship
between the believer and his Lord, we must turn to the interpretation of God's redemptive acts toward men ("salvation-history," as we shall call it) which is held by Pseudo-
Barnabas and his gnostic tradition. The events of the past
—that is, of Jewish religious history—hold the key to what is
happening and what will happen (see 1:7; 5:3; 17:1–2). The
very language employed throughout Barnabas to describe
the *Christian* hope is directly and thoroughly rooted in the
language of God's dealings with Israel. Thus Christians are
the *new* (or younger) *people* (3:6; 5:7; 7:5; 13:1–6), the
true heirs of the *promise* (5:7; 6:17; 15:7; 16:9) and of the
covenant (4:6–8 = 14:1–5; 6:19; 13:1–6), God's *sons* (4:9)
and *holy people* (14:6); the Christian community is God's
new creation (6:11–14; 16:8) which inherits the *good land*
(6:8–18) and is God's dwelling place—his *pneumatic Temple*
(4:11; 6:15; 16:10). Similarly, Jesus is the *Isaac offering*
(7:3), the *Atonement goat(s)* (7:4–10; cf. 5:2*; 6:1*; 9:2*,
"suffering Servant"), the *red heifer* (8:2), the *new Moses*
(?14:4–5), and the victorious *Joshua* who leads the people
into the land (6:9, 16b) after conquering the adversary,
Amalek (12:8–10a). The cross was revealed beforehand in
the *household of Abraham* (9:8), in *Moses' prayer* stance
(12:2–4) and Moses' *bronze serpent* image (12:5–7), in the
wood of the red heifer ritual (8:5), in the *apocalyptic sign*
of the tree (12:1*), and so on (see 11:6 ff.).

The history of Israel is the reverse of what God has now
done through Jesus: God tried to give the covenant to the
"older/former people" but they proved themselves to be
unworthy by various sins and errors, especially their failure
to understand correctly (i.e., gnostically—see §5:1–2) what
God intended (2:9; 9:4 f.; 10:1–12; 12:10; 16:1 f.). Thus
they never really received the covenant (4:7 f. = 14:1 ff.),
but it was reserved for the "new people." They are "men in
whom sins are complete" (8:1 f., cf. 5:11; 12:2a, 5b; 14:5a),
forsaken by God (4:14) because they have forsaken him

(11:2*; cf. 8:7). The history of the "new people" is just the opposite—although formerly full of sins (5:9; 11:11; 14:5; 16:7), they are now "a people of inheritance" (6:19; 13:1–6; 14:4) who receive the covenant through Jesus (14:4–5). Thus Christians operate under the "new law of our Lord Jesus Christ" (2:6—an interpolated context?), which is in fact *the true law,* and is "new" only by way of contrast to the incorrect, literal (cultic) interpretation of Mosaic law which prevailed in Israel (3:6 "their law") through the work of a "wicked angel" (9:4b; cf. 10:9). This true law does not impose itself as a yoke which necessitates mechanical obedience (2:6), but is a matter of correct (gnostic, pneumatic; §5: 1–2) understanding—understanding which Moses himself exhibited when he received God's covenant of righteous ordinances (10:1–2, 9; cf. 4:7 f. = 14:2 f.), and which also was granted David (10:10; cf. 12:10). Whereas God never really found a dwelling place in his old creation Israel—they put their hope on a building, not in him (16:1 f.)—the newly created people are becoming his habitation through Jesus' indwelling the believer and the community (6:14–16; 16: 7–10). Israel rejected God, the foundation of life which could provide "baptism which conveys forgiveness of sins" and built their own cistern which leads to death (11:1–2); but Christians wash away their sins and filth in the water which leads to eternal life (11:11a). Israel jumped to the conclusion that the covenant God had given Moses (but which they lost before Moses could give it to them [4:7]) was irrevocably theirs—that it was a sure thing, forever valid (4:6b). But Pseudo-Barnabas warns his readers that Israel was rejected despite all God did for her, and that Christians must *never* adopt this attitude that salvation is assured without question (4:14; see §5:4).

7. *Jesus: His Role in Salvation and Titles.* The decisive fact which has made it possible for the once-sinful people to become God's new people is the appearance of Jesus "in flesh" (5:6, 10, 11; 6:7, 9, 14; see 12:10) to suffer "for us" (5:1–5; 7:2[9]; 14:4) and provide forgiveness "for our sins"

(5:1 f.; 7:3). So also his apostles were sent out with the message of "forgiveness of sins" (8:3), by which the heart is purified from its corruption (5:1; 8:1-3; 11:11; cf. 14:5) and the recipient becomes a new creature (6:11; 16:8) in whom Jesus actually dwells (6:14-16; 16:9 f.). Strangely enough, Barnabas nowhere suggests that subjective "repentance" is a prerequisite for such forgiveness. The word "repentance" occurs only in 16:9 (and 5:9 var.—a scribal addition?), where it seems to be a gift bestowed on the believer (at baptism?) when he turns to the Lord.

Pseudo-Barnabas shows little interest in or awareness of Jesus' earthly life. The birth and baptism receive no mention, although there is a general reference to Jesus' ministry (5:8; cf. 4:14), to his choice of apostles (5:9), and to the drink offered him on the cross (7:3). Most important, however, is the fact that he "endured suffering in the flesh" at the hands of men, to bring forgiveness (5:1), to destroy death and exhibit the resurrection (5:5; see 15:9, where Easter Day and the ascension are noted), to fulfill the promise to the fathers and prepare the new people (5:7; 14:1b, 6), and to bring to a grand total the sins of those who oppose God's agents (5:11; 14:5a).

Jesus is no ordinary man or prophet. He is "Son of God" and "Lord" who had been active in creation (5:5, 10; 6:12) and will ultimately judge (5:7; 7:2, 9; 12:9*; 15:5; cf. 4:12; 21:3)—yet he suffered in the flesh "for us" (5:1-2, 9-11; 7:2[9]; 14:4). He was "prepared" with this end in view, to appear and liberate enslaved sinners, and to establish God's covenant with them (14:5b). Because Jesus is the "beloved heir" (4:3; 14:5), the Christians in whom he dwells are the "true heirs" of the promise (§5:6). Indeed, there is a sense in which Jesus not only receives and inherits the covenant, but he *is* the covenant in us, established by a word (see 14:4b-7; §5:8). Just as Jesus participated in the old creation (5:5* = 6:12*; 5:10), he is active as creator now (6:11 ff.) and will ultimately "make all things new" (15:5, 7 f.; see 6:13).

The most frequent designation for Jesus is "Lord," especially in the material that emphasizes his suffering (chs. 5–8;
see also 1:1; 2:6; 14:4, etc.), although the same title also is
freely used for God (see §5:9)—a fact which makes precise
interpretation difficult in many passages (e.g., 8:7; 16:8; 19:
9b, etc.). As we shall see (§5:9), Jesus' functions often seem
to overlap with those of God. Among other titles for Jesus,
"Beloved One" is the most notable (3:6; 4:3, 8).[11] "Christ"
occurs as a name (with Jesus) in the Greek textual tradition
only at 2:6, where it might well be secondary, although **L**
includes it also at 1:1 (so also **CO**) and 17:2—the salutation
and conclusion! In 12:10–11* the Greek *Christos* clearly
carries its original force of "Messiah." The contrast drawn in
12:10 between "man's son" and "Son of God" is not necessarily a conscious reflection of the (Synoptic Gospels') title
"Son of man," although such a possibility cannot be excluded
entirely. Notice that in the same context, "Son of David" is
rejected as an appropriate title! "Servant" is applied to Jesus
only in quotations (6:1*; 9:2*; cf. 5:2*), and quotations also
supply such titles as "Stone/Rock" (6:2 f.*), "Day" (? 6:4*),
and "Righteous One" (6:7*). The shorthand title "the Name"
(see §9:8) is employed only in 16:8b; other references to
"the Name" are more clearly defined: "of the Lord" (1:1;
16:6*, 7, 8*; 19:5), and, by implication, "of Jesus" (= Joshua,
12:8 f.).

8. *The Function of the "Word."* Although Jesus is never
called *Logos,* or "Word," as such, the epistle exhibits a fairly
developed "theology of the Word." It is by his word (*logos*)
that the Lord (Jesus?) established the covenant with (or in)
"us" (14:5). It is through the word (*logos*) that "we" have
been made alive (6:17), and that others will obtain the hope
(11:8 [*rhema,* not *logos*], 19:10c [*logos;* cf. Did. 4:2]). The
Christian is to honor those who spoke the word to him (19:9
= Did. 4:1), to observe the words he has heard (19:4d =

---

[11] See also Eph. 1:6; Ign. Smyrn. (start); Odes Sol. 3:8; 8:24; 38:11 (cf.
1 Clem. 59:2 f.); Hermas, Sim. 9:12:5; Justin, *Dial.* 137:2.

Did. 3:8), and to avoid speaking God's word in unworthy
situations (19:4b). The indwelling Lord speaks out through
us with words (*rhemata*) which astound the listener (16:10;
cf. 6:14 f.; 10:11c). Although the seeds of this approach are
already present in the Two Ways tradition, Barnabas places
greater emphasis on the role of the "word" in salvation.[12]

9. *God: Creator and Sovereign.* The eternality (18:2) and
universal sovereignty of God (16:2*; 21:5) are not compro-
mised in Barnabas, despite the warning that Satan has "authority" during the present eschatological crisis (§5:3). God
is the creator of universe and man (2:10*; 5:5 = 6:12 [in
connection with the Son]; 15:3; 16:1; 19:2a [cf. Did. 1:2];
20:2h–i [= Did. 5:2h–i]), and he both rules the course of history—past (e.g., 12:5), present (e.g., 19:6c), and future (e.g.,
4:3; 15:4)—and is the true Lord of all men, without prejudice
(19:7c; 20:2h). The title of "Lord" is widely applied to God
(as also to Jesus, §5:7), especially in scriptural quotations
(e.g., chs. 2–3). He is also called the "Father" (2:9; 12:8;
14:6), "Master" (1:7; 4:3), and the "Patient One" (3:6). He
has sent his Son Jesus for man's salvation (see 14:7 f.; §5:7),
and both "Lord Jesus" and "Lord God" seem to be involved
in such functions as creating (5:5 = 6:12; 15:8; 16:8, etc.),
revealing gnosis of salvation-history (see 1:7; 5:3; 6:10; 12:8;
17:1; 5:6 seems to indicate Jesus; Spirit is also active here—
see §5:2:20), dwelling in the Christian (see 6:14b [Jesus];
16:8 [God]), judging (see 4:12; 7:2, etc.), reigning (4:13;
8:5 [Jesus]; 11:5*, etc.)—in fact, almost the same formula is
used of each in 5:5 (Jesus) and 21:5 (God), "Lord over the
whole world." Probably neither Pseudo-Barnabas nor his tradition saw any need to exercise much care in such matters.
Pragmatically speaking at least, Jesus' acts were God's acts,

---

[12] For similar emphases in other early Christian authors, see also Rom.
10:8 ff., 1 Pet. 1:23 ff., Jas. 1:18. Much of the impetus for this approach
seems to derive from Deut. 30:11–14, which provides the background for
Paul as for the author of Baruch 3:29 f. (on "wisdom"), and which links the
idea of God's present, indwelling word (LXX, *rhema*) with the Two Ways
symbolism (cf. Deut. 6:6 f.; 11:18 f., 26 ff.).

and a general use of the title "Lord" included both figures in the picture.

10. *"Spirit" and "spirit."* One expects, at this point, a summary of the role of the "Holy Spirit" in Barnabas. Almost everything that can be said has been said in another connection (§5:2:20). Nowhere in Barnabas is there an unambiguous reference to the "Spirit" as a separate entity/person/hypostasis of the Godhead. The best possibilities seem to be 6:14 (an ambiguous parenthetical comment concerning the Lord's foreknowledge), 9:2 var. (where the text is corrupt and the "spirit" reference probably is a gloss), 12:2 (the "spirit" prompts Moses), 14:9* (citing Isa. 61:1, the prophetic spirit), and 19:7 = Did. 4:10 (a translation/interpretation problem, see §9:10). All but the last instance are clearly connected with revelation/prophecy, which (as we have seen) characterizes the general use of the concept in Barnabas.

11. *The Community: Its Organization, Practices, and Background.* Finally, what clues can we gather from Barnabas concerning the background, practices, and beliefs of the recipients? Clearly they are a community (or group of communities), a fellowship of believers—and are exhorted to remain so and not to slip into individualism (4:10; 6:16; 16:8; 19:10 [= Did. 4:2]; 21:2, 4). If the Two Ways tradition is characteristic of this community—and this cannot be taken for granted—their social concern approached the communal life of Acts 2–5, at least in terms of sharing possessions (19:8 f. [= Did. 4:8, 5]; cf. 21:2b). It is doubtful that much weight should be placed on the allusion to slaves and masters (19:7), etc. There is nothing in the epistle that enables us to determine how the community was organized, or how its worship was conducted. Apart from the references to the ministry of the "teachers" (see §4:3, §9:3—"prophetic" figures? [cf. 16:9]), there are only vague allusions to "those in authority" (or perhaps, "those economically prosperous"? [21:2]) and to those "who proclaim the Lord's word" (19:9b [= Did. 4:1]; cf. 10:11c; 16:10). Sunday seems to have been

observed (weekly?) as a "day of rejoicing" in commemora-
tion of Jesus' resurrection, apparently to the exclusion of the
traditional Jewish Sabbath-rest (15:8 f.). Of the "sacra-
ments," only baptism is mentioned. It is the occasion for
remission of sins (§5:7) and entrance into new life (11:1, 11;
cf. 6:11; 16:8). Apparently immersion was practiced (11:
11), but no other details are given. With respect to ethnic
background, both Pseudo-Barnabas and his recipients seem
to be non-Jewish. The contrast between "us" and "them"
(Israel, the [cultic] Jews) is repeatedly drawn (see esp. 3:6;
4:6–8; 5:2–8, 12; 6:7; 8:1–3; 9:4 f.), and the community is
expressly identified with uncircumcised Gentiles (13:7; 14:
5–8; cf. 3:6; 16:7–9). Nowhere does the author-editor attempt to distinguish himself from them in this respect (see
e.g., 16:7), but he writes as one of them (1:8; 4:6).

§6. Questions of Higher Criticism: Date, Authorship, Origin

It is customary for commentaries to deal with such matters as date, author, destination, place of origin, and so forth,
somewhere near the outset of the introductory remarks. Once
the general category of "evolved literature" (§1) is taken
seriously, however, these (frequently enigmatic) problems
are seen to be of less than primary importance. In fact, for
writings such as Barnabas and the Didache, such questions
can receive adequate treatment only after problems of
sources and approach have been examined. The complex
background of evolved literature requires that at least three
kinds of higher critical examination be made: (1) to determine the background of each of the various tradition blocks
employed in the writing—to some extent, the commentary
attempts to deal with this problem; (2) to examine any inter-
mediate stages of compilation between the various individual
blocks and the present form—see §4:4; cf. §8; and (3) to ask
the more usual questions of authorship, date, and so on,
about the "final" form of the writing which has been preserved for us. In the limited space available here, we cannot

hope to pursue each line of approach with the necessary
detail. Nevertheless, it is worthwhile to summarize the direc-
tion(s) in which the present research points.

1. *Undisputed Early Use in the East.* Although it has
sometimes been argued that earlier writers used Barnabas
(esp. Justin, Irenaeus; see §6:8, 10), Clement of Alexandria
(*ca.* 190) is the first indisputable witness to the existence of
the epistle. Not only does Clement claim to quote from Barnabas on eight different occasions in his *Stromateis* ("Miscel-
lanies"),[13] but he identifies the author as the "apostle" Barnabas (see Acts 14:4, 14), "one of the seventy [see Luke
10:1 ff.] and a co-worker with Paul" (see Acts 11:25–15:39;
1 Cor. 9:6; Gal. 2:1; Ps.-Clem. *Hom.* 1:9, etc.). According to
Eusebius (*ca.* 325), Clement's (now lost) *Hypotyposeis*
("Outlines") included commentary on "Jude and the other
general epistles, and Barnabas and the Apocalypse attributed
to Peter" (*H.E.* 6:14:1). Origen, who re-established the
Alexandrian "catechetical school" after Clement fled from
Egypt (see also §6:7), calls Barnabas "a general epistle" and
cites Barnabas 5:9 (*Contra Celsus* 1:63) as well as comment-
ing on the "Hebrew names" in the epistle. Eusebius, who also
represents the Alexandrian school tradition, classifies the
epistle both among the "disputed writings" (*H.E.* 6:13:6–
6:14:1) and among the "illegitimate" (3:25:4; see §10:2) in
his discussions of religiously authoritative literature (NT
"canon"). Indeed, in the mid-fourth century, Serapion of
Thmuis (in the Nile Delta) also cites Barnabas (5:5 or 6:12)
as by the "apostle," and apparently considers the epistle to
be in some sense authoritative.[14] Barnabas' near-canonical

---

[13] Actually, *Str.* 6:(8):64:3 cites 1 Clem. 48:4, not Barnabas. The other
seven quotations occur in 2:(6):31:2 (Barn. 1:5, 2:2 f.), 2:(7):35:5 (Barn.
4:11), 2:(15):67:1–3 (Barn. 10:10, 1), 2:(18):84:3 (Barn. 21:5–6, 9),
2:(20):116:3–117:4 (Barn. 16:7–9), 5:(8):51:2–52:2 (Barn. 10:11 f., 4),
5:(10):63:1–6 (Barn. 6:5, 8–10).
[14] Text in G. Wobbermin, *TU* 17:3b (1899), 21 (frg. 31:2). It has also
been claimed that Anastasius of Sinai (*ca.* 700) referred to the epistle by
name, but I have not yet been able to locate the exact passage.

status in early Eastern Christianity also finds support in Codex Sinaiticus (§3:2).

2. *Evidence from the West and in Lists of Books.* Among Western Christian fathers, the epistle has left almost no impact. Jerome (*ca.* 400) knew it as the work of the "apostle" and classified it among New Testament apocrypha (*Vir. Illust.* 6). He also commented on the symbolism of various "Hebrew names" in Barnabas, following Origen's treatment (§6:1). Once he expressly refers to Barnabas 8:2 (*In Ezek.* 43:19), and elsewhere he attributes a saying about the hypersinfulness of the apostles (Barn. 5:9; see also Origen!) to "Ignatius" (*Adv. Pelagius* 3:2). But at best, Jerome is an Eastern-oriented Westerner. The only other clear evidence that Barnabas was known in the early Latin-speaking church comes from the Latin version (§3:5), which might have existed as early as the third century (from North Africa?). Although Tertullian (*ca.* 200, North Africa) and his admirer Novatian (*ca.* 250, Rome) believed that the "apostle" Barnabas had written an epistle dealing with things Jewish, they identified Hebrews, not Barnabas (if they even knew the latter) with that supposed author. Possibly the "Epistle of Barnabas" mentioned in the Latin stichometric canonical list of Codex Claromontanus (sixth century) actually refers to Hebrews (but see C. F. Andry, *JBL* 70 [1951], 233 ff.; and §10:2). Two Greek lists also mention the "Epistle of Barnabas"—the "List of Sixty Books" (*ca.* 600) places it among the "apocrypha," and the "Stichometry of Nicephorus" (*ca.* 820) among the "disputed books"—and almost certainly have our Barnabas in view (see also §10:2). Finally, the Armenian chronicler Mkhitar (thirteenth century) lists Barnabas as a "disputed" general epistle.

3. *Summary of the Traditional View.* In summary, then, the dominant (i.e., Eastern) traditional view of Barnabas is that (1) it is a "general epistle" (Origen, Mkhitar; cf. Clement, Eusebius) rather than a letter addressed to a particular community (cf. §4:3; §5:11), (2) written by the (Hellen-

istic) Jewish Levite of Cyprus (see Acts 4:36) who had received his commission from Jesus himself as one of the "seventy" (Clement) and had subsequently ministered as a companion of Paul—the "apostle" Barnabas (Clement, Eusebius, Jerome, Serapion, MSS of family **G**, cf. Origen). The date implied by this view would necessarily be in the middle or late first century. None of the known traditions provide information as to place of origin or general sphere of circulation of this "general epistle." Acts 15:39 leaves Barnabas in Cyprus, his alleged homeland, while 1 Cor. 9:6 implies that he reached Corinth. Eusebius and Jerome are silent about his subsequent ministry, although a later tradition associates his name with the beginnings of Christianity at Milan. Alternatively, the Pseudo-Clementine *Homilies* pictures Barnabas as the founder of Alexandrian Christianity (! compare §6:7, 12).

4. *Date: The Epistle's Evidence and Its Interpretation.* For the past three centuries critical scholarship has struggled to evaluate the traditional view and to suggest new solutions where they seemed to be necessary. The epistle itself proved to be of little assistance here. About the only precise piece of evidence it contains that is directly relevant for this discussion is found in 16:3–5, which presupposes that "the city and the Temple" have been destroyed "because of their making war," and that the Temple site was still in ruins. Thus our form of Barnabas 1–17 seems to have been published after the Jewish revolt in 66–70, when the Temple fell, and before Hadrian's workmen erected a Roman Temple to Zeus-Jupiter on the same site around the year 135.

Attempts to pinpoint the date of writing with more precision on the basis of 16:4, which anticipates the rebuilding of the "Temple" in some sense, are beset with difficulties: (1) the text of 16:4 is in some doubt, although probably it refers only to the efforts of "the servants of the enemies," and not to Jewish participation (so MS **S**) in the project; (2) although it is doubtful, it is not impossible that 16:4 is speaking of the *spiritual* Temple built in Gentile hearts (16:6–10) rather than the physical building; (3) but even if it is taken to refer to an expected rebuilding of a physical temple at Jerusalem, it is not clear whether this is viewed as a Jewish or a Roman temple. In either case, our knowledge of the rumors, threats, and promises which may have circulated between the years 70–135 is insufficient to inspire confident speculation, although if a Roman temple is meant, the latter part of that period becomes more probable.[15]

Finally, the mention of kings and kingdoms in Barnabas 4:4–5 has sometimes been scoured for indications of date. This is a futile quest, however, for several reasons: (1) the "evidence" is contained in stock apocalyptic phraseology which was applied over and over again at various periods of history from the time of "Daniel" onward—usually "history" was made to fit the symbolism, and not vice versa; (2) even if it were possible to identify some clear historical situation behind the symbolism, that would not necessarily be the situation of the final form of Barnabas, but only of the apocalyptic source quoted; (3) the lack of editorial comment in 4:4–5 and the vague exhortation at the end of the section (4:6a) inspire little confidence that Pseudo-Barnabas had in mind any precise historical identifications for this material.

Indeed, even if an exact date for the writing of the final form of Barnabas could be established, we would still be faced with the equally, if not more, important task of determining the age of *the materials* used by the final author-editor. Some of these certainly antedate the year 70, and are in some sense "timeless" traditions of Hellenistic Judaism (e.g., the food law allegories of ch. 10, the Two Ways). It is with such materials that much of the importance of the epistle for our understanding of early Christianity and its late-Jewish heritage rests.

---

[15] Specific treatments of the problem of date include A. L. Williams, *JTS* 34 (1933), 337 ff.; L. W. Barnard, *Journal of Egyptian Archaeology* 44 (1958), 101 ff.

5. *Authorship: The Traditional View and Its Critics.* On the problem of authorship, the epistle is as good as silent. Apart from the title and subscription in the various manuscripts, no name is mentioned. As we have seen, the author was probably an itinerant "Teacher" (§4:3; cf. §9:3) who was trained in a school tradition closely related to Hellenistic Judaism (§4:1–2), and who wished to instruct his recipients in how to live during these perilous last times (§5:3–4). He is especially concerned that his readers correctly understand God's historical dealings with man lest they be tempted to lapse into cultic Judaism (?) or become overconfident in their Christianity (§5:4, 6, 11). Despite this Jewish atmosphere, however, there is reason to believe that both the author and the recipients were ethnically non-Jewish (§5:11). But not all commentators subscribe to this interpretation; Pseudo-Barnabas has even been pictured as a converted Rabbi.[16]

One view that is almost universally shared by recent scholarship is that the "apostle" Barnabas did not write the epistle. Although some of the reasons advanced have been less than "scientific" (e.g., Barn. 10 is "unworthy of an apostle"!), it can scarcely be denied that the cumulative evidence does not favor the traditional attribution—the post-70 date and the possibly non-Jewish authorship are probably the strongest single obstacles. But it should also be emphasized that the "apostle" Barnabas is an almost unknown figure to us, and that even what little information is contained in Acts is not entirely above suspicion. There is no legitimate way to exclude the possibility that an early missionary-apostle named Barnabas who once traveled with Paul is responsible for transmitting some, or even much, of the material now contained in the epistle, perhaps by way of a sort of "Barnabean school," which preserved and promulgated his teachings

---

[16] So J. Muilenburg, K. Thieme, L. W. Barnard; J. V. Bartlet held a sort of "compromise" view that Pseudo-Barnabas was a former proselyte to Judaism who later became a Christian.

(and from which Hebrews also came?; see §6:2, 12). But this can neither be "proved" nor "disproved" with the available evidence, and it best accords with both the situation and the modern critical temperament to refer to the author-editor as Pseudo-Barnabas.

6. *The Problem of Background and Origin.* There remains one large and important problem area for which the traditional view has not formulated a clear answer. In what part of the early Christian world was this Barnabean approach to Christianity popular? Where was Pseudo-Barnabas trained in his ethical-eschatological-gnostic approach? Where did this community (or these communities, if it was sent as a general letter) exist which believed in such a way? And furthermore, whence did the various traditions which are now united in Barnabas originate?

It is impossible to deal adequately with such interrelated questions in the brief scope of this introduction. A complete investigation would require detailed comparison, both positive and negative, between the epistle and nearly every piece of literature preserved from the Judeo-Christian world of the first three centuries or so. But at least a survey of the material is in order, and since our basic question is one of location, a geographical approach seems to be the most satisfactory.

7. *Alexandrian Affinities.* The most obvious starting point for this investigation is the Near Eastern world in general and Alexandria in particular. It is in the Alexandrian school tradition that we first hear of the epistle, and it is with Clement of Alexandria that Barnabas reached its highest known plateau of popularity and influence (§6:1). There is a real sense in which Clement is still the best commentary on Barnabas. Not only does he quote from the epistle, but he breathes the same atmosphere of gnosis [17] (§5:1–2), ethical

---

[17] Note the excerpt from Clement's *Hypotyposeis* cited by Eusebius, *H.E.* 2:1:4 f.–"To James the Just and John and Peter, the Lord after the resurrection committed the 'gnosis'; they committed it to the other apostles, and the other apostles to 'the 70,' of whom Barnabas also was one." Elsewhere, Clement refers to Barn. 6:8–10 as containing a trace of "gnostic tradition" which few have been privileged to approach (*Str.* 5:[10]:63:1–6).

parenesis in the quest for salvation (§5:4–5), Hellenistic
Jewish interests and methods (§4:1–2), and so forth. Sometimes he presents material which is quite similar to Barnabas
but for which he does not seem to be entirely dependent on
the epistle (see Barn. 2:4—3:6; 6:10b, ch. 10, etc.). Sometimes he expands on the Barnabas material in such a way as
to suggest that he knows a living school tradition of which
Barnabas represents an earlier stage (esp. ch. 10). In short,
although it would not be amiss to call Clement a student of
Barnabas, it might be even more to the point to describe
them as earlier and later products of the same Christian en-
vironment/school. That is to say, even if Clement had never
read the epistle, he probably would have thought in the same
ethical-gnostic-Jewish categories. This was his training, as it
was Pseudo-Barnabas'. The main point of difference between
them (apart from Clement's obviously superior literary tal-
ents and philosophical orientation) seems to be in the area
of eschatology (§5:3), which is present in Clement but is not
nearly so vivid and so vital as in Barnabas.

So far so good. But whence did Clement derive this approach to Christianity? And where did he come across the
epistle? It is doubtful that he was a native of Alexandria
(although one tradition claims this), and his early life, by
his own confession, brought him into contact with both the
western (Southern Italy, Greece) and the eastern (Syria,
Palestine) Hellenistic world in search of the best available
teachers of his day. He claims to have studied under teachers
from Ionia, Egypt, Palestine (a Hebrew!), and East Syria
(Str. 1:1:11). It is not clear when Clement finally settled in
Alexandria, but he found there his favorite—and last—teacher,
Pantaenus, a former Stoic philosopher (of Sicilian origin?)
who came to Alexandria after a period of "missionary work"
in the East ("India"!) and became leader of the catechetical
school during the last two decades of the second century.
Clement taught in the school and ultimately succeeded Pantaenus as its head. Soon after the turn of the third century

(*ca.* 203), he found it expedient to leave Egypt because of
Roman persecution, and spent the final decade or so of his
life in Cappadocia and Antioch.[18]

The following considerations suggest that, wherever Clement first came across Barnabas, he was not responsible for
introducing the "Barnabean approach" to the catechetical
school at Alexandria: (1) Clement considered Pantaenus to
be the greatest of his several teachers, and he came into
contact with him in Alexandria—thus it is extremely unlikely
that Clement's mature thought disagreed seriously with Pantaenus; (2) Clement succeeded Pantaenus as head of this
school, which had existed from early times (if we can believe
Eusebius)—thus his mature ideas probably accorded not only
with those of Pantaenus, but with the traditional approach
of the Alexandrian Christianity represented by the school;
(3) finally, the youthful Origen, a native Egyptian (from
Alexandria?) who stepped into the gap created by Clement's
voluntary exile and whose earliest contacts with the Alexandrian school (through his father?) must have taken place
when both Pantaenus and Clement were active, continued
to employ the general approach to Christianity which domi-
nates Barnabas-Clement. This tends to confirm the impression that the common denominator here is the "ancient tradition" of the Alexandrian catechetical school, not any peculiar importation of ideas by individual teachers such as
Clement or even Pantaenus.

Unfortunately, there is no undisputed literary evidence
from this Christian catechetical school prior to Clement.
Nevertheless, the thread of "sacred studies" at Alexandria
does become visible at a much earlier date and in a Jewish
setting in the figures of Philo (*ca.* A.D. 30) and his Alexandrian predecessors such as Aristobulus (*ca.* 150 B.C.) and

---

[18] See Eusebius, *H.E.* 5:10–11 and the notes in the edition of H. J. Lawlor
and J. E. L. Oulton (London, 1927–1928). Also J. Quasten, *Patrology* 2
(Westminster, Md., 1953), 4–6. Probably Clement was born in Athens, *ca.*
150, of "pagan" parents, and died *ca.* 215.

Pseudo-Aristeas (second century B.C.?). Not only do Clement and Origen know of these authors, but the Christian school shares the approach of the Hellenistic Jewish school on such matters as the emphasis on special understanding, ethical instruction, and "allegorical" exegesis. It is mainly on the matter of eschatology that Philo and the Christian Alexandrians part company. Whether the lack of eschatological interest is an idiosyncrasy of Philo, or was also shared by the tradition in which he stands, is difficult to determine because of the scarcity of sources. Despite this difference, it seems probable that there was some sort of rough continuity between the Alexandrian Jewish school of sacred studies represented by Philo, and the Alexandrian Christian catechetical school of Pantaenus-Clement-Origen.

How does Barnabas relate to this situation? The epistle is best known at Alexandria and its approach can be called Alexandrian in such matters as exegetical gnosis and ethical parenesis. Eschatology, however, plays a much larger role, relatively speaking, in Barnabas than among the Alexandrians (Jewish or Christian). Furthermore, the absence of a personalized "Logos" theology in Barnabas (cf. §5:8), and indeed, Pseudo-Barnabas' lack of philosophical orientation, would be strange if Barnabas represents a continuing Alexandrian school tradition such as has been outlined above. In terms of specific traditions, Barnabas has its closest affinities with the Alexandrians in chapters 2–3, 9–10, and 12–13; possibly also 6:8–19; 11:8–11; 16:6–10, and the Two Ways (see §10:7) could be considered Alexandrian, but this is less clear (cf. §6:9).

8. *Palestinian Affinities.* As we move farther to the East in search of parallels, there is also reason to suggest Palestinian and Syrian affinities for some of the epistle's material. The recent discoveries at Qumran, for example, reveal a type of Semitic-speaking Judaism which existed in the first century of our era and which shares with Barnabas a vital concern for attaining "knowledge" of the past, present, and

future by means of enlightened study of "scripture." [19] Furthermore, eschatology is of great interest at Qumran (including apocalptic imagery), and a Two Ways approach similar to Barnabas 18 is attested.[20] Finally, both the Qumranites and Barnabas' tradition show a wide acquaintance with other revered Jewish writings alongside the Old Testament. Judaism in general, and Semitic Judaism in particular, emphasized a strongly ethical approach such as we find in Barnabas (cf. Tobit, Sirach, the Rabbis, etc.), while Barnabas' apocalyptic materials resemble the late-Jewish apocalyptic traditions which seem to have been nourished in Semitic-speaking Judaism, although they soon blossomed out into the world at large (see esp. the Daniel, Enoch, and Ezra cycles). Indeed, the combination of ethical parenesis in an apocalyptic setting can also be amply illustrated in this literature (see esp. the Testaments of the Twelve Patriarchs, 2 Enoch). In another direction, the *halakic* material used in Barnabas 7–8, and the Moses *haggada* in 12:1–7 are closely paralleled in extant Rabbinic literature.

Thus far, the more or less "Palestinian" parallels mentioned derive from a Semitic-speaking Judaism (although many of the ethical and apocalyptic writings were quickly translated into Greek, where their evolution continued). But there is no reason to think that Pseudo-Barnabas knew a Semitic language, or that any of his immediate sources were not in Greek. Thus it is important to uncover whatever scant information has been preserved from *Hellenistic* Palestinian thought. Probably Paul would have included himself in this category (see Gal. 1:14; Phil. 3:5 f.; cf. Acts 22:3), and in-

---

[19] See, e.g., the Qumran *Hymns* (1:21; 2:13; 4:27 ff.; 11:3 f., etc.) on how God grants knowledge of the wonderful mysteries, or the *Habakkuk Commentary* 7:1–5 on the things to come (cf. *Damascus Document* 1:10–12). Concerning "knowledge" in the Dead Sea Scrolls, see W. D. Davies, *Harvard Theological Review* 46 (1953), 113 ff. (reprinted in his *Christian Origins and Judaism*, Philadelphia, 1962); on the use of scripture, see F. F. Bruce, *Biblical Exegesis in the Qumran Texts* (London, 1959).

[20] See J.-P. Audet, *Revue Biblique* 59–60 (1952–1953), 219 ff., 41 ff.

deed, he shares with Barnabas ideas such as a special "gnosis"
for believers whose hearts are "circumcised" (Rom. 2:28–29;
1 Cor. 8:1 ff.; 14:6; 2 Cor. 11:6, etc.; cf. Luke 11:52), and an
eschatology in which Satan's present power is acknowledged
(2 Cor. 2:11; cf. Eph. 2:2 f.), although Christians are already
participating in the "new creation" (2 Cor. 5:17) as "temples"
of God (1 Cor. 3:16; 6:19). "Stephen's Speech" in Acts 7
also resembles Barnabas in its picture of Moses on Sinai,
Jewish rebelliousness, and the significance of the Temple,
although one cannot be sure that the "Speech" actually represents the views of a Palestinian Hellenistic Jewish Christian.[21] Finally, in the second century the figure of Justin
emerges from a non-Jewish, Palestinian background. Unfortunately, we cannot tell what role (if any) his homeland
played in the development of his Christian thought. After
his conversion to Christianity, Justin traveled as an itinerant
"philosopher"-teacher. He was especially active in the area
of Ephesus, and ultimately founded a school in Rome where
he met his death as a martyr (ca. 165). His affinities with
Barnabas include not only the use of similar traditional materials [22] (see esp. ch. 7; 11:2 f.; ch. 12), but a gnostic approach to exegesis like that of the Alexandrian tradition (e.g.,
Dial. 99:3, 112:3), a breadth of available sources, and similar
ethical emphases.

The differences between Barnabas and these various types
of "Palestinian"(?) thought should not be neglected. Qumranic eschatological exegesis is much more concrete (or "his-
toricized") than what we find in Barnabas, and sometimes
seems to be carried out for its own sake (contrast §5:3–4).
Nor is Qumran anticultic to the same extent (or for the same
reasons) as Barnabas. The Rabbis tend to suppress apocalyptic ideas to concentrate on law, which deviates sharply from
Barnabas' approach. Pauline concepts of how salvation is

[21] L. W. Barnard has made some comparisons between "Stephen's Speech"
and Barnabas in New Testament Studies 7 (1960/61), 31 ff.

[22] Windisch and others argue that Justin had read Barnabas, but the evidence is not compelling.

obtained (cf. §5:4, 7), why Moses' legislation was given (2 Cor. 3; Gal. 3; cf. §5:6), and so forth, also are foreign to Barnabas. "Stephen's Speech" can refer without comment to Abraham's "covenant of circumcision" (Acts 7:8; contrast Barn. 9:6 ff.), and Justin's Christianity is far more "developed" (including a personalized "Logos" theology as at Alexandria, §6:7) than that of Barnabas. Nevertheless, especially the ethical-apocalyptic emphases of Barnabas and the specific traditions behind Barnabas 7–8 and 12:1–7 could be said to have a somewhat "Palestinian" flavor about them.

9. *Syrian Affinities.* Apart from the Hellenistic city of Antioch, there are few sources that can confidently be cited as products of Syrian Christianity before the end of the second century. (Tatian, who studied under Justin at Rome, is only a partial exception.) If we can accept the proposed East Syrian origin of the Odes of Solomon (probably from the second century; an Alexandrian origin also has been suggested), however, it will provide an excellent point of comparison with Barnabas. The rather "mystical" approach of the Odes is especially close to Barnabas 6:8–19, 11:8–11, and 16:6–10, while 5:6–7 also is paralleled in Ode 31:10 f., and such Christological titles as "Beloved One," "Rock," and "Righteous One" occur (cf. §5:7). Furthermore, there is evidence of Two Ways imagery in the Odes (see the commentary on Barn. 18:1). On the negative side, there is little in the Odes to resemble Barnabas' use of quotations and Old Testament sources, anticultic polemic, eschatological-apocalyptic atmosphere, and highly developed ethical emphases.

With respect to early Antiochene Christianity, Barnabas shares with Ignatius (*ca.* 110) a general ethical-eschatological orientation as well as some specific concepts like God indwelling believers as temples (Ign. Eph. 15:3; but see also Paul), but differs widely on the use of quoted materials interpreted gnostically and on specifics like the widespread "Son of David" Christology in Ignatius (contrast Barn. 12:10 f.). Further "Syrian" parallels of interest could be discussed if the suggestions that such documents as Matthew, the Gospel of Peter, the Gospel of Thomas, Didache, and so forth, may represent Syria were more firmly established. Also relevant would be a comparison between the ideas of Barnabas and the Syrian Acts of Thomas (third century?), with its poetic-mystical approach (like the Odes of Solomon).

10. *Affinities with Asia Minor.* The source situation with respect to Asia Minor is much better, with the "Johannine school" flourishing there at the end of the first century, and with Irenaeus recalling the words of his Asian teachers at the end of the second. In his two preserved writings, *Against Heresies* and the *Exhibition* (or *Demonstration*) *of the Apostolic Preaching*, Irenaeus shows numerous points of agreement with Barnabas, although he writes in a situation far different from the epistle. With reference to specific traditional materials embedded in Barnabas, Irenaeus is especially close to 2:4–3:6; 5:6 f., 13; 10:10 f. (?); 13:2; 14:5; 15:3–5, 8; and 18:1–2 (cf. also 1:5; 17:1). From a more theological viewpoint, there are definite similarities on such ideas as "recapitulation" (Barn. 5:11 uses this word) and its relation to salvation-history (§5:6); the relationship between "spirit," man, and revelation (§5:2:20); and millennial eschatology. It is no wonder that some commentators feel that Irenaeus may have read Barnabas (or heard Pseudo-Barnabas).[23] But equally possible is the suggestion that Barnabas reflects an earlier stage of the Christian approach which flowered in Irenaeus (via Asia Minor). It is unfortunate that only a few scraps of writing are preserved from the earlier Asian "Elders" such as Papias (*ca.* 130) and Polycarp (*ca.* 70–156). In his millennarian approach, Papias probably would have agreed to some extent with Barnabas 15:3–8. Similarly, general passages such as chapters 2 and 7 of Polycarp's preserved epistle(s) to the Philippians encourage the belief that he may have had an outlook similar to that of Barnabas. But this is mainly an argument from silence. Similarities between

---

[23] See H. Windisch (who thinks that the Asian "Mark the Gnostic" also may have known Barnabas); L.-M. Froidevaux, *Recherches de science religieuse* 44 (1956), 408 ff.

Barnabas and the Johannine literature are less striking, and need not be discussed here.

11. *Affinities with the West (Rome, North Africa)*. Finally, there are certain affinities between Barnabas and the West (Rome, North Africa) that should be mentioned. Nothing certain is known about the background of Clement of Rome (*ca.* 95), but the epistle which circulates under his name is like Barnabas in its frequent use of the Old Testament and related material (e.g., cf. Barn. 4:7 f.), which helps to give 1 Clement a definite Hellenistic Jewish cast, its references to special "gnosis" (1:2b; 36:2; 40:1; 41:4; 48:5; 59:2), and its ethical emphasis (including Two Ways ideas; see §2:7) with the promise of eschatological reward (e.g., chs. 33 ff.). A similar emphasis on conduct and promised reward permeates the (Roman) Shepherd of Hermas (early second century, including a Two Ways background)—and if the homily known as 2 Clement can be considered Roman (but Corinth and Alexandria also are claimed), the same might be said of it (note also the use of quotations and symbolic exegesis in 2 Clement; contrast Hermas). Perhaps this is the place to mention that especially in its apocalyptic materials (and gnostic exegesis), Barnabas shows some relationship to Hippolytus "of Rome" (*ca.* 225)—but it is almost certain that Hippolytus was trained in the East (Alexandria?), and thus he can scarcely be used as evidence for native (?) Roman ideas. Barnabas' attitude to Jewish law also could be compared to that of the Valentinian Gnostic Ptolemy (Rome?, late second century).

Of North African authors, only Tertullian (*ca.* 220) is directly relevant for this survey, although Cyprian's collection of *Testimonies* (*ca.* 250) sometimes resembles Barnabas in its use of proof-texts. In general, Tertullian's rigorous ethical approach can be compared with Barnabas; more specifically, Tertullian uses "scapegoat" and "cross" symbolism similar to Barnabas 7 and 12, and expects a millennium (see Barn. 15: 3 ff.). Otherwise the epistle has little in common with the Carthage lawyer who also had spent some time in Rome.

12. *Summary and Suggestions Concerning Origin.* Obviously this evidence does not justify dogmatic statements about the origin and background of the epistle. A large part of the problem is the fact that almost from the very beginning, Christian preachers and teachers crisscrossed the Mediterranean world in their travels. And already in the second century it apparently was not uncommon for young Christian students to search out famous teachers throughout the world. Thus Tatian the Syrian studied under Justin (from Palestine) in Rome, and Clement "of Alexandria" can tell of studying under a Syrian teacher in Greece. Undoubtedly this kind of mobility has contributed greatly to the "school" background of Pseudo-Barnabas, whether we picture various teachers coming to a fixed location where he encountered their teachings, or Pseudo-Barnabas himself seeking out various teachers (or something of each).

The most satisfactory explanation for the gnostic and parenetic focus of Barnabas' approach (§5:1–2, 4–5) would appear to involve Alexandrian influence. Similarly, it is tempting to link the anticultic thrust of Barnabas with the like-minded Judaism known to Philo (*Migr. Abr.* 89–93; see the commentary on Barn. 9–10; 15–16), apparently in the Alexandrian area. But it should be emphasized that this is *partly* because most of our knowledge about Hellenistic Jewish thought comes from Alexandria, and thus we can construct general theories about that city (as in §6:7); *partly* also, perhaps, because Alexandria exerted such a wide influence on the general intellectual climate of the Mediterranean world (including Rome). If we must look outside of Alexandria to explain certain other features such as the apocalyptic-eschatological atmosphere, and it is not at all certain that we must, Palestine and Asia Minor seem to be the leading contenders. There are also some other writings which might shed helpful light on this problem if we only knew their background: for example, the New Testament "Epistle" called "to the Hebrews" (from Alexandria? Rome?) uses Old Testament texts similarly and deals, on a more "philosophical" level, with the problems of Jewish history and cult. Even more striking are the similarities between Barnabas and the brief document preserved in 4 Ezra 1–2, which emphasizes Israel's rejection of God's covenant commandments, God's rejection of cultic law, the call of a new people to observe God's statutes, the imminence of the eschatological consummation which will bring "rest" to the righteous, and so forth. But what is the background of 4 Ezra 1–2? And what is its relationship to early Christian thought? Nor have we paid sufficient attention to the types of heterodox thought which were developing in the second century and which might possibly cast additional light on the epistle (e.g., G. Truth, G. Thomas, G. Philip—all recently discovered at Nag Hammadi).

Since the above evidence does not suggest a simple solution to the problem of Pseudo-Barnabas' background, the following hypothesis is offered by way of conclusion. Barnabas is the work of a Christian teacher whose thought, in general, is oriented toward Alexandria, and whose area of ministry is in northeast Egypt. He was not trained in the "classical" Philonic tradition, however, but in a related "school" which had both profited from that approach (or vice versa) and which was steeped in apocalyptic eschatology—a school which had access to a large stock of "ancient" Jewish sources alongside of the Old Testament. Perhaps it was a Christianized offspring of a Qumranlike Judaism in Greek dress—Philo attests the existence of certain Hellenistic Jews living near Alexandria (and elsewhere—also in Asia Minor?) who had several such "Qumranic" traits (the "Therapeutae" of De Vita Contemplativa), and the Qumran caves themselves have produced a few scraps of Greek literature, which suggests the existence of Greek-speaking sister communities. Barnabas' relationship to Asia Minor may then be explained by positing a widespread influence of such a school, or by suggesting that Pseudo-Barnabas had also studied (directly or indirectly) under an Asian teacher. Whatever the worth of this hypothesis, there does not appear

to be any simple solution to the problem of how, where, and
when so many different materials came to be combined in
such a peculiar way in the epistle. The western Mediterranean world does not particularly fit the situation, but we
have much to learn about the development of eastern Christianity at this early period.

THE DIDACHE

OR

TEACHING OF THE APOSTLES

§7. Various Forms of the Didache Tradition

In addition to the witnesses to the separate Two Ways tradition (§2:5) the following manuscripts and documents contain or are closely related to the form of the Didache with which we are directly concerned.

(1) **H** (Codex Hierosolymitanus) is the Bryennios manuscript described in §3:1, which contains the only known form of the full Didache in Greek. Its text of the Didache was first published by Bryennios in 1883, and facsimiles appeared in 1887, edited by J. R. Harris.

(2) **P.Ox** is the Greek Oxyrhynchus Papyrus No. 1782, dating from the late fourth century, which consists of two fragments of a codex, and preserves Didache 1:3b–4a and 2:7b–3:2a in a slightly variant form (with some significant expansion) from **H.**

(3) **Cop** is a fragment of a Coptic version (or possibly of an extract from such a version) from the fifth century and contains Didache 10:3b–12:2a, including the prayer for the oil in 10:8 (= **ApCo**).

(4) **Georg** is a complete Gregorian version preserved in a nineteenth-century manuscript at Constantinople (the translation itself may be as early as the fifth century). It lacks any equivalent to Didache 1:5–6 (cf. **ApCo**) and 13: 5–7. Although the complete **Georg** text has never been published, some variant readings were made available in 1932 (*Zeitschrift für die neutestamentliche Wissenschaft*, 31,

111 ff.). The title of the Didache in this manuscript includes the words "written in the year 90 or 100 after the Lord Christ"!

(5) **ApCo** is the Greek *Apostolic Constitutions* 7:1–32, which seems to derive from fourth-century Egypt and builds on an adapted form of the whole Didache. It is difficult to determine the precise relationship between **H** and the Didache tradition known to **ApCo**. It seems probable that **ApCo** or its immediate predecessors have reworked and streamlined the Didache, as well as adding numerous comments (especially scriptural quotations/allusions) to the basic Didache tradition. For example, the liturgical portions of the Didache appear in **ApCo** in a form which presents fewer problems to the fourth-century user: nothing is said of the alternative modes of baptism (Did. 7); the prayers of Didache 9–10 are reworked to fit a sacramental Eucharist with the more usual order of bread-cup, and the frequent repetition of "yours is the glory forever" is drastically curtailed. Similarly, the archaic rules governing prophets and apostles in Didache 11–13; 15 are removed, while "priests" and "presbyters" are introduced into these contexts. The apocalyptic material of chapter 16 is also streamlined—thus **ApCo** lacks the Barnabas parallel to Didache 16:2, as well as details about the "anti-Christ" figure in 16:4b and the conflagration of 16:5a. Numerous vague references to what is "said" (Did. 14:3a; 16:7) or to "the commandment" (1:5b; 13:5, 7) or to the words of "the Lord" and "the gospel" (11:3; 14:3; 15:4) are lacking in **ApCo**, along with such an explicit and identifiable reference as 9:5b. Only in Didache 11:2 does **ApCo** retain the term "didache" (teaching) itself. Finally, most allusions to "gnosis" and perfection/blamelessness (1:4; 1:5b; 6:2; 9:3; 11:2) have been removed along with the parenthetic address "my child" (3:1–6; 4:1). Some of these features may derive from the form of the Didache used by **ApCo**, but it would be risky to conjecture which. For the rest, it is clear that **ApCo** knows a form of the Didache quite close to **H**—it includes at least the first part of the "interpola-

tion" in Didache 1:3b ff. (but **ApCo** lacks 1:5b–2:1; cf.
Georg), and follows the general order of **H**'s text (the most
notable exception is 3:1–4, where the material of 3:3 *follows*
3:4). **ApCo** agrees with **Cop** in including the prayer for the
oil in 10:8, and has a few agreements with **P.Ox** against **H**.
Thus, for all its problems, **ApCo** also has some demonstrable
value in discussions of the textual history of the Didache.

(6) **Eth** indicates the Ethiopic version of the "Ecclesiastical Canons of the Apostles" (see §2:5:2), one of the many
church manuals derived, in one way or another, from the
Apostolic Tradition of Hippolytus which became so popular
in the East. Known from late manuscripts (fifteenth to eight-
eenth centuries), the Ethiopic Apostolic Tradition contains
an interpolated section (it is absent from the exactly parallel
contexts in the Sahidic and Arabic versions) as follows:
Ethiopic 52 (= Arabic 51, Sahidic 63b) deals with false
bishops, which leads to a discussion of false and true prophets. At this point the Ethiopic alone introduces a section (1)
admonishing the reader to avoid idolatry, corpses, blood,
things strangled, broken bones (in food?); (2) then Didache
11:3–13:7 (except for 11:6; 13:2) on false and true prophets; (3) then Didache 8:1–2a on "the hypocrites"; (4) then
on sabbath conduct of presbyters and lesser church officials,
the congregation at large, and reception of visitors. Thereafter the text resumes its agreement with Sahidic and Arabic
concerning gifts and false prophets, and promises to speak
next of how bishops are to be ordained.

§8. The Didache as a Community Tradition

1. *Kinds of Redactional Evidence.* Because the impersonal, composite character of the Didache is even more obvious than that of Barnabas (at least Barnabas provides some
personal glimpses of the author-editor, §4:3–4), the task of
distinguishing between the various traditional materials now
incorporated into the Didache is sometimes slightly less difficult. Three kinds of evidence are especially helpful: (1)

actual writings which obviously are closely related to the
Didache but which show a slightly different stage in the
development of the tradition (e.g., §2:5)—thus problems of
text as well as of redactional levels may be involved here;
(2) internal evidence from the present form(s) of the Didache itself that a certain amount of adaptation to changing
circumstances already has occurred; and (3) more subtle
matters of style and content which suggest the existence of
older, smaller units of tradition behind the present form of
the Didache.[1]

2. *Development as Attested by the Various Forms of the
Didache.* Not only is it true that the Didache and its materials are preserved and reworked into larger collections by
the church manual tradition in which it stands (see §2:5:2,
§7:5–6), but it sometimes happens that our extant witnesses to
this kind of use and reuse of traditional materials provide a
firsthand view of how the tradition evolved. We have already
mentioned certain features of the Two Ways section in the
Didache which seem to have developed independently from
the form known to Barnabas (§2:4). For the most part, we
have no real way of telling which of the modifications have
emerged only in the *final* stage of the editing of the Didache
(or of Barnabas, for that matter), which had already taken
place in the tradition *before* it came to the final author-
editor, and which are subsequent glosses. But occasionally
a passage can throw some clear light on the process. Didache
1:3b–2:1 is a case in point. For all practical purposes, this
"interpolation" is lacking in Dctr, Barnabas, and CO (also
Syntagma-Fides and Shenuti?). The more or less "non-
Synoptic" portion (1:5–6) is lacking in Georg and is greatly
abridged in ApCo. P.Ox contained at least the "Synoptic"
materials (1:3b–4a), and even knows a significantly *longer*
form of 1:4a! It is most probable, then, that this interpolation
into the Two Ways material is the responsibility of one of

---

[1] For a summary of J.-P. Audet's approach to these problems, see Robert
M. Grant, *The Apostolic Fathers: An Introduction* (New York, 1964), 73–74.

the most recent if not the final redactional level before the **H-Georg-P.Ox-ApCo** form of the Didache appeared. A similar piece of evidence is the "Prayer for the Ointment" in some witnesses (**Cop, ApCo**) to Didache 10:8. If this prayer was not already known to the **H-Georg** form of the Didache (which does not include it), it represents one of the very next redactional stages in the *continuing* evolution of the Didache.

3. *Major Internal Evidence of Development.* Certain other of the more recent stages of development in the Didache are indicated by such concessions and/or adaptations as the following:

6:2—the ideal is the "perfect" man who can "bear the entire yoke of the Lord," but this ideal has been adapted to a more realistic position: "do the best you can."

6:3 reads similarly—the ideal is to keep the food laws. But in the light of changing conditions and attitudes, at least "avoid food consecrated in pagan temples"!

7:2–3 shows a concession caused by external circumstances. The ideal, and thus probably the earliest form of this baptismal instruction called for immersion (?) in "running water." But other modes came to be accepted as new situations arose. There may also be such a concession in 7:4, where the whole community is no longer required to fast before catechumens are baptized.

10:7—the hitherto unmentioned prophets (see 11:3, 7–12) receive a concessional footnote with reference to their freedom in prayer practices, which helps link (awkwardly) two separate blocks of material which have been brought together in the developing Didache tradition.

15:1–2—as Didache 11–13 indicates, the kind of Christian ministry with which the Didache is mainly concerned is that of itinerant apostles, prophets, and teachers. But a more settled ministry gradually came about (see already 13:1), and thus 15:1–2 was introduced to cover the new situation.

4. *Supplementary Evidence from Style and Content.* Finally, other more subtle evidence from style and/or content

can be introduced to support the above clues and to indicate additional lines of development behind the form of the Didache preserved for us. For example, within the Two Ways section, 3:1–6 clearly has its own style in comparison to its context. But if it is an insertion into the Two Ways tradition, it is a more ancient one than Didache 1:3b—2:1 since it is present in **Dctr** and **CO**, but not in Barnabas (see also §2:4). Again, it could be argued that Didache 8, which differs both in *general* style and in content from its surrounding context, is an insertion (by way of the idea of "fasting") into a formerly more unified section on Baptism-Eucharist (chs. 7, 9–10). Indeed, **Eth** attests a (reworked?) form of Didache material in which 8:1–2a (fasting-prayer) has been appended to 11:3—13:7 (prophets-apostles-teachers) to form a unit dealing with "false prophets and hypocrites" (see §7:6). It is unlikely that 11:3—13:7 plus 8:1–2a existed as a unit before the present form of the Didache took shape. But it is at least probable that certain smaller components such as 8:1–2a once circulated apart from their present Didache context (Matt. 6:1–5, 16–18 is based on similar material). The "Lord's Prayer" in 8:2b has been added after the analogy of Matthew 6:9 ff. (its original independence is supported by Luke 11:1 ff.), but it is impossible to tell at what stage in the development behind the Didache this took place (note that 11:3 and 15:3–4 have not been filled out so neatly with the appropriate "Gospel" texts!).

In fact, chapters 11–13 also show indications of having been constructed from smaller, separate blocks of material. The heart of this section is the instruction on itinerant (apostles and) prophets (11:3–12), which has its own separate rubric (11:3), and has extended its influence into previous (10:7) and subsequent (13:1; 15:1–2) material. Less extensive but also influential is the similar concern for itinerant "teachers" (11:1–2; 13:2; 15:1–2). Apparently traveling prophets and teachers represent the main type of ministry respected by the Didache tradition (15:1–2; see §9:3). But into this context has been introduced a section on traveling

Christians in general (12:1–5), and, as a way of implement-
ing the admonition of 13:1–2, a block of Jewish *halaka* on
offering the "first fruits" as support for God's ministers and
the needy (13:3–7). This last section has been made to apply
to the prophets by symbolically identifying them with the
original "high priests" (13:3b—later developments of this
tradition substitute "bishop" and other clergy, or retain
"priests" in a Christian context; see §7:5). Any attempt to
explain in detail how all these materials came together
would be even more conjectural than the above analysis. But
one feature stands out—11:1–2 is not entirely natural in its
present position (11:3 is the stylistic parallel to 7:1; 9:1) but
would make an admirable *concluding section* to the Two
Ways. It is thus tempting to speculate that, in various stages,
Didache 6:3—10:8 was added to the Two Ways until a longer
manual dealing with the reception of catechumens into the
congregation (at Easter) was formed, with 11:1–2 displaced
from its original position but retained at the conclusion to
the expanded manual. This, in turn, led to the gradual incor-
poration of 11:3—13:7, and ultimately to the form of the
Didache known to us.

5. *Toward a Reconstruction of the Stages of Development
Behind Our Didache.* Although the present evidence is insufficient to permit a confident, concrete, and detailed reconstruction of all the stages of development behind the
Didache, some observations are possible by way of summary.

(1) The oldest controllable material is the originally Jewish Two Ways tradition, which had already been subject to
a great deal of development (see §2:4–5) before it became
part of the larger Didache—3:1–6 represents an older, pre-
Didache and perhaps pre-Christian addition to this base,
while 1:3b—2:1 is a Christian contribution that may have
been added by the Didachist himself.

(2) The Two Ways instruction was united with teaching
about baptism (7:1–4) to provide a manual covering the reception of catechumens. Probably the prayers of chapters
9–10 (including 10:8, for the "ointment") also found their

place in this manual because they were relevant for the
Baptismal-Eucharist service at which catechumens were received. It is possible that this manual once circulated separately, with 11:1–2 as its conclusion (so also Audet). It is not
clear when 8:1–3 was added, but the idea of fasting in 7:4
furnished the necessary link (the "Lord's Prayer" in 8:2b
may have been an even later addition). Apparently 10:7 is
an adjustment made in the light of 11:3–12. The food laws
of 6:3 reflect Jewish-Christian interest and seem to have
been added (at a relatively early date?) to supplement the
Two Ways, as another aspect of the "Lord's yoke" (6:2).

(3) The material in 11:3—15:4 is loosely unified around
the theme of community relationships—toward traveling ministers (11:3–12), migrant Christians (12:1–5) ministers who
settle (13:1–2), indigenous clergy (15:1–2), and fellow
Christians (15:3–4). The instructions of 13:3–7 have been
introduced to show how the settled ministers (and the needy;
see 15:4) can be supported, and this "first fruits" context
had probably influenced the inclusion of 14:1–3 (on Christian "sacrifice") at this point. It may well be that this entire
block had its own separate development (paralleling 1:1—
11:2), and at a later date came to be appended to 11:2 because 11:1–2 also mentioned itinerant Christian ministers.
Certainly 15:1–2 is one of the most recent stages of the
developing tradition.

(4) The background of the apocalyptic-parenetic section
in Didache 16 is especially vague, although it may have some
relationship to older Two Ways thinking (see §2:3, 7). As it
now stands, it forms an appendix with few clear ties to what
precedes.

If this all seems overly complex, let the reader consider
the subsequent history of the Didache materials (§7, §10).
Neither simplicity nor straight-line development characterize
the production of such church manuals. We are not dealing
with a copyrighted document, which is the result of one
man's endeavors, but with a conservative, *living* community

tradition which can occasionally (sometimes rather acciden-
tally) be glimpsed in a state of suspended animation, as it
were, by means of the various pieces of surviving Christian
"literature" which represent these interests. The Doctrina
gives us one (early?) glimpse, the Didache another, and the
Apostolic Constitutions another (later). But for the most
part we are left to conjecture if we wish to explain in detail
how the various developments came about. Not only is such
conjecture legitimate, but occasionally it may also be accu-
rate.

§9. The Christianity Represented by the Didache

1. *Ethno-Religious Background.* Our knowledge of the
kind of Christianity represented by the Didache is severely
limited because of the nature of the document. Theology, in
even a rudimentary sense, is almost completely lacking. We
are dealing with liturgy and polity—with church orders—and
with only a small sampling of that. And we must constantly
be aware of the fact that ideas which are simply reproduced
from older materials preserved, with little change, in the
present form of the Didache do not necessarily represent the
main interests and beliefs of the community for which *this*
form of the Didache manual was produced. Repetition of
traditional beliefs does not always imply conscious agreement with what the originators of the tradition had in mind.

The pronounced (Hellenistic) Jewish background of this
Christianity is obvious from the Didache's use of particularly
Jewish source materials (especially the Two Ways), and its
concern for Jewish-Christian problems (food laws [6:3],
fasts and prayers of the "hypocrites" [8:1–2a], high priestly
office and contribution of "first fruits" in the church [13:3–7],
and the Christian "sacrifices" [14:1–3]). But Christianity in
general, and Eastern (including Egypt and Asia Minor)
Christianity in particular, retained such more or less conscious vestiges of its Jewish heritage for decades and cen-

turies after the "victory" of Gentile Christianity. This tells us nothing about the ethnic background of the Didache community or its leaders. They were Christians building on a Jewish base—and more than just an Old Testament base. But this does not mean they were necessarily of Jewish descent. The subtitle of the Didache, ". . . to the nations/Gentiles" is no more decisive here than are the references in 9:4 and 10:5 to the church scattered throughout the entire world, although such allusions may weigh the scales in the direction of predominantly Gentile recipients for the present form of the Didache.

2. *Practices of the Community.* The practices of the community seem to have included the following: (1) careful (ethical) catechetical instruction preceding baptism (7:1; 11:1); (2) prebaptismal fasting by the initiants and the one who will baptize them (7:4); (3) baptism in the threefold name (7:1, 3; but cf. 9:5) by the best available means (7:1–3); (4) probably baptism was followed by a special Eucharistic meal with the initiants (9:1—10:6); (5) possibly an anointing with oil followed this meal—or perhaps came directly after baptism (10:8 var.); (6) regular fasts on Wednesdays and Fridays (8:1; see 1:3b); (7) weekly(?) meetings on the "Lord's Day" (= Sunday? see 14:1–3; 16:2), which included a meal of some sort, prayer, and confession (private? cf. 4:14); (8) recitation of the "Lord's Prayer" thrice daily (8:2–3); (9) possibly also a daily community gathering (4:2; see 16:2); (10) regular attention to inner-community discipline and prayer (15:3 f.; see 1:3b; 2:7; 4:3; 4:14), as well as the performance of "works" such as alms-giving (15:4; see 1:5–6; 4:4–8; 11:12; 13:4) and systematic contributions (13:3–7); and (11) attention to hospitality for the traveling Christian, whether layman or leader (11:3—12:5). From all indications, the community was not (or its background had not been) particularly rich and thus was rather careful about economic matters (11:5 f., 9, 12; 12:2–5; 13:1–7).

3. *Leadership.* With respect to leadership,[2] the Didache community not only remembers but has preserved rules governing the days of itinerant apostles and prophets who would minister for one or two days without asking any pay (11:3–12). It also is concerned with prophets and teachers who decide to settle for a more or less permanent period, and with their means of support (13:1–7; cf. 11:1–2). The most recent development, however, seems to have been the rise of a settled ministry through bishops and deacons appointed by the community itself (15:1–2). It is possible that some sort of itinerant ministry still survived, but it has become the exception rather than the rule. It should be noted that in discussing these various types of ministry, the Didache pictures the community as self-governing and as exercising authority over its ministers (see 6:1; 11:1–2; 12:1; 15:1, etc.) —in fact, it must be warned not to exercise too much control over prophets (10:7; 11:7; 11:11 f.) and not to despise native leaders (15:2)!

It is not entirely clear how the functions of these various leaders were related one to another and to the community at large. Apparently the teachers were at least in charge of moral instruction like the Two Ways (11:1–2). The "apostles" seem to be roughly synonymous with "prophets" (11:5–6). The prophets receive the most emphasis, and can play a definite role in leading liturgy (10:7)—"they are your high priests" (13:3b). We do not know how liturgy was conducted in the absence of a prophet or teacher (cf. 13:4), but presumably the manual was written partly to solve such a dilemma.

4. *Commandments, Gospel, and Christian Conduct.* The general attitude of Didache Christianity toward Christian conduct, insofar as it can be recovered, is similar to the rigorous ethical approach evident in Barnabas (§5:4–5). This is,

---

[2] For an extended discussion of early Christian leadership, see Grant, *op. cit.*, 141 ff.

of course, almost self-understood in that the Two Ways catechism is extremely important for both traditions. In the Didache version of this approach, however, "the gospel" (see
11:3; 15:3–4) and its prescriptions are much more in evidence [3]—for example, the summary of Torah in terms of love
for God and neighbor and the (negative) "golden rule"
(1:2); love even for enemies (1:3); active submission to
antagonism of various sorts (1:4); threefold baptism (7:1,
3); "Lord's Prayer" (8:2); sayings of Jesus (9:5); sin against
the prophetic spirit (11:7); workman worth his wages (13:
1); apocalyptic exhortation (16:1 ff.). Nevertheless, the characteristically Barnabean emphasis is also present in exhortations to observe the righteous commands (3:8b; 4:13; 11:2;
cf. 1:5; 13:5, 7) and in the allusion to the "Lord's yoke" (6:2;
cf. Barn. 2:6). Furthermore, the function of the "word" in
the Christian proclamation is attested in 4:1 (see §5:8),
almost side by side with the emphasis on one's labor in behalf of salvation (4:6; see §5:4).

5. *Eschatology and Future Salvation.* It is only in chapter
16 that the Didache approaches the eschatological orientation which pervades Barnabas (§2:2–3, §5:3). It is true that
the Two Ways section alludes to "the reward" (4:7b; 5:2c
= Barn. 19:11a; 20:2c), and the prayers repeat traditional
language about the coming "kingdom" and the activity of
"evil" or the "Evil One" (8:2; 9:4; 10:5), the passing away
of "this world" and the coming of the Lord (10:6), but these
are extremely faint echoes and inspire no confidence that the
community which used them was waiting with bated breath
for the consummation. Apart from chapter 16 we find that
such matters as "the Lord's return," resurrection, judgment,
and final salvation have no real role in the Didache. There
are a few references to "judgment" in Didache 1–15, but none
of them are strictly eschatological (4:3; 5:2; 11:11 f.). The
"resurrection" is mentioned only in 16:6 f. There is no clear

---

[3] The relationship between the Didache and the "gospel tradition" is discussed in detail by H. Koester. See also §10:5:5.

concept of a new creation in the last days (cf. 4:10b[?]), but only general exhortations to "watch" and "be ready" (16:1) so as to be "perfect" (16:2; see 1:4; 6:2; 10:5) and "endure" to salvation (16:5; cf. 1:4 var.; 5:2m; 8:2; 10:5).

6. *Absence of "Traditional" Soteriology.* The Didache says very little about the traditional soteriological categories of sin, repentance, and satisfaction. The Two Ways section seems to approach this subject in 4:6, "If you should appropriate something through your labor, give it [i.e., to the needy] as a ransom for your sins" (cf. the form in Barn. 19: 10d), but the thrust here seems to be that social justice in a communal society is included in the road to salvation—the way of righteousness. In 4:14 and again in 14:1, confession of transgressions is treated as a prerequisite for meaningful community worship—but not as a presupposition for salvation. Similarly, repentance in 15:3 is more a matter of community discipline than of soteriology in the modern sense. This also seems to be true of 10:6, where lack of "holiness" calls for "repentance." The general prerequisite to participation in the community life appears to have been baptism "in the Lord's Name" (9:5; cf. §9:2:3), but the theological significance of baptism is never treated (explicitly or implicitly). There is no indication in the Didache that an initial repentance connected with the idea of personal sinfulness for which Jesus' death atones was considered basic to the Christian life (cf. §5:7).

7. *Gnosis, Revelation, and Exegesis.* As for any overtones of "gnosis," exegetical or otherwise (§5:1–2), they are quite incidental in the Didache. The prayers refer to "life and *gnosis*" (9:3) and "*gnosis*, faith and immortality" (10:2) which God has "*made known*" (see §5:2:5) through Jesus. Again, in 11:2 we find a general reference to the "righteousness and *gnosis* of the Lord," which apparently is identified with (at least) the Two Ways instruction (also called "gnosis" in Barn. 18:1). Otherwise we read about "knowing" (i.e., discerning) the true character of a prophet (11:8) or a recipient of hospitality (12:1), or of "knowing" who rewards

the almsgiver (4:7). Nor is there any emphasis on "pneumatic" exegesis, although 10:3 alludes to "pneumatic food
and drink" (apparently the Eucharist), and the prophets of
11:7–12 are said to speak out "in the spirit" (see §5:2:20).
The Didache does contain a few explicit quotations of various sorts (1:6; 8:2; 9:5b; 14:3; 16:7; cf. §9:4 and the Indexes)
but there is no indication that special insight is required to
understand them.[4]

8. *Jesus the Lord.* The references to "Jesus" by name are
limited to the prayers of 9:2 f. and 10:2(f.), where the
frozen liturgical phrase "Jesus your child/servant" is repeated in several places [5] (see also 10:8)—in 9:2 it is parallel
to "David your child/servant." In the same context (9:4),
the title "Jesus Christ" is involved liturgically. "Christ" occurs nowhere else in the Didache (but **Georg** includes it in
1:4; 10:3; 15:4; 16:8), although in 12:4 f. reference is made to
"Christian" and to "Christ-peddler." By far the favorite
Christological title in the Didache is *kyrios*—Lord. It is un-
ambiguously applied to Jesus in the preserved subtitle of the
Didache as well as in 8:2; 9:5 (twice); 11:2b (second occurrence); 11:4; 12:1; 15:4; 16:1; 16:7 f. The tradition also probably had Jesus in mind in such (ambiguous) passages as 4:1;
6:2; 10:5; 14:1, 3 (twice); and 15:1. Quite ambiguous are
4:12 f.; 11:2 (first occurrence); 11:8, although probably
the final author-editor of the Didache also applied these to
Jesus. Finally, on one clear occasion Jesus is referred to as
"your holy Name" (10:2–cf. 9:5; 10:3; 12:1).[6] It is only in
the "trinitarian" formulas of 7:1, 3 that the title "Son" is
applied to Jesus (cf. 16:4 on the deceiver). Thus, the most
that can be said is that Christology is incidental to the Didache—it is echoed, in various forms, especially in the liturgi-

---

[4] On the problem of the Didache's use of biblical sources, see Grant, *op.
cit.*, 74–75.

[5] Cf. Acts 3:13, 26; 4:27, 30; 1 Clem. 59:2 ff.; Mart. Polyc. 14:1, 3; 20:2;
Diognetus 8:9, 11; 9:1; see Grant, *op. cit.*, 110 f.

[6] Cf. 1 Clem. 58:1; 59:3; 60:4; Barn. 16:8 (§5:7); Hermas, Sim. 9:14:5 f.;
see Grant, *op. cit.*, 111–112.

cal passages, but this cannot be called "theological reflection." In general, the identity of "Jesus" and "Lord" is simply assumed. He is never explicitly called "God," and his functions are seldom defined with any precision (e.g., 16:7 f. describes his apocalyptic role, but nowhere is he pictured as creator or revealer or savior—there is no reference to his blood, suffering, death, etc.).

9. *God the Father.* References to "God" are frequent: he is the creator (1:2; see also 5:2i), the God of David (10:6), whose word has gone forth (4:1; cf. 6:1), who exercises judgment on his prophetic agents (11:11), who is God of slaves as well as of masters (4:10 f.). In 10:3, this creator God is called "Almighty Master." Nor is the concept of the divine "Father" lacking—but it occurs primarily in the liturgical portions of the Didache—in prayers (8:2; 9:2 f.; 10:2; 10:8) and in the "trinitarian" formulas (7:1, 3) and also in the almsgiving interpolation of 1:5 (the **Dctr** parallel has "Lord"; Hermas has "God"). We have already noted (§9:8) passages in which "Lord" might refer to God.

10. *"Spirit" and "spirits."* Apart from the "trinitarian" formulas of Didache 7, Holy Spirit as a divine agent (person?) is scarcely to be found (but see **Georg** in 11:7–8). Perhaps the majority of older translations are correct in reading 4:10b in this light—"he comes not to call preferentially, but (to call those) whom the (Holy) Spirit prepared"—but it is also possible that the text means ". . . to call those for [in?] whom he prepared the spirit [of righteousness?]" (cf. §5:10). In any case, this reflects Two Ways theology and not necessarily that of the Didache community. It should at least be noted here that elsewhere in the Didache, "spirit" is anthropomorphic (**P.Ox** at 1:4), or refers to the characteristic "pneumatic-prophetic" form of discourse (*en pneumati* 11:7–12; cf. §5:2:20 on the "gnostic" use of this phrase in Barnabas).

§10. Questions of Higher Criticism: Date, Authorship, Origin (see also §6, Introduction)

1. *Alleged Use of Didache Materials.* Because of its extremely complicated background and its continuing evolution even after the present form had been reached, it is difficult to trace (and thus localize) with any confidence the use of *this precise form* of the Didache tradition by ancient authors.[7] For example, one of the fragments traditionally ascribed to Irenaeus cites a passage that in content resembles Didache 14:3 as coming from "the second of the Apostolic constitutions."[8] Undoubtedly this is an allusion to *some form* of the church manual tradition with which we are concerned, but *which form?* And was it really a form known in Asia Minor-Rome-Gaul in the last half of the second century (i.e., can we accept the Irenaeus identification)? It would be exciting to build up some theories about how Didache 14 once was in "the second" of the constitutions, while the Two Ways (or 1:1–11:2?; see §8:5:3) formed "the first," but such hypotheses are only as solid as their foundations, which in this case are quite shaky. Similarly, there are several references in Clement of Alexandria to Didache-like material which cannot be explained as allusions based on Barnabas. Nevertheless, Clement does not cite enough such material to provide sufficient control for determining his relationship to *our* form of the Didache, nor does he attach any helpful label to this material (once it may be called "scripture"). There is no doubt that various forms of the Didache tradition (and its sources) existed long before Clement and were already being reworked in various ways (Barnabas, Hermas). Thus Clement's evidence must be used with caution and the same must be said of other alleged "quotations" and allusions, as,

---

[7] For a general survey of the possibilities, see Grant, *op. cit.*, 13–33.

[8] In Stieren's ed., frg. 38 (Harvey, frg. 36). The background of this fragment is mysterious, and it is impossible to say whether it is authentically from Irenaeus.

for example, the occasional parallels to the Didache in the
third-century Didascalia manual.

2. *References to Documents Known as "Didache."* This
much is clear: several writers and lists from the beginning
of the fourth century and onward refer to a writing known
as the "Teaching" (*Didache, Doctrina*) or "Teachings"
(*Didachai, Doctrinae*) of the Apostles. Unfortunately
they do not cite exact excerpts, and thus there is no way of
telling what the precise relationship might have been between what they cite and our Didache. For example, Eusebius (*ca.* 325) refers to "the alleged Teaching*s* [plural] of
the Apostles" as among the illegitimate (*notha*) candidates
for New Testament Scripture (*H.E.* 3:25:4; see also §6:1).
Did he have our form of the Didache in mind? Similarly,
the Pseudo-Cyprianic tract *Adversus aleatores* 4 from about
the same date (?) loosely alludes to material allegedly found
"in doctrinis apostolorum," but precision of quotation seems
lacking. In his festal letter of 367, Athanasius of Alexandria
includes reference to "the so-called Teaching of the Apostles"
among noncanonical literature considered suitable for use in
instructing new Christians. Probably *our* document or something very similar to it is meant. Much later, the "List of Sixty
Books" (*ca.* 600) contains an entry which appears to refer to
a *single* apocryphal work called "The Travels and Teachings
of the Apostles" (cf. Ps.-Clem. literature!), while the stichometric listing of Nicephorus (*ca.* 820) refers to "The Teaching of the Apostles" under the category of New Testament
Apocrypha. The fact that Nicephorus lists its "Didache" as
having some 200 stichoi (lines of relatively fixed length)
does not help us at all in determining the precise identity of
the work, since we have no way of telling how this number
was determined, or whether the number itself has been corrupted in transmission.[9] By drawing generalizations from the
other figures listed in the *Stichometry* for known New Testament books, we would *expect* the extant form of the Didache

---

[9] On this matter, see also Grant, *op. cit.,* 74.

to have about 300 stichoi (not 200—there seem to have been about 35 letters per stichos). Comparison in another direction is even more striking: "Barnabas," according to Nicephorus, has 1,360 stichoi (we would expect only about 850–900 [as in the Claromontanus list; see §6:2] for the present form of the epistle), while the extant text of the Didache is about one third the length of Barnabas (thus much more than "200 stichoi")! There are a few other references to a "Didache" apocryphon in the later fathers (sixth to fourteenth centuries), but they all seem to depend on such lists as the above.

3. *Undisputed Use of the Didache.* Our quest for a *terminus ante quem,* a date before which our Didache must have been in circulation, and for a localized sphere of influence (to assist in determining whence the Didache originated) is somewhat advanced when the various versions and adaptations of the tradition are introduced into the discussion. Certainly the fourth century provides ample evidence that our form of the Didache is not only in existence, but is influential in the East, especially in Egypt—see **P. Ox, ApCo.** And from the fifth century we have the Coptic fragment and possibly the Georgian version. Thus it is safe to say that third-century Egypt (and Eastern Christianity) knew our form of the Didache—as well as related materials (see **CO, Eth, Syntagma-Fides, Shenuti,** etc.).

4. *Internal Clues as to Place of Origin.* When we search the words of the Didache itself for clear indications of origin and date, the result is almost complete frustration. In the prayer of 9:4, the allusion to wheat gathered from the "mountains" in order to make a loaf of bread would seem to preclude Egypt as the basis of the analogy, since in ancient Egypt the fertile regions were located in the Nile Valley (nourished by the annual flooding), and not on hillsides or mountains. Thus many commentators have seen Syria, or more particularly Palestine, as the home of this imagery. It is noteworthy that the (Egyptian?) **ApCo** lacks this reference to mountains in its reworked form of the Didache. Another possible geographical clue in the Didache has some-

times been seen in the reference to "warm" water in 7:2. But it is by no means clear that the text has warm *baths* in mind, such as one might find more readily in Syria than in Egypt, and thus this "evidence" is negligible (again, **ApCo** lacks this reference).

5. *Alleged "Primitive" Elements in the Didache.* Thus we are reduced to talking about the relative "primitiveness" or "development" of the Christianity reflected in the Didache, of its relation to identifiable sources or movements, and of the "most likely" location(s) from which such an approach to Christianity might have emerged. As the commentaries and studies of the Didache well attest, this is an extremely tenuous approach.[10] Some of the most frequently discussed items in this context are the following:

(1) Church government in the Didache (chs. 11–13, 15) looks "primitive" with its concern for itinerant apostles, prophets, and teachers, and with its lack of any indication that ecclesiastical authority rests in a monarchial bishop (cf. the emphasis placed on the bishop by Ignatius of Antioch, *ca.* 110) or even in a college of presbyters (cf. 1 Clem. 42; from *ca.* 95).

(2) The prophetism of Didache 11 has variously been assessed as "early" (cf. 1 John, Hermas), or perhaps related to the Montanist revival of prophecy in the later second century (*ca.* 155/170) in Asia Minor.

(3) The language of the prayers in Didache 9–10 sounds "early" (cf. the early chapters of Acts; see §9:8).

(4) At numerous points the Didache tradition shows its Jewish background and Jewish-Christian interests (see §9: 1). On the other hand, 8:1 f. is critical of certain Pharisaic-Jewish (?) practices. Thus it is sometimes argued that the Didache was written (soon) after the "break" between church and synagogue (*ca.* 70–135).

(5) In its present form, the Didache appears to have a rather wide acquaintance with the Synoptic tradition (1:2–5;

---

[10] See also the discussion in Grant, *op. cit.,* 75 f.

7:1/3 [?]; 8:1–2; 9:5b; 11:7; 14:2 [?]; 15:3 [?]; 16:1, 3–8; see §9:4), often in a "harmonized" text form. This tends to suggest a date in the later second century (around the time of Justin and his student Tatian, who composed a "harmony" [ca. 170]) rather than an early second- or late first-century date.

(6) In two passages, outside of the Two Ways tradition proper, the Didache has material which clearly is related to, and possibly derived from, Hermas (see Did. 1:5) and Barnabas (Did. 16:2). If the Didache has used Hermas and Barnabas here, of course, it must be dated later than those sources (whenever one dates them and whichever stage of their development was known to the Didachist).

(7) The Didache shows almost no interest in doctrine, even in Christocentric soteriology (§9:6), nor in polemic against heterodoxy (cf. 8:1–2a), and thus seems more primitive than (or remote from) later second-century interests.

6. *Conclusions Concerning Date.* This list could be swelled by discussion of more detailed problems such as the doxology to the Lord's Prayer (8:2), which has been claimed as Syrian in origin but also shows affinities with Egyptian witnesses, or the use of certain words which are not well attested in earliest Christian literature (12:5 "Christ-peddler," 13:5 "bread dough") or which are used in a different (more "primitive") way from later Christian vocabulary (15:1 "appoint"). But there is little value in multiplying such "evidence." All that can emerge is the twofold impression: the Didache contains a great deal of material which derives from very early (i.e., first-century and early second-century) forms of (Jewish-)Christianity; but it would be difficult to argue convincingly that the *present form* of the Didache is earlier than mid-second century. The very conservative nature of the church manual tradition, which is especially obvious in its later development (e.g., **Eth** continues to refer to itinerant prophets, although **ApCo** has reworked and abridged this section; **ApCo** retains the "archaic" prayer forms, etc.), is sufficient explanation for the "primitive" factors in the Did-

ache. And the corollary of this observation is that the date ascribed to the extant form of the Didache is largely irrelevant when particular items in the tradition are discussed.

7. *Probable Place of Origin.* As for the location at which our form of the Didache was composed, similar problems are present. Perhaps the prayers derive ultimately from Syria-Palestine (§10:4); this does not allow us to say that the entire compilation has the same background. It seems clear that the Didache represents Eastern Christianity. Probably it also comes from a semirural rather than a large urban environment—thus the itinerant ministry, the basically agricultural-pastoral symbolism and economy (esp. ch. 13), although "trades" are also in view (12:3 f.). If Egypt seems somewhat more probable than Syria, it is because the later uses of the Didache tradition (**ApCo, Eth**) and the earliest direct textual evidence (**P.Ox, Cop**) point most strongly to that area.

8. *The Author-Editor.* Nothing definite can be said concerning the identity of the editor responsible for the Didache. He may have been an itinerant "teacher" himself, but his whole aim is to let the "apostolic" teachings speak for themselves. There is no evidence to indicate his ethnic background.

TRANSLATION
AND
COMMENTARY

OUTLINE OF BARNABAS AND THE DIDACHE

78

The Didache 6:3–16:8

I. Instruction and reception of catechumens (6:3–11:2) [continuation of the Two Ways Catechism (Did. 1:1–6:2)]
    Concerning food (6:3)
    Concerning baptism, fasting, and prayer (7:1–8:3)
    Concerning the giving of thanks—in connection with the Eucharist (9:1–10:8)
    The approved teacher (11:1–2)

II. Intracommunity relationships (11:3–15:4)
    Concerning apostles and prophets (11:3–12)
    Hospitality toward traveling Christians (12:1–5)
    Material support for God's ministers (13:1–7)
    The community "sacrifice" (14:1–3)
    Respect for indigenous leaders (15:1–2)
    Community discipline and conduct (15:3–4)

III. Eschatological admonition (16:1–8)

Barnabas 1:1–17:2

Introduction (1:1–2:3)

Salutation (1:1)

1 Greetings, sons and daughters [§4:3], in the Name of the Lord *a* who loved us, in peace.

a So HS: but CO and L agree in reading "of (our) Lord Jesus Christ"; see §5:7.

1:1–8. Although in *content* Barnabas is more accurately a catechetical tractate than an epistle, there is nothing necessarily artificial about the epistolary salutation in **1:1.** Christian and secular parallels are cited by Goodspeed, *JBL* 34 (1915), 162–165. In general, the language and style of this entire introductory section is very stilted, which magnifies the usual problems of translation and interpretation. It may be that, in part, Pseudo-Barnabas is following accepted literary patterns here—compare **1:2** with Cyprian's opening words in *On*

Commendation (1:2–3)

2. Seeing that God's righteous acts [§5:5:2] toward you are so extraordinary and abundant, my joy over your favored and illustrious spirits [§5:2:20] is unbounded—you have received such grace [§5:2:26], such an implantation of the pneumatic gift! [§5:2:20, 9.] 3. Wherefore I, who also hope to be saved [§5:4], inwardly rejoice all the more because I can actually see that the spirit [§5:2:20] which is on you has been poured out in your midst from the abundance of the fountain *b* of the Lord [see 11:2*]. My eagerly anticipated visit to you has so wonderfully exceeded all expectations concerning you!

Purpose and themes (1:4–8)

4. Therefore, I am convinced of this—indeed, I am all the more conscious of it because I know that he who spoke *c* many things in your midst was my traveling companion in the Way of Righteousness [§2:2], the Lord; *c* and for this reason I myself am constrained at all times to love you more than my own soul [§5:5:5]—

b So HL (pēgē); but S has "love" (agapē).
c So H; but S (cf. L) reads "when I spoke . . . my traveling companion . . . was the Lord."

Works and Almsgiving (*ca.* 254): "Most beloved brethren, manifold and extraordinary are the divine benefactions by which, for our salvation, the bountiful and copious mercy of God the Father and of Christ both have been and always will be exercised"; or 1:5, 8 (4:9a; 17:1; 21:9) with the first section of Irenaeus' *Apostolic Preaching* (see to 17:1); or 1:8 with Ign. Eph. 3:1, etc. There is no persuasive evidence that Ignatius or Cyprian knew Barnabas, although Irenaeus has some affinities with the epistle (§6:10).

Whatever its literary background, the introduction pictures Pseudo-Barnabas as an itinerant teacher (§4:3) whose recent visit to the recipients has convinced him that they are worthy (cf. 9:9) to receive his "gnostic" instruction, since they have been prepared with the proper "spirit." The "fountain of the Lord" (or ". . . which is the Lord"?) imagery is often connected elsewhere with the idea of divine guidance and/or the divine spirit: see Philo, *Quod Det. Pot.* 83; G.

for great faith and love dwell in you, with hope [§5:5:1] of obtaining the life he gives! 5. Therefore, since it has occurred to me that if I am diligent in imparting to you a measure of what I have received [§4:3] it will be to my credit for having ministered to such spirits [§5:2:20], I have hastened to send you this brief communication [§1:2, n.2] so that along with your faith [§5:5:1] you might also have perfect gnosis [§5:1–2].

6. There are, then, three basic doctrines [§5:5:3] of the Lord of life: [d] Hope, the beginning and end of our faith [§5:5:1]; and Righteousness [§5:5:2], the beginning and end of judgment [§5:3–4]; (and) Love, a witness of the joy and gladness [e] [§5:5:5] of works done in righteousness [§5:4].

7. For the Master [§5:9] has made known [§5:2:5] to us through the prophets what already has come to pass and what is now occurring, and he has given us a foretaste of what is about to happen [§5:1–2]. Thus as we observe each of these things being worked out as he said, we ought all the more abundantly

---

[d] So H(L); but S reads "... Lord: Life, Faith, Hope—our beginning and end." As is common, L is a great deal shorter here and mentions only "hope." L could be rendered "... Lord: Hope of Life ..." (cf. 1:4b, which literally reads "hope of his life"), and so might H if it were not for the punctuation marks and marginal comment in that manuscript.

[e] So H; but S has "Love which is joyfulness and a witness of the gladness ...."

Hebrews on Jesus' baptism; Odes Sol. 11:6; 30:1 f.; Qumran *Manual* 10–11.

As it now stands, 1:6 is rather parenthetical, although it deals with basic themes that will recur throughout the epistle. Possibly it was inserted here because of its similarity to the passing references to faith-love-hope-life in 1:4b (see also 1:5b on that which accompanies faith). Numerous parallels could be cited—cf. esp. 1 Cor. 13; Ign. Eph. 14:1; Polycarp, Phil. 3:3. The primary purpose of Barn. 2–16 is enunciated in 1:7 f.—to pass along exegetical "gnosis" which can help the recipients interpret the course of salvation-history (§5:6) as it speeds toward the consummation (§5:3). The formula in 1:7a (see 5:3; 17:1 f.) probably has a traditional background—many similar passages occur in late Jewish and early Christian literature: e.g., Qumran *Mysteries* 1:3 ff; Philo, *Spec. leg.* 1:334; Theophilus, *Ad Autol.* 1:14; 2:9,33; Irenaeus, *Adv. haer.* 4:33:1; Hippolytus, *Antichrist* 2.

and enthusiastically draw near in fear of him *f* [§5:5:6]. 8. And now, not as a Teacher [§4:3] but as one from your very midst, I will point out [§5:2:7] a few things [§1:2, n.2] which will enable you to rejoice in the present circumstances [§5:3].

Transition to the first main section (2:1–3)

2 Since, then, the present days are evil and he who is now at work possesses the power [§5:3], we ought to walk circumspectly [§5:2:21] and seek out the Lord's righteous requirements [§5:4, §5:5:2]. 2. The auxiliaries of our faith [§5:5:1], then, are Fear [see §5:5:6] and Endurance, while Patience and Self-control also fight along at our side. 3. Thus while these allies remain in a pure state [see 19:8c] in relation to the Lord, there rejoice with them Wisdom, Understanding, Knowledge, and Gnosis [= 21:5; see §5:2:22, 23, 11, 6].

---

f So HS; but L has "to his altar," possibly because the verb "to draw near" can also mean "to bring an offering" (cf. 2:9).

2:1–3. There is a sense in which **2:1–3** sets the stage for the whole of Barn. 2–16 (and ch. 21), since the idea of eschatological warfare permeates the epistle (§5:3). But in a more direct way, **2:1** serves as a transition from the general goals of 1:7–8 to the specific theme of 2:4–3:6—the gnosis of "What the Lord Requires." Not only does 3:6 provide a clear conclusion to that section, but 4:1 clearly reiterates the ideas of **2:1** and thus seems to introduce a parallel section with similarly strong eschatological orientation. The lists of ethical/practical and mental/gnostic virtues in **2:2–3**, which are typical of Barnabas and its Hellenistic Jewish background (cf. Philo), seem rather parenthetical here, but this is characteristic of Pseudo-Barnabas' "method" (cf. 1:6; §4:4). The reference to evil days in **2:1** may reflect the Jewish concept of the "Messianic Woes" which immediately precede the Lord's victory (cf. 8:6). On Satan as the present worker who has some measure of authority, cf. 2 Thess. 2:7; Luke 4:6; 12:5; 22:53; Acts 26:18; John 14:30; Col. 1:13; Eph. 2:2; the "Freer Logion" which is appended to Mark 16:14 in one Greek manuscript ("And they replied, saying that this aeon of lawlessness and faithlessness is under Satan, who through unclean spirits does not allow the truth of God to be grasped.... Christ replied to them that the limit of the years of the authority of Satan has been fulfilled, but other fearful things are at hand....").

I. WHAT THE LORD REQUIRES (2:4–3:6)

4. For he made it clear to us through all the prophets [§5:2:25; see 1:7; 5:3] that he needs neither sacrifices nor whole burnt offerings nor offerings in general—as he says in one place:

5. What good is the multitude of your sacrifices to me? says the Lord.

I am satiated with burnt offerings of rams and the fat of lambs, and I do not want the blood of bulls and goats—
not even if you come and appear before me!
For who has required these things from your hands?
Do not continue to tread my (Temple) court.
If you bring finely ground flour, it is vain;
offering of incense is an abomination to me,
I cannot bear your new moon festivals and sabbaths [see 15:8; Isa. 1:11–13].

2:4–3:6. The contention that God has no need of anything, including cultic acts such as sacrifice and fasting, had wide circulation in Hellenistic Judaism (Philo, Josephus, 2 Macc. 14:35, 3 Macc. 2:9)—and in the Hellenistic world at large (Pythagoreans, Epicureans, Stoics, Neo-Platonists)—as well as among early Christian writers (Acts 17:25; 1 Clem. 52:1; Justin, *Apol.* 13:1; *Dial.* 23:2, etc.). Thus it is quite strange to call Pseudo-Barnabas "anti-Jewish" on the basis of this context. He is certainly anticultic, but there were many Jews among his contemporaries who shared his attitude. It is also important to note that the passage under consideration is positive as well as negative in its teaching—true sacrifice involves a person's attitudes toward his neighbor and his God (2:8, 10a; cf. the Two Ways approach, and esp. 19:2); true fasting *is* social justice (3:3, 5; cf. 20:2, etc.). These positive emphases also have a long history in Jewish literature (e.g., 1 Sam. 15:22; Ps. 50:14 f.; Isa. 1:17; Amos 5:24; Mic. 6:8, etc.), especially in periods when the cultic center, the Temple, was in ruins (see also the Rabbis on sacrifice = prayer [cf. *Did.* 14], charity, justice, etc.).

Of the quotation contexts employed here, those from Isaiah in **2:5** and **3:1–5** are relatively straightforward LXX citations, while those in **2:7–8** and **2:10a** cannot be explained as direct literal use of particular single texts now preserved in our Old Testament. It is probable that Pseudo-Barnabas took these strange text forms from a source that dealt with "true sacrifices." This suggestion gains considerable strength from the fact that both Irenaeus (*Adv. haer.* 4:17:1–4) and Clement (*Paed.*

6. Therefore he set these things aside [9:4b; 16:2], so that the new law of our Lord Jesus Christ [§5:7], which is not tied to a yoke of necessity [cf. Acts 15:10], might have its own offering which is not man-made [see 16:7b].

7. And again he says to them:

Did I command your fathers, when they were coming out of the land of Egypt, to offer burnt offerings and sacrifices to me? 8. But, rather, this is what I commanded them [see Jer. 7:22 f.]—

Let none of you hold a grudge in his heart against his neighbor,

And love not a false oath [see Zech. 7:9 f. = 8:16 f.].

9. Therefore, since we are not without understanding [§5:2:23], we ought to perceive [§5:2:1] the gracious intention of our Father [§5:9]. For he is speaking to us, desiring that we who are not misled as they were [§5:6] should seek [§5:2:13] how we might approach him with our offering.

3:[12]:89–91) use the **2:10a** material in contexts dealing with basically the same matters as Barn. **2:4–3:6**—contexts in which Isa. 1:11 ff. and 58:4 ff. also play a large role along with Jer. 7:22 and Zech. 7:10; 8:17. Furthermore, Pseudo-Gregory of Nyssa (*Testimonies* 12) uses the **2:7 f.** material in connection with Isa. 1:11 ff. Although Clement knew Barnabas well and often referred to it by name (§3:4, §6:1), there is very little reason to believe that he is making direct use of Barnabas here. Nor is it clear that Irenaeus or Pseudo-Gregory knew the epistle. In short, there is excellent reason to believe that **2:4—3:6** is based on a Hellenistic Jewish anthology of texts united around the theme "What the Lord Requires." This tractate once circulated independently, and, in various forms, came into the hands of Pseudo-Barnabas, Irenaeus, Clement, Pseudo-Gregory (?), and probably others (cf. Justin, *Apol.* 37). As Barnabas now stands, the editorial comments that hold these quotations together show ample evidence of the influence of Pseudo-Barnabas' Christian tradition. But there is nothing necessarily "Christian" about the main emphases of the section, and its strong parenetic background—similar to that of the Two Ways (§2)—is quite apparent.

Some of the editorial portions merit brief comment: **2:6** raises some minor problems when viewed in the light of the rest of the epistle—this is the only well-attested occurrence of the full name of "Jesus Christ" (§5:7), and with **3:6**, the only place where a clear contrast is made between "their Law" and the Christian "new law" (§5:6). This could be used as supporting evidence for the contention that **2:4—3:6** is a

10a. To us, then, he speaks thus: [g]

A sacrifice to God is a broken heart [see Ps. 51:17];
An odor well pleasing to the Lord is a heart which glorifies its
    creator [§5:9].

10b. Therefore, brethren, we ought to pay strict attention to the matters which concern our salvation [§5:4], lest the Wicked One causes error [4:1; 12:10; 14:5] to slip in among us and hurls us away from our life! [§2:7; §5:3–4.]

3 Therefore he speaks again concerning these things to them:
Why do you make a fast to me, says the Lord,
    so that today your voice is heard wailing?
This is not the sort of fast I have chosen, says the Lord,
    not a man humiliating his soul.[h]

2. Not even if you bend your neck in the shape of a circle,
    and deck yourselves out in [i] sackcloth and ashes—
        you cannot even call such conduct an acceptable fast! [Isa.
        58:4b–5.]

3. But to us he says:
Behold, this is the fast which I have chosen, says the Lord.[j]
Loose every bond of injustice,
    untie the knots of forcibly extracted agreements.

---

[g] H [mg.] notes here "Ps. 50 [LXX] and in the Apocalypse of Adam." On the "Adam" reference, see M. R. James, *JTS* 16 (1915), 409f.

[h] So S; but H (= Cl.A.) lacks "says the Lord" and reads "a day for a man to humiliate his soul" (see LXX). L has ". . . says the Lord, that someone should humiliate his soul without cause."

[i] So H; but S (= Cl.A.) and LXX have "spread under you," while L has both readings (perhaps correctly?): "put on sackcloth and strew ashes beneath you."

[j] S adds, probably under the influence of 3:1b, "not a man humiliating his soul but . . . ."

---

tradition block appropriated by Pseudo-Barnabas with only minor adaptations, and that he elsewhere uses materials that display slightly different backgrounds and attitudes (e.g., 4:7 f. = 14:1 ff.). However, it is not clear whether he or someone else (his source? or a later copyist?) is responsible for the "Jesus Christ" and "new law" references. On the "yoke" allusion in **2:6**, see also Matt. 11:29 f.; 1 Clem. 16:17; Did. 6:2. In **2:9b** the final verb can mean simply "to draw near" or "to bring an offering" (cf. 1:7b)—the sacrificial setting seems to require the latter.

Release the downtrodden with forgiveness,
>   and tear up every unjust contract.
Distribute your food to the hungry,
>   and [k] if you see someone naked, clothe him.
Bring the homeless into your home,
>   and if you see someone of lowly estate, do not despise him,
>   nor (despise) anyone of your own household.[k]

4. Then your light will break forth early,
>   and your healing [l] will arise quickly.
And your righteousness will go before you,
>   and the glory of God will surround you.

5. Then you will cry out, and God will listen to you;
While you are still speaking, he will say "Here I am"—
>   if you put away from you bonds and scornful gestures and
>   words of complaint,
>   and give your food to the hungry without hypocrisy,
>   and have mercy on [m] the person of lowly estate [Isa.
>   58:6–10a].

6. For this reason, therefore, brethren [§4:3], when he foresaw how the people whom he prepared [§5:6] in his Beloved One [§5:7] would believe in childlike innocence [see 6:11], the Patient One [§5:9] gave us a preview [§5:2:25] concerning everything [2:4], lest we be shattered to pieces as "proselytes" to their law [§5:6].

---

[k] So HS; but L (see Cl.A.) follows the usual LXX text more closely: ". . . and lead the homeless poor into your home. If you see someone naked, clothe him, and do not despise those of your household." Possibly an earlier form of Barnabas did not include the final words ("nor . . . household"), which interrupt the stylistic balance of the passage and may have been supplied later from the better-known LXX text.

[l] So HS[1(?)]; but L presupposes the similar Greek word "garments" (cf. Cl.A.), which is a widely attested variant reading in LXX witnesses to Isa. 58:8 (see also, and correct, *JBL* 79 [1960], 342). S* is of no help here because of a scribal error.

[m] So S; but H and LXX have "satisfy (with food)." L lacks the entire clause.

II. READINESS IN THE SHADOW OF CRISIS
(4:1-14)

Transition to the new section (4:1-2)

4 We must, then, carefully investigate the present situation [cf. 17:2] and seek out the things which are able to save us [§5:4; cf. 2:1].

1b. Therefore let us completely flee from all the works of lawlessness,
    lest the works of lawlessness ensnare us [5:4];
And let us hate the error of the present age [4:10a],
    so that we might be loved in the age to come [§5:3].
2. Let us give no leisure to our own soul so that it has opportunity to associate with the wicked and sinful—lest we become like them! [Cf. 10:3-8.]

The imminent eschatological crisis (4:3-6a) [§5:3]

3. The great final scandal is at hand, concerning which it has been written—as Enoch [n] says. 3b. For the Master [§5:9] cut short the times and the days [see 15:5] for this reason, that his Beloved

---

[n] So HS; but L has "Daniel" (see 4:5, §4:1-2), perhaps thinking of Dan. 8:13; 9:26 f.; 11:31; 12:11 (see Mark 13:14 and par.). The words "as Enoch/Daniel says" may be an early scribal gloss (Windisch, *ad loc.*).

4:1-6a. Little comment is required at this point for **4:1-2** beyond noting its close relationship to 4:9b-14 and to Two Ways thought in general (§2:3, 7). The section in **4:3-6a**, however, presents several problems. Pseudo-Barnabas appears to be making two main points: (1) the "final scandal," which has long been expected in apocalyptic literature, may come at any time (i.e., the "little horn"); and (2) the "times" have been abridged in order to speed up this final crisis and its results (i.e., the simultaneous fall of the three? Cf. Mark 13:20 = Matt. 24:22; 4 Ezra 2:13; 2 Baruch 20:1; 83:1). But there is no reason to think that he has a clear sequence of contemporary events in view. He is using a living apocalyptic tradition based on Dan. 7:7-8, 19-24 (see also Rev. 13; 4 Ezra 11-12); it has provided the imagery, and thus we cannot press the imagery for exact evidence about Pseudo-Barnabas' date and situation (§6:4).
Although there seem to be three quotation formulas here, only two

One might hasten and come into his inheritance [§5:7]. 4. And the prophet speaks thus: ^{o}

Ten kingdoms ^{p} will reign on the earth.

And afterward there will arise a little king,

   who will humiliate three of the kingdoms ^{q} simultaneously.

5. Similarly, Daniel says concerning the same one:

And I saw the fourth beast, wicked and powerful

   and more dangerous than all the beasts of the sea; ^{r}

And how that ten horns sprouted from him,

   and from them budded a little offshoot of a horn;

And how that it humiliated three of the great horns simul-

   taneously.

6. Therefore you ought to understand! [§5:2:23; cf. Mark 13:14.]

Danger of misplaced security in the covenant (4:6b–8)

6b. Furthermore, I also urge you [21:2, 4, 8] as one of your own, and especially as one who loves you all more than I love my own self [§4:3, §5:5:5], walk circumspectly ^{s} [§5:2:21] and do not be like certain people [4:2], compounding your sins

   ^{o} H$^{mg.}$ comments "Apocrypha of Daniel and Esdras"—see §4:1–2.

   ^{p} So SL; but H has "kings" as in most Greek MSS of Dan. 7:24 (see 2:44)—the same problem exists in Hippolytus, *Antichrist* 27.

   ^{q} So L; but HS have "kings"—note the similar problem in 4 Ezra 12:23 (cf. Dan. 7:17).

   ^{r} So HL (see Dan. 7:3; Rev. 13:1; 4 Ezra 11:1); but S has "earth" (Dan. 7:17, 23).

   ^{s} So HL; but S adds "now" (see 4:9b).

---

unambiguous citations appear. The "Enoch" allusion in 4:3a probably refers back to the general theme of the "final scandal." The style and content of 4:3b strongly suggest that it is editorial comment, not an Enoch text. If Pseudo-Barnabas had a precise Enoch passage in mind, it apparently is no longer preserved in extant Enoch literature (the best candidates are 1 Enoch 89:61–64; 90:17 f.; 2 Enoch 34:1–3, but they are not very satisfactory). It is possible that "the prophet" of 4:4 is supposed to be Enoch—apparently 4:4 is not attributed to Daniel as is 4:5. In any case, presently known apocalyptic texts contain neither of these alleged quotations. They probably come from elaborations of the Daniel tradition, such as we find in Hippolytus, *Antichrist* 25 (cf. *Orac. Sib.* 3:396 ff.): "As Daniel says [cf. Dan. 7:7–8, 19 ff.]: 'I beheld the beast, and behold ten horns followed him, among which there arose another little one as an offshoot. And it rooted up three of its predecessors.'"

by claiming that your covenant is irrevocably yours.[t] 6c. But they
lost it completely in the following manner, after Moses already
had received it— 7. *for* the scripture *says:*
And Moses was on the *mountain fasting for forty days and forty*
nights, and he received the covenant from the *Lord,*
  stone *tablets inscribed by the finger of the Lord's hand.*
But when they turned to idols, they lost it. 8. For the *Lord* speaks
thus:
Moses, Moses, descend immediately, for your people whom *you*
led out from the land of Egypt have sinned.
And Moses understood [§5:2:23], *and he hurled the* two *tablets*
from his *hands.* 8b. *And* the covenant (of the tablets) was
smashed to bits so that the covenant of Jesus, the Beloved One
[§5:7], might be sealed in our heart, in hope of his faith [§5:5:1].

Parenthetical personal note (4:9a) [§4:3]

9. But since I wish to write many things—not as a Teacher
would, but as is fitting for a friend to do—and to omit nothing of
what we have received [see 17:1], I hurry along. I am your
devoted slave [§1:2, n. 2].

[t] This important text is badly corrupt. The above translation follows H,
with minor adjustments based on S. L is quite different: "do not be like
those who heap up your sins and say that their covenant is also ours. But it is
ours." L seems to miss the point of the argument, that Christians should
beware of the attitude of false security which developed in Judaism and led
to the heaping up of sins (§5:6).

4:6b–9a. The close correspondence between **4:6c–8** and **14:1–4**
(italics indicate common wording) shows that we are once more in the
presence of familiar traditional material. The general contents resemble, but do not verbally reproduce, Deut. 9:9–16 (cf. Exod. 3:4;
24:18; 31:18; 32:7 f., 19; 34:28), and the form of presentation is very
similar to the reworked form of the Sinai story in 1 Clem. 53. The
emphases of the tradition are that Moses understood (see Acts 7:25)
and received the covenant, but that the people lost it without ever
receiving it (14:1b, 4a) when they made the golden calf. The setting
in chapter 14 is by far the more natural (see the problem of the "two
people" in ch. 13), and the tradition has been inserted into chapter 4
as a warning against overconfidence (the theme of 4:9b–14), *not* primarily (if at all) as a warning against Jewish proselytizing activity
(see L). In these last times there is a real danger of failure. Although
Christians have received *the* covenant (not a *new* covenant; see §5:6)

Warnings against overconfidence (4:9b–14) [§2:7]

9b. Wherefore let us walk circumspectly [§5:2:21] in these last days [§5:3]. For the entire period of our life and faith *u* will be wasted unless now, in the lawless time and in the impending scandals, we resist as befits God's sons [§2:3]. 10. Therefore,*v* lest the Black One [§5:3] make deceitful entrance [2:10b], let us flee from all that is irrelevant, let us hate completely [4:1b] the works of the wicked way [§2:2]. 10b. Do not live monastic lives by retiring to yourselves as though you have already attained the righteous state, but by assembling together, seek out together what is to your mutual advantage [§2:3]. 11. For the scripture says:

Woe to those who are wise [see §5:2:23] in their own eyes,
   and understanding [see §5:2:11] in their own sight [Isa. 5:21].

u So L; but H has only "our life" and S, "your faith" (= Did. 16:2b).

v So H; but S lacks "therefore," which could change the whole construction. L lacks the whole clause. Thus many editions put the verse division before the words "let us flee. . . ."

---

through Jesus, they must not cease striving for ultimate salvation (§5:4). Apparently Jewish cultic law was viewed by Pseudo-Barnabas and his tradition as the misconceived substitute for the lost covenant—similar ideas seem to have been present in Hellenistic Judaism (see Strabo, *Geog.* 16:35–37) and in early Christianity (cf. Acts 7:38 ff.; the Ebionites).

4:9b–14. This combination of Two Ways and eschatological imagery to warn against complacency in these last times is the real goal of what has preceded in chapter 4 (see 4:1–2, 6b). Its relationship to Didache 16 and the Two Ways has been discussed in §2:3, 7. In many ways this section summarizes some of the key attitudes of Pseudo-Barnabas (§5:3–6), and reflects themes which elsewhere are treated at greater length—for example, Temple (4:11b; 6:15, 16:7–10), meditating (4:11b; 10:11). It is one of the longest primarily editorial contexts in Barnabas 2–16, but even at that it leaves the impression of a string of familiar traditional platitudes. If 4:14b intends to quote Matthew, this is the only such New Testament citation in Barnabas (§4:1). It is possible that Pseudo-Barnabas here used a popular Jewish apocalyptic saying also known to (Jesus and) the author of Matthew (see also Matt. 20:16 var.; cf. 4 Ezra 8:1–3).

11b. Let us be pneumatics [§5:2:20]; let us be a perfect Temple to God [§5:6]. To the best of our ability let us meditate [§5:2:17] on the fear of God [§5:5:6] and strive to keep his commandments [§5:5:4], so that we might rejoice in his ordinances [§5:5:2, 5]. 12. The Lord will judge the world impartially. Each man will receive payment in accord with his deeds—if he was good, his righteousness precedes him; if he was wicked, the reward of wickedness goes before him! [§5:3–4, 7.] 13. Thus on no account should we slumber in our sins [4:2; cf. 4:6b] by relaxing as "those who have been called"—and the wicked Archon [§5:3] will take advantage of his power over us [2:1] and push us away from the kingdom of the Lord [2:10b]. 14. And finally, my brethren [§4:3], understand this [§5:2:18]: When you notice what great signs and wonders were performed in Israel [5:8] and still they have been abandoned [§5:6], let us take heed [§5:2:21] lest we be found to be, as it is written, "many called but few chosen" [see Matt. 22:14].

III. WHY THE LORD ENDURED SUFFERING (5:1–8:7)

The Lord endured fleshly suffering to purify us (5:1–2) [§5:7]

5 For it was for this reason that the Lord submitted to deliver his flesh to destruction, that by the forgiveness of sins we might be purified [8:1]—that is, by the sprinkling (for purification) of his

---

5:1–8:7. With 5:1, Pseudo-Barnabas introduces a lengthy section (chs. 5–8) that deals with the problem of why the Lord (1) came in the flesh and (2) passively submitted to (or "endured") a humiliating death at the hands of sinful men, despite the fact that he is God's Son who assisted in creation and will execute judgment on mankind (see also 14:4–5). In presenting his argument, Pseudo-Barnabas often interweaves traditional materials, and occasionally he goes off on a tangent (see 6:1–4, 8–19) or inserts personal parenthetical comments (5:3–4; 6:5, 10b; 7:1). Early Christian concern for the theme of the Lord's enduring is well illustrated by Justin (*Apol.* 50:1; 63:10, 16; *Dial.* 68:1)—cf. also Ign. Polyc. 3:2; Polycarp, Phil. 1:2; 8:1; 2 Clem. 1:2, etc. To some extent, the way in which the material has been subdivided for present purposes is artificial—Pseudo-Barnabas was not so systematic (§4:4)—but perhaps it will help in tracing the general drift of the argument.

blood.[w] 2. For it is written concerning him—partly with reference
to Israel [6:7b] and partly to us [§5:11]—and it says thus:
  He was wounded because of our lawless actions,
    and he was rendered helpless because of our sins;
      by his wounds we were healed [Isa. 53:5].
  As a sheep to the slaughter was he led,
    and as a lamb he was silent before his shearer [Isa. 53:7b].

Parenthetical admonition to exercise gnosis (5:3–4) [§5:1–2]

3. We ought, therefore, to give heartfelt thanks to the Lord
because he has both given us gnosis [§5:2:6] of the things which
have come to pass, and has given us wisdom [§5:2:22] in the
present events—nor are we without understanding [§5:2:23] concerning what is about to happen [1:7; 17:1 f.]. 4. But the scripture
says:
  It is not unjust to spread out nets for capturing birds [Prov.
  1:17].
4b. This is what it is saying: It is just that a man should perish
if, although he has gnosis [§5:2:6] of the Way of Righteousness,
he becomes ensnared in the Way of Darkness [§2:2; see 4:1 f.,
9b ff.].

The Lord endured to fulfill the promise(s) (5:5–7) [§5:7]

5. And furthermore, my brethren [§4:3], consider this: if the
Lord submitted to suffer for our souls—he who is Lord of the

---

  [w] So HL (see 1 Pet. 1:2); but S has "by his blood which is sprinkled"
(see Heb. 12:24).

5:1–4. The Lord's presence *in the flesh* is emphasized throughout
chapters 5–7: he *had to* (5:6) or was *about to* (6:7, 9, 14) come in
the flesh (see 12:10); he *came* in flesh (5:10, 11); his flesh was afflicted (5:12–13) and offered up (7:5), but it has been firmly established (6:3) and he will return in flesh (7:9 ?). The theme of (ritual)
purification (5:1) is also treated in 8:1–3. On the form of the quotation in 5:2 and its background, see *JBL* 80 (1961), 372 f. The aptness
of the proverb cited in 5:4 for a Two Ways context is apparent not
only from its original Old Testament setting but from the use of
"birds" elsewhere in Pseudo-Barnabas' tradition (10:4, 10) to symbolize pestilent plunderers like those "sinners" described in Prov. 1:10–19.

whole world, to whom God said at the foundation of the world [§5:7, 9; see 6:12]:

Let us make man in accord with our image and likeness [Gen. 1:26a]

—then how is it that he submitted to suffer at the hand of men? [Cf. 7:2.] Learn! [§5:2:15.] 6. The prophets, after they had received special insight from him [§5:2:26], prophesied concerning him. And he submitted so that he might break the power of Death and demonstrate [§5:2:7] the resurrection from the dead—thus it was necessary for him to be manifested [§5:2:25] in flesh. 7. Also (he submitted) so that he might fulfill the promise to the fathers [14:1] and, while he was preparing *ᵃ* the new people for himself [§5:6] and while he was still on earth, to prove [§5:2:7] that after he has brought about the resurrection he will judge.

The Lord endured in flesh so that sinners could see him (5:8–10) [§5:7]

8. Furthermore, although he was teaching Israel and doing such great wonders and signs [4:14], the result was not that they loved him dearly for his preaching! *ʸ* 9. But when he chose his

---

ᵃ The MSS of family G begin here (§3:3).

ʸ So H, cf. L: "they neither believed nor loved him"; but the negative idea is lacking in S ("he preached and they dearly loved him") and in G ("he preached and he dearly loved him [Israel]").

5:5–10. The dialoguelike setting of **5:5** suggests that this has been a disputed problem in Pseudo-Barnabas' school background—how can the Lord's humiliation by and for men be reconciled with his exalted nature? Possibly **5:5** should be translated: "could the Lord actually submit . . . since he is Lord of the whole world . . . how could he submit?" In any case, Pseudo-Barnabas neither denies Jesus' exalted Lordship (as the extreme Ebionites) nor his real passion (as the Docetists). Early Christian literature preserves several parallels to one or more of the items enumerated in **5:6b–7**—see esp. Odes Sol. 31:10 f.; Irenaeus, *Ap. Preach.* 35–39; Hippolytus, *Ap. Trad.* 4. In **5:8–10** the argument seems to be this: before God's Son became flesh, men continually failed to follow him because they could not actually see him (as Logos?). Thus he had to come in flesh so that sinful man could see him and be saved. The sun analogy was common in Judaism as a proof that no man could see God (cf. b.*Hullin* 60; Philo, *Spec. leg.* 1:40), and was widely adopted by Christians to illustrate the necessity of the Logos becoming incarnate (see Windisch, 330 f.).

own apostles who were destined to preach his gospel [8:3]—men
who were sinful beyond measure so that he might prove [§5:2:7]
that he came not to call righteous but sinners ᶻ [Mark 2:17b parr.]
—it was then that he revealed himself [§5:2:25] as God's Son
[12:10]. 10. For if he had not come in flesh, how could men be
saved by looking at him? ᵃ They cannot even gaze directly into
the rays of the sun, even though it is a work of his hands and is
destined to cease existing! [15:5.]

The Lord endured to complete the number of Israel's sins (5:11–14) [§5:6–7]

11. Thus the Son of God came in flesh for this reason, that he
might bring to summation the total of sins [8:1–2; 14:5] of those
who persecuted his prophets to death. 12. So also he submitted
for this reason. 12b. For God says that the afflicting of his flesh
[7:2] came from them:

> ᶻ So HSL; but G adds "to repentance" (Luke 5:32).
> ᵃ Or perhaps, "how could men survive when they looked at him?"

5:11–6:7. There is a rough unity to 5:11—6:7 in that the main
theme, supported by various quotations, is Jesus' rejection by Israel
(already suggested in 5:2; cf. 5:8). The tangential section on Jesus'
ultimate exaltation as victorious judge (6:1–4–"Servant," "Stone,"
"Day"—note the strong dialogue flavor) apparently was suggested by
the abridged form of Isa. 50:6–7 in 5:14, with its reference to a "solid
rock" (see 6:3c). It is not clear what is meant by the "commandment"
(§5:5:4) of 6:1, but it accords well with the juridical terminology of
the ensuing quotation.

Several of the quotations are extremely interesting as evidence of
how Old Testament and related materials circulated: e.g., in 5:13b
and 6:6 we have Psalm phraseology strung together to form a new
passage (cf. Qumran *Hymns,* Psalms of Solomon, Luke 1–2)—Irenaeus
also knows the first of these psalmic passages (*Ap. Preach.* 79). The
unique form of Isa. 50:8–9 cited in 6:1 also is reproduced by Irenaeus
(*Ap. Preach.* 88 = *Adv. haer* 4:33:13; see *JBL* 79 [1960], 346), who
also does a great deal with the idea that Jesus brings things "to summation" (5:11—the "recapitulation" theory). It may be that Irenaeus knew
Barnabas, but a more likely situation is that both are influenced by an
(Asian) Teacher (Elder?) who used these "proofs" similarly (see
§6:10, 12). Other quotations in this section also have a long history
in Christian apologetic: Jesus often received such Old Testament titles
as "Stone" (6:2b–4a; see Justin, *Dial.* 34:2; 86:3, etc.; *JBL* 79 [1960],

When they smite their own Shepherd,
   then the sheep of the flock will be lost [b] [see Zech. 13:7].
13. And he desired to suffer in such a manner, for it was necessary
so that he might suffer on the wood [7:5; 8:5; 12:1, 5]. 13b. For
one who prophesies concerning him says:
   Spare my soul from the sword [Ps. 22:20a]
   and affix my flesh with nails [see Ps. 119:120a (but in LXX text
      form)],
      for a synagogue [c] of wicked men have come upon me [d] [see
      Ps. 22:16b].
14. And again he says:
   Behold, I have bared my back for stripes,
      and my cheeks for smiting [Isa. 50:6a],
   but I have set my face as a solid rock [Isa. 50:7b].

Vindication of the Lord who endured (6:1-4)

6 When, therefore, he made the commandment, what does
he say?

Who disputes my judgment? Let him oppose me.
Or who vindicates himself in my presence?
   Let him draw near to the Lord's Servant.
2. Woe to you, for you all will grow old like a garment,
   and a moth will devour you! [Isa. 50:8b-9.]

[b] So, for the most part, HS* (but it is not entirely clear where the quotation begins). L finds two quotations here: "And Isaiah [!] says, 'by the
afflicting of his body we are all healed' [Isa. 53:5b]. And another prophet: 'I
will smite the shepherd and the sheep of the fold will be dispersed.' " G
mostly agrees with HS* at the start of 5:12b, but agrees with L on the form
of the shepherd quotation (see Matt. 26:31; Mark 14:27). S²mg. expands the
S* quotation to read: ". . . then the sheep of the fold will be scattered and
lost." The verb "be lost" also could be rendered "perish" (see 5:4b; 11:7*).
   [c] So HSL (see 6:6); but G has the plural "synagogues," perhaps because
the verb is plural.
   [d] So SGL; but H reads "has encompassed me," probably under the influence of LXX (see Barn. 6:6).

───

344 f.), "Day" (? **6:4b**; see Justin, *Dial.* 108:4; Clement, *Eclog. Proph.*
53:1), "Righteous One" (**6:7**; see Justin, *Dial.* 17, 133-137). Pseudo-
Barnabas certainly is no innovator here, and is undoubtedly using
proof-texts made available by his school tradition. How much of the
present setting is also traditional is difficult to determine.

2b. And again, since he was established as a mighty Stone which crushes, the prophet says of him:

Behold, I will insert into the foundations of Zion a Stone which is precious, chosen, a cornerstone, prized [Isa. 28:16a].

3. Then what does he say?

And whoever trusts in him ᵉ will live forever [8:5b; 11:10 f.].

3b. Is our hope, then, on a stone? Not in the least! But he speaks in such a way since the Lord has established his flesh in strength.

3c. For he says:

And he established me as a solid Rock [see Isa. 50:7b].

4. And again the prophet says:

The very Stone which the builders rejected has become the cornerstone! [Ps. 118:22.]

4b. And again he says:

This is the great and awesome Day which the Lord made [Ps. 118:24a (see 118:23)].

Summary statement about the Lord's suffering (6:5–7) [§5:7]

5. I write to you more clearly so that you might understand [§5:2:22]. I am a slave devoted to your love [4:9a; §4:3; §5:5:5].

6. What, then, does the prophet say again?

A synagogue of wicked men encompasses me [Ps. 22:16b],
they surround me as bees around honey [Ps. 118:12a],
and for my garments they cast lots [Ps. 22:18b].

7. Thus, since he was about to be manifested [§5:2:25] in flesh and to suffer [12:2a], his passion was revealed beforehand [§5:2:25]. 7b. For the prophet says concerning Israel [5:2]:

Woe to them, for they devised a wicked plot against themselves when they said, "Let us bind the Righteous One, for he is displeasing to us" [Isa. 3:9b–10a; see Wisd. Sol. 2:12].

ᵉ G has "whoever hopes on," while HSL have "whoever believes in" (Isa. 28:16b; see §5:5:1).

The good land of the new creation (6:8–19) [§5:6]

8. What does the other prophet, Moses, say to them? *f*

Behold, thus says the Lord God: Enter into the good land, which the Lord promised [5:7] to Abraham and Isaac and Jacob, and make it your inheritance—a land flowing milk and honey [see Exod. 33:1, 3; Deut. 6:18, etc.].

f So S Cl.A. (H lacks the interrogative "what . . . ?"); but GL have "and Moses also says to them."

6:8–19. The connection between this eschatological-allegorical "midrash" on the "good land" and its surroundings is not obvious. The foremost possibilities are (1) that Pseudo-Barnabas intends to show how "the promise" of 5:7 is being fulfilled (see **6:8, 17b**) and/or (2) he is drawing a sharp contrast between "suffering" humanity (**6:9**) —for whom Jesus suffered (5:5)—and the "new creation" which results from Jesus' endurance. Clearly **6:8–19** is a basic unit, and its traditional background is betrayed by the several unique quotations used and by the occasional awkward constructions that remain alongside the more recent editorial comments—e.g., in **6:12b** the verbs in the quotation are plural and obviously "to us," not "to the Son," and in **6:13a** the "you" is singular (!), despite the subsequent "us" (possibly this is a vestige of the older dialogue setting which still permeates this section?).

The argument of **6:8–19** is often subtle and/or evasive to a modern reader. The main contrast in **6:8–12** is between "suffering land" or the old creation, formed from the "face of the land" (see Gen. 2:7), and the "good land" or the new creation, formed in God's image (Gen. 1:26 ff.). Behind this contrast lies the (Hellenistic) Jewish idea (which was widely adopted in early Christian thought, both "orthodox" and heterodox) that Genesis 1–2 speaks of two men being created, the "heavenly" and the "earthly." Somewhere in the remote background of the "gnosis" quotation (?) in **6:9** lies a Semitic play on the words "Adam" and "land" (*adama*). Also in the background of that strange verse is the contrast between the ancient "Jesus" (for that is the Greek form of the Hebrew "Joshua") who led the older people into the land, and the eschatological Jesus who fulfills the promise (see **6:16c; 12:8–10!**). **6:10b** is a parenthetical admonition similar to 5:3–4; the source of the quotation is unknown, although Clement also cites it in two places (once clearly from Barnabas, once linked to Job 11:2).

In **6:13–19**, some of the implications of the new creation are spelled out: it is eschatological (cf. 15:8)—as the "old" creation was to have lordship over Eden, so the "new" will ultimately rule. The apocalyptic quotation in **6:13b** is paralleled in Didascalia 26 (= Lat. 6:18:15),

9. And what does "gnosis" [§5:2:6] say? Learn! [§5:2:15.]
Hope [§5:5:1], it says, on that Jesus who is about to appear
to you [§5:2:25] in flesh [5:1]. For man is land suffering, for
Adam was formed [6:11–14] from the face of the land.
10. What, then, does he say? "Into the good land—a land flowing
milk and honey" [6:8].
10b. Blessed be our Lord, brethren [§4:3], who has placed in
us wisdom [§5:2:22] and understanding [§5:2:18] of his secrets.
For the prophet says:
Who can understand a parable of the Lord *g* [§5:2:19], except
he who is wise and understanding [§5:2:11], and who loves his
Lord? [§5:5:5.]
11. Since, then, he renovated us by the forgiveness of sins
[§5:7], he made us to be another sort (of creation), as though

g The Greek is ambiguous and could be punctuated "the prophet speaks
a parable of the Lord: 'Who can . . .'" (see L). Cl. A., however, and probably H, understood it as above.

---

and is similar to Rev. 21:5, and Hippolytus, *Commentary in Daniel*
4:37. The quotation in **6:14b** resembles Ezek. 11:19; 36:26, but verbally is quite different from all known texts of Ezekiel. Its meaning
for Barnabas is that Jesus replaces the "strong hearts" with *himself*
(see §5:6). This is also the clue to **6:16**—Jesus appears before God as
he indwells his new people, the eschatological Temple. He is the heart
of the new creation (see 16:7–10; cf. Odes Sol. 4:5; 17:3), he is inside
the Temple (see 16:9–10). The milk-and-honey analogy of **6:17** reflects the ancient custom of feeding newborn babies honey before they
took milk. In later Christian baptismal practice, this symbolism became
part of the service (see Hippolytus, *Ap. Trad.* 23:2).
It is always possible that Barnabas **6:8–19** is to be understood in
terms of baptismal liturgy (so N. A. Dahl, in the Goguel *Festschrift*
[Neuchâtel, 1950], 62 ff.; G. Schille, *ZNW* 49 [1958], 31 ff.; L. W.
Barnard, *TU* 79 [1961], 263 ff.; Prigent, 84 ff.), but it should be
emphasized that there is nothing in the text itself that demands, or
even strongly suggests, this interpretation. It is true that the sole explicit baptism passage in Barnabas (11:6–11) contains similarities to
6:8–19—for example, eschatological Eden setting (11:10), the idea of
the fair "land" (11:9)—but they are not strong enough to be con-
vincing. Nor are they as strong as the relationship between **6:8–19**
and 16:6–10. Thus Barnabas **6:8–19** is *primarily* a block of eschatological commentary on a synthetic Pentateuchal passage (6:8; cf. 4:7 f.
= 14:2 f.) dealing with the new creation. Whatever else it may be is
secondary.

we had a child's soul [cf. 3:6]—he fashioned us again [cf. 6:9b], as it were. 12. For the scripture is speaking about us when he says to the Son [5:5]:

Let us make man in accord with our image and likeness, and let them rule over the beasts of the earth and the birds of heaven and the fish of the sea [Gen. 1:26].

12b. And when he saw how well we were formed [6:9b], the Lord said:

Increase and multiply and fill the earth [Gen. 1:28].

These things (he said) to the Son.[h]

13. Again, I will show you [§5:2:7] how he says to us that he made a second fashioning in the last times. 13b. And the Lord says:

Behold, I make the last things like the first.

13c. It is for this reason, therefore, that the prophet proclaimed: "Enter into the land flowing milk and honey, and exercise lordship over it" [see 6:8]. 14. See [§5:2:10], then, we have been fashioned anew! 14b. As he says again in another prophet:

Behold, says the Lord, I will remove from them—

that is, from those on whom he foresaw the Lord's spirit [i]—

their stony hearts, and I will insert fleshly hearts.

14c. Because he was about to be manifested [§5:2:25] in flesh [5:1] and to dwell in us. 15. For, my brethren [§4:3], our heart being thus inhabited constitutes a holy Temple to the Lord! [16:6–10.] 16. for the Lord says again:

And in what manner shall I appear before the Lord my God and be glorified? [See Ps. 42:2b.]

16b. He says:

I will confess you in the assembly [j] of my brethren,
and I will praise you in the midst of the assembly [j] of saints [Ps. 22:22].

16c. Therefore we are those whom he conducts into the good land! [§5:6.]

17. What, then, is the "milk and honey"? Because the infant is

---

[h] This (awkward) comment is lacking in HL, but present in SG (cf. 5:5); L also lacks the parallel phrase in 6:12a. Possibly this is a gloss (cf. 9:3a, "these are for a witness," which L also lacks).

[i] Or, "from those whom the Lord's spirit foresaw" (see §5:10). L lacks 6:14a–b.

[j] Or, "congregation," "church."

initiated into life first by honey, then by milk. 17b. Thus also, in a similar way, when we have been initiated into life by faith [§5:5:1] in the promise [6:8, 14:1b] and by the word [§5:8], we will live exercising lordship over the land. 18. But as it was already said above [see 6:12]: "And they shall increase, and multiply, and rule over the fish. . . ." 18b. Who, then, is presently able to rule over beasts or fish or birds of heaven? [Cf. 10:3–5, 10.] For we ought to understand [§5:2:1] that "to rule" implies that one is in control [see 2:1], so that he who gives the orders exercises dominion. 19. If, then, this is not the present situation, he has told us when it will be—when we ourselves have been perfected as heirs of the Lord's covenant [14:5].

Transition back to the main theme of suffering (7:1–2)

7 Understand [§5:2:18], therefore, children of joy,[k] that the good Lord revealed everything to us beforehand [§5:2:25] so that we might know [§5:2:4] whom we ought to praise continually with thanksgiving.

[k] So HSG; but L has "of love" (see 9:7; 21:9; §4:3; §5:5:5).

7:1–8:7. The lengthy section begun in 5:1 is brought to a close with examples of how certain Jewish cultic rituals typified what would happen to Jesus. The basic source for chapters 7–8 seems to be a (Hellenistic) Jewish *halakic* (legal) treatment of such matters as the Atonement Fast (7:3–5), the two goats at the Atonement (7:[4], 6–11), and the red heifer ritual (8:1–6; see esp. G. Allon, summarized in *Journal of Jewish Studies* 11 [1960], 24). Chapter 7 actually quotes from such a source on several occasions, but chapter 8 contains only a paraphrase summary of the ritual. In fact, the Talmud (Mishna *Yoma* 4–8) knows some of the nonbiblical details mentioned in chapter 7—the fasting (7:5), similarity of the goats (7:6, 10), crimson wool and maltreatment of the scapegoat (7:8a, 9b), and the removal of the wool (7:8b, but in *Yoma*, only half the wool [thread] is removed and is placed on a rock or on the Temple [not on a bush], then the goat is shoved to its death over a cliff—despite Lev. 16:22). Comparable Jewish elaborations on the red heifer rite are almost completely lacking. Philo claims to have treated its symbolic meaning in a treatise which is no longer extant (see *Spec. leg.* 1:268 f.), and a Rabbinic tradition states that only Moses was shown its significance (so L. Ginzberg, *Legends of the Jews,* vol. 3 [Philadelphia, 1911], 216). The Yemenite Jewish *Midrash ha-Gadol,* I am told (by Rabbi P. Weis of

2. If, then, the Son of God, who is Lord and is about to judge
the living and dead, suffered so that his being afflicted [5:2, 12b]
might bring us life [12:5], let us believe that it was not possible
for the Son of God to suffer except on our behalf [§5:7; cf. 5:5].

Lessons from the Atonement ritual: the Fast and the scapegoat (7:3–11) [§5:6]

3. But he also drank vinegar and gall [see Ps. 69:21] when he
was crucified. 3b. Hear [§5:2:2] how the priests of the Temple
made even this clear [§5:2:25], when the commandment was
written:

Whoever does not fast during the (Atonement) Fast must
surely die [see Lev. 23:29].

3c. The Lord gave such a commandment since he was destined
to offer the vessel of the spirit [§5:2:20] as a sacrifice for our
sins, so that the "type" [§5:2:24] which is based on Isaac's having
been offered up on the altar [Gen. 22:9] also might be fulfilled.
4. What, then, does he say in the prophet?

And they shall eat from the goat which is offered up during the
Fast for all sins [cf. Lev. 16:9, 27]—

pay attention [§5:2:21] more diligently—

and the priests alone shall all eat the entrails unwashed, with
vinegar.

Manchester, England), contains details about "children" who sprinkle
(8:1, 3a).

From an early date Christian apologetic incorporated the Atonement
symbolism (see Heb. 9:25; 10:19; 13:11, etc.). Both Justin (*Dial.*
40:4) and Tertullian (*Adv. Marcion.* 3:7:7) employ a form of the
tradition similar to Barnabas, but which scarcely seems to be directly
dependent on Barnabas. For both of them the scapegoat represents
Jesus' humiliation and rejection, while the similar goat that is burned
as an offering *after* the scapegoat is dispatched (Lev. 16:27) depicts
the triumphal Jesus who can be recognized by those who rejected him
(cf. 7:10a)—and upon whom, according to Tertullian, the church now
feasts while others fast (cf. 7:3–5). Tertullian also knows about the
scarlet wool (but does not develop that theme) and the detailed maltreatment of the scapegoat, but for him the goat is hurled to destruction as in *Yoma*. Barnabas, on the other hand, sees in both goats a type
of Jesus' suffering (7:4–5, 9), while the scapegoat also symbolizes his
exaltation (7:9). Barnabas' exact meaning is not always clear (does

5. For what reason?

Since I am destined to offer my flesh [5:1] for the sins of my new people [§5:6], you (priests) are about to drink gall mixed with vinegar—you alone will eat while the people fast and smite themselves on sackcloth and ashes.

This is to demonstrate [§5:2:7] that he must suffer at their hands [l] [5:11 ff.; 12:5].

6. Pay attention [§5:2:21] to what he commanded:

Take two goats which are handsome and alike, and present them; and let the priest take one for a burnt offering for sins [Lev. 16:7, 9].

7. But what do they do with the other?

Accursed, he says, is the other [see Lev. 16:8].

7b. Pay attention [§5:2:21] to how the type [§5:2:24] of Jesus is made clear! [§5:2:25.]

8. And you shall all spit on and prick (that goat), and encircle its head with scarlet wool, and thus let it be cast out into the desert [see Lev. 16:10].

8b. And when this has been done, the one who bears the goat brings (it) into the desert [m] and takes the wool and places it upon a bush which is called *rachē*,[n] the buds of which we are

[l] So HL (S adds "many things"—see 7:11; Mark 8:31, etc.); but G has "for them" (i.e., the "new people"?).

[m] The text is difficult, but apparently pictures the goat being carried (?) into the wilderness at the head of a procession (see Lev. 16:21 f.).

[n] Apparently a thorny bush (7:11) like the blackberry. The witnesses vary somewhat as to its exact name.

7:10a also equate the offered goat with the victorious Lord?), and is not limited to symbols of Jesus but also to his followers—those who wish to grasp the "crown" of the kingdom (7:11; cf. 8:5).

The material on the Atonement Fast in 7:3–5 is more difficult to analyze because of the scarcity of parallel reports. The connection between fasting and Atonement Day was well known (although it is not called a "fast" in the OT)—e.g., Philo, Josephus, *Yoma* 8—and Mishna *Menahoth* 11:7 even refers to the priests eating the "he-goat" on that day (cf. 7:4 f.; Tertullian). Similarly, 7:3b may reflect the Jewish tradition that Atonement Day coincides with the day Isaac was offered up (see Ginzberg, *Legends,* vol. 1 [Philadelphia, 1909], 283). But despite the fact that the basic *halakic* midrash here revolves around the idea of *fasting*—and it is not at all clear how the quotations of 7:3–4 were supposed to relate to one another (e.g., do the *people* eat in 7:4a or only the *priests,* as in 7:4b–5; are the priests, therefore,

accustomed to eat when we find them in the countryside. Thus
of the *rachē* alone are the fruits sweet.

9. What, then, does it mean—pay attention [§5:2:21]—that the
one is placed on the altar [7:6] and the other is accursed [7:7a],
and that the accursed one is crowned? [7:8a.] 9b. Because they
will see him then, on that day, wearing the scarlet robe around
his flesh [5:1], and they will say:

Is not this he whom we once crucified, despising and piercing
and spitting on him? [7:8a.] Surely this was the one who then
said he was God's Son! [See Mark 15:39b, parr.]

10. Now how is this like that situation? For this reason the goats
were alike and handsome [7:6], equal, so that when they see it
coming then [7:8b, 9b], they will be amazed at the similarity of
the goat. 10b. Therefore notice here the type [§5:2:10, 24] of
Jesus who was destined to suffer.

11. And what does it mean that they place the wool in the midst
of the thorns? [7:8b.] It is a type [§5:2:24] of Jesus placed in the
church, so that whoever desires to snatch away the scarlet wool
must suffer many things because the thornbush is treacherous,
and he must obtain it through affliction [§5:4].

---

condemned by the "commandment" in 7:3b; why is 7:3b mentioned
at all?)—Pseudo-Barnabas seems to have appropriated the tradition
solely to illustrate that Jesus drank "vinegar and gall" (cf. esp. G. Peter
5:16; Matt. 27:34, 48 parr.). The fact that the "quotation" attributed
to Jesus in 7:5 contains the fasting emphasis along with the "vinegar
and gall" detail suggests that Pseudo-Barnabas is not responsible for
the "Christianizing" of these materials, but that they have come, with
little adjustment, from his Christian school background. Similar "quotations" attributed to Jesus and his adversaries recur in the scapegoat
midrash (7:11b, 9b), indicating that 7:6–11 derives from basically
the same "Christianized" source as 7:3–5. (For a detailed discussion
of the "Gospel tradition" in chs. 7–8, see Koester, 127 f., 149–156,
263.)

There are even fewer relevant parallels to chapter 8 (see Heb.
9:13), although some later Christian authors drew (different) lessons
from the red heifer symbolism. Probably 8:5 is a conscious reflection of
a Greek variant to Ps. 96:10—"the Lord reigned *from the tree/wood*"
—which had wide currency in the early Christian apologetic (Justin
[*Dial.* 73; *Apol.* 41], Tertullian, etc.). The words of 8:7 act not only
as a conclusion to chapters 5–8, but as an excellent transition to the
gnosis of chapters 9–10.

11b. In such a way, he says, those who desire to see me and
to take hold of my kingdom [8:5] ought to take me through
affliction and suffering [see Acts 14:22].

Lessons from the red heifer ritual (8:1–7) [see Num. 19:1–10]

8 And what do you suppose is the type [§5:2:24] involved here,
in that he commanded to Israel that those men in whom sins are
complete [§5:6] should offer a heifer; and when they had slaughtered it, to burn it; and then the children should take the ashes
and put them into a container; and the scarlet wool should be
wrapped around a piece of wood—again, note the type [§5:2:10,
24] of the cross [see 12:1–7], and the scarlet wool [7:8–11] and
the hyssop; and thus the children sprinkle the people individually
in order to purify them from sins? [5:1.] 2. Understand [§5:2:18]
how it is told to you in such simplicity: the calf is Jesus; the sinful
men who offer it are those who offered him to be slaughtered
[5:2]. Then men (appear) no longer, (it is) no longer (concerned
with) the "glory" of sinners! [Cf. 5:11.] 3. Those who sprinkle are
children [cf. 6:11], they are those who preach to us forgiveness
of sins and purification of the heart,[o] to whom he entrusted the
authority to proclaim the gospel [5:9]. 3b. There are twelve (of
the latter), for a witness to the tribes, since there are twelve
tribes of Israel. 4. But why are there (only) three children who
sprinkle? This is for a witness to Abraham, Isaac, and Jacob, because they are great before God.
   5. And the fact that the wool is on the wood [8:1] signifies that
the kingdom of Jesus [7:11b] is on the wood, and that those who
hope on him will live forever [6:3a]. 6. But why are the wool and
the hyssop together? Because in his kingdom there shall be
wicked and vile days, in which we shall be saved [§5:4]. For the
one whose flesh is distressed is cured by means of the hyssop's
vileness!
   7. Wherefore, the things which have come to pass [1:7] are
clear to us, but hidden to them, because they did not hearken
[§5:2:2] to the Lord's voice [§5:6, 11].

   [o] So GS[2] mg· L; but HS* lack "of the heart" [cf. 5:1].

IV. CONCERNING CIRCUMCISED
UNDERSTANDING (9:1–10:12)

Exhortations to "hear" (9:1–4a) [§5:2:2]

9 For again, he speaks concerning the ears, how he circumcised the ears of *ᵖ* our heart. 1b. The Lord says in the prophet:
By listening with the ear, they hearkened to me [Ps. 18:44a].
1c. And again he says:
By hearing, those who are far off shall hearken;
The things I have done will become known [Isa. 33:13].
And circumcise, says the Lord, your hearts *q* [cf. Deut. 10:16; Jer. 4:4].
2. And again he says:
Hear, Israel, for thus says the Lord your God [see OT *passim*]; *r*
Who is he who desires to live forever? [See Ps. 34:12a.]
By hearing, let him hearken to the voice of my servant [see Isa. 50:10a].

ᵖ So L (cf. 9:4a; 10:12); but HSG lack "the ears of" (see 9:1c).
q So HSG (cf. 9:1a); but L has, perhaps correctly (see 9:4a), "your ears."
r So HS; but GL add another, somewhat unique, formula—"and again, the Lord's spirit [§5:10] prophesies" (cf. 12:2; see 11:5).

9:1–9. The Old Testament prophets frequently warn that a barrier of disobedience exists which prevents Israel from "hearing" the Lord (e.g., Isa. 6:9–10; Jer. 5:21–23; Ezek. 12:2). Similarly, several Old Testament passages refer to "circumcision of the heart" (Lev. 26:41; Deut. 10:16; 30:6; Jer. 4:4; 9:26; Ezek. 44:7, 9) and "of the ear" (Jer. 6:10; cf. Exod. 6:12, "of the lips") as the solution to this problem. This type of approach was extended especially to the thought life, which controls a man's ethical obedience, in the Judaism represented by Philo—circumcision of the understanding (ears, heart) thus became prime for him (see *Spec. leg.* 1:1–12; 1:304 ff.; *Quest. in Gen.* 3:46–52). Although Philo himself also continued to support circumcision as a physical rite, other Jews of his day accepted only the symbolic meaning and rejected physical circumcision (*Migr. Abr.* 89–93).
It is against such a background that Barnabas **9–10** must be understood. With the exception of **9:7–9**, this section contains little that is necessarily "Christian." Pseudo-Barnabas is neither rejecting the idea

3. And again he says:

Hear, heaven, and give ear, earth; for the Lord has spoken
   [Isa. 1:2a]—

these are mentioned as a witness [cf. Deut. 4:26].

3b. And again he says:

Hear the Lord's word, rulers of this people [Isa. 28:14;
   1:10].

3c. And again he says:

Hear, children, a voice crying in the desert [Isa. 40:3].

4. Therefore he circumcised our ears, so that when we hear
[§5:2:2] the word [§5:8], we might believe [§5:5:1].

False and true circumcision (9:4b–5)

4b. But he also set aside [2:6; 16:2] the circumcision on which
they relied. For he said that circumcision was not a matter of the
flesh, but they became transgressors [5:11] because a wicked
angel [18:1] "enlightened" them [§5:2:22].

5. And he says to them:

Thus says the Lord your God—

here I find [§5:2:12] a commandment [§5:5:4]—

Woe [8] to those who sow among thorns;
Be circumcised to your Lord [Jer. 4:3–4].

---

[8] So L; but HSG read "Do not sow" (= Jer. 4:3b LXX).

---

of circumcision nor substituting a Christian rite such as baptism for it—
instead, he argues that true circumcision is a matter of understanding
and obedience (cf. 2:4–3:6). There is nothing unique about the physical operation (9:6; cf. Philo) in which cultic Judaism misguidedly put
its trust (9:4b; cf. 4:6b), but the circumcision that the Lord desires
involves special insight (§5:1–2) which produces an upright life. The
section is prefaced by an anthology of brief excerpts calling all kinds
of men to "hear"—those afar, Israel, rulers, children (9:1–4a). Then
the basis of true circumcision is described (9:4b–5), followed by a
Christian "gematria" explaining the real significance of the institution
of the rite by Abraham (9:6–8). Finally, chapter 10 applies the theme
of circumcised understanding to the cultic food laws, and ties the
whole section together in the comments of 10:12 (cf. 8:7).

The "lesson" (literally "word"—see §5:8) in 9:7–8, of which Pseudo-
Barnabas is so proud (9:9), also is known to several later Christian
authors (Clement, Ambrose, Pseudo-Cyprian), but they do not relate
it to the problem of circumcision (cf. 13:7). Probably the unique

5b. And what is he saying?

Circumcise the wickedness from your heart! [t]

5c. And again he says: [u]

Behold, the Lord says, all the nations have uncircumcised foreskins,

but this people is uncircumcised in heart! [See Jer. 9:26.]

The meaning of Abraham's circumcision (9:6–9)

6. But you will say: And yet the people received circumcision as a special sign [Gen. 17:11]. But every Syrian and Arab, and all the priests of the idols also (are circumcised). Are they also, then, from their covenant? But even the Egyptians are in circumcision! [See Jer. 9:25 f.]

7. Learn [§5:2:15], then, abundantly concerning everything, children of love [7:1; 21:9]; for when Abraham first gave circumcision, he circumcised while looking forward in the spirit [§5:2:20] to Jesus, and he received the teachings [§5:5:3] of the three letters. **8.** For it says:

And Abraham circumcised the men of his household [Gen. 17:23], 18 and 300 (in number) [Gen. 14:14].

[t] The Greek witnesses here give a quotation from Deut. 10:16—"circumcise the hardness of your heart and do not stiffen your neck." L, however, differs both in the introductory formula and in what follows: "That is, hear your Lord and circumcise the wickedness from your heart." The last idea is echoed in several early fathers and fits the context admirably (see also Isa. 1:16; Symmachus [?] to Jer. 4:4). Possibly the entire L text should be adopted here.

[u] So L; but HS have the unparalleled formula "take it again," while G has simply "(and) again."

contribution of Pseudo-Barnabas here is not that he is the originator of 9:7–8, but that he has taken an already traditional Christian "gematria" based on Gen. 14:14 and has joined it to the circumcision discussion by means of Gen. 17:23—both of the Genesis passages refer to Abraham's "household." Notice that circumcision plays no role between 9:8b—10:11; rather, the idea of "three doctrines" (§5:5:3) now becomes central—doctrines received by Abraham (9:7), Moses (10:1, 9), and David (10:10). It should also be mentioned that the symbolism of "T" = the cross (9:8b) was not unknown in the Hellenistic world at large—Lucian (second century), *Judicium Vocalium* 12, mentions that the cross is constructed in the form of a "T," and "is so named by men"!

8b. What, then, is the gnosis [§5:2:6] which was given him? (See 19:1c.) Learn! [9:7.] For a distinction is made in that the 18 comes first, then it says 300. Now the (number) 18 (is represented by two letters), J = 10 and E = 8—thus you have "JE," (the abbreviation for) "JEsus." *v* And because the cross, represented by the letter T (= 300), was destined to convey special significance [§5:2:26], it also says 300. He makes clear [§5:2:8], then, that JEsus is symbolized by the two letters (JE = 18), while in the one letter (T = 300) is symbolized the cross.

9. He who placed the implanted gift of his teaching *w* in us knows! [§5:2:9–10.] No one has learned [§5:2:15] from me a more trustworthy lesson! But I know that you are worthy [cf. 14:1b, 4a].

The intention of Mosaic food restrictions (10:1–2)

10 Now when Moses said:

Eat neither pig [10:3], nor eagle nor hawk nor crow [10:4],
nor any fish which is without scales [10:5; see Lev. 11:7–15;
Deut. 14:8–14],

he received in his understanding [§5:2:23] three doctrines [§5:5:3]. 2. Further, he says to them in Deuteronomy [§4:1]:

v Because of the repeated numbers (symbolized by letters in Greek) and abbreviations, there is a great deal of confusion among the witnesses to 9:8b— especially L, which had to attempt a translation of this cryptic section. Thus the above translation sometimes takes minor liberties with the text for the sake of the English reader (e.g., the Greek IH [= 18] is transliterated to JE).
w So GL; but HS have "of his covenant," perhaps correctly (see 14:5).

10:1–12. The heart of chapter 10 is the material on "Moses' three doctrines" in **10:1, 3–5** (and vs. 9?). To it have been added, in various stages: (1) the complementary tradition about David's gnosis (**10:10**), which obviously parallels **10:3–5**, and might be of equal age with that tradition; (2) the interpretation of Moses' positive food laws in **10:11**, which goes beyond the "three doctrines" idea but otherwise accords well with **10:1–5** (and vs. 9), and is filled with stock ideas from Pseudo-Barnabas' tradition; (3) the additional "three doctrines" material on sexual abnormalities in **10:6–8**, which breaks the continuity of **10:3–5, 9** and is a unity in terms of style, content, and background; (4) various editorial comments that may represent diverse stages in the development of this tradition block—**10:9** sounds like the "original" conclusion (with **10:10e**?) to **10:3–5**, while **10:2** seems to be an

And I will ordain as a covenant [14:5b] for this people
my righteous ordinances [§5:5:2; see Deut. 4:10, 13].
2b. Therefore it is not God's commandment [§5:5:4] that they
(literally) should not eat, but Moses spoke in the spirit [§5:2:20].

The three doctrines of Moses (10:3–5)
[tradition 1, see 10:1]

3. For this reason, then, he mentions the "pig": Do not associate, he is saying, with such men—men who are like pigs. That is,
men who forget their Lord when they are well off, but when they
are in need, they acknowledge the Lord; 3b. just as when the pig
is feeding it ignores its keeper, but when it is hungry it makes a
din, and after it partakes it is quiet again [10:10c].
4. "Neither eat the eagle nor the hawk nor the kite nor the
crow." Do not, he is saying, associate with nor be like such men—
men who do not know how to procure their own food by honest
labor and sweat, but in their lawlessness they plunder the possessions of others, and they keep sharp watch as they walk around
in apparent innocence, and spy out whom they might despoil by
plundering; 4b. just as those birds are unique in not procuring
their own food, but as they perch idly by, they seek how they
might devour the flesh of others—pestilent creatures in their
wickedness! [10:10d.]

(early?) expansion on the pattern of 10:9. The comments in 10:11e–12
draw the whole matter to a close, and relate back to 8:7 and 9:1, 4a.
Similar ethical interpretations of the negative and positive food laws
were well known in Hellenistic Judaism, if the "Epistle of Aristeas"
and Philo are representative (see §6:7). The former argues that Moses,
who had "understanding of all things," gave these laws as moral lessons
for the sake of righteousness (139, 144, 150, 168 f.). Thus certain
rapacious birds (cf. 10:4) are forbidden for food as a sign that a
righteous person must not tyrannize (145–148), and the "unclean"
weasel, which conceives through the ear and gives birth by the mouth
(cf. 10:8b), symbolizes informers who transmit hearsay evidence
(163–167). The "divided hoof" (cf. 10:11d) signifies discernment
between right and wrong, and distinction between God's righteous
people and the immoral nations (150–152); to "ruminate" (cf. 10:11c)
means to remember God and to meditate on his creative acts (153–
160). Philo elaborates on the positive injunctions in a similar vein, and
at one point compares men who indulge their passions to the "unclean"
pig (Agric. 131–145, Spec. leg. 4:100–118). Similarly, T. Asher 2:8

5. "And do not eat," he says, "sea eel nor octopus nor cuttlefish." Do not, he is saying, be like *a* such men—men who are completely impious and have already been condemned to death [see 11:7 *]; 5b. just as those fish are uniquely cursed and loiter in the depths, not swimming about as do the rest but inhabiting the murky region beneath the deep water [10:10b].

The three doctrines on sexual sins (10:6–8) [tradition 2]

6. But neither shall you eat the hairy-footed animal [Lev. 11:5; Deut. 14:7]. Why not? Do not be, he is saying, one who corrupts children, nor be like such people; 6b. because the hare increases unduly its discharge each year, and thus has as many holes as it is years old.*y*

   a So HS; but GL add "by associating with" (see 10:3a, 4a).
   y Although no serious *textual* problem exists here, neither the wording of this passage nor the point of the analogy is clear. The main problems are: (1) a "corrupter of children/boys" (see 19:4a; cf. 10:7a) usually means a sodomist or homosexual of some sort (so Cl. A. takes this passage), but might also mean an abortionist here; (2) the yearly increase in bodily emission probably refers to excrement, although seminal ejaculations and even birth of young are not impossible; (3) the number of "holes" could refer to anal or womb openings, or even to dens (or passages to the main den). See the commentary.

---

compares immoral men who obey ritual laws with the "half clean" hare. The Christian authors were not lax in adopting this approach, as is amply illustrated by Theophilus, Irenaeus, Tertullian, Novatian, Lactantius, Aphrahat, Chrysostom, Methodius, and so on. It is in the writings of Clement, however, that it reaches its apex—not only does he know and use Barnabas 10, but he incorporates into that framework a wealth of related traditions and observations known to him. Barnabas 10 represents one stage along the way from Hellenistic Jewish interpretation to the catechetical school of Clement (see §6:7, 12). On early interpretation of the dietary laws in general, see S. Stein, *TU* 64 (1957), 141 ff.

The special tradition in 10:6–8 is an especially interesting specimen from such a milieu. Whereas 10:3–5 deals with the three categories of creatures forbidden in the Pentateuch (land-air-water [cf. 6:18!]; but not all of the exact names mentioned in Barnabas occur in the extant Greek OT MSS), 10:6–8 speaks of three land animals that were considered "unclean" (but "hyena" is not specifically forbidden in the OT) and concerning which some rather unique tales had been told by ancient Greek naturalists. Despite the attempts of Aristotle and

7. But neither shall you eat the hyena [cf. Jer. 12:9 LXX].
Do not, he is saying, be an adulterer nor a corrupter,[z] nor be like
such people. 7b. Why? Because this animal changes its nature
each year, and at one time it is male while at another it is female.
8. But also he hated the weasel [see Lev. 11:29], fittingly. Do
not, he is saying, be such a person. We hear of such men, who
perform a lawless deed uncleanly with the mouth. Neither associate with those unclean women who perform the lawless deed
with the mouth.[a] 8b. For this animal conceives through its mouth.

Summary and support from David (10:9–10d)

9. Concerning foods, then, when Moses received the three doctrines [10:1] he spoke out thus, in the spirit [10:2b]. But because
of fleshly desires they accepted his words as though they concerned actual food [10:2b; cf. 9:4b].

[z] Probably this means "homosexual" (cf. 10:6a; 19:4a).
[a] Although the text is in poor condition here, the meaning is fairly clear.
H lacks reference to the female offenders, and L has "do not be ... such a
one who hears iniquity and speaks uncleanness..." (!). SG read approximately as above.

---

others to correct some of these stories, it was fairly common knowledge
that the hare (1) adds a new anal opening each year to accommodate
its excessive defecation; (2) is hermaphroditic; (3) simultaneously
carries different sets of young in different stages of development in its
womb ("superfetation"), and thus can conceive when it already is
pregnant; and (4) has many exits to its home. In the light of such
ideas, it is difficult to determine what 10:6 is about—excessive sexual
activity? homosexuality? abortion? general filthiness? The foremost
popular story that circulated concerning the hyena (10:7) was that it
had both male and female genital organs by which it reproduced
(denied by Aristotle, the elder Pliny, Clement, etc.)—thus it became
a symbol of adultery and homosexuality (?). Finally, the weasel was
listed by many natural historians among the several creatures that
conceive through the ears or mouth. Although the lesson which was
sometimes drawn from this belief concerned minding one's tongue,
10:8 applies it to "fellatores" and "fellatrices" who induce sexual or-
gasm with the mouth. In short, the special background of 10:6–8 is
popular Hellenistic natural history which has been transformed into
moral lessons in association with Mosaic food prohibitions. This process
had already begun centuries before in Hellenistic Judaism (see Pseudo-
Aristeas, above).
Early Christian writers found a very congenial base for symbolism

10. And David also received gnosis [§5:2:6] of the same three doctrines [10:1]—and he says [Ps. 1:1]:

10b. Blessed is the man who has not walked according to the counsel of impious men—

just as the fish which grope in darkness in the depths [10:5b]—

10c. nor stood in the way of sinners—

just as those who appear to fear the Lord sin like the pig [10:3]—

10d. nor sat in the seat of pestilent fellows—

just like the birds perched for plundering [10:4b].

Moses' positive food laws, conclusion (10:10e–12)

10e. Now receive complete (understanding) concerning food.[b]
11. Moses says again:

Eat every split-hooved and cud-chewing animal [Lev. 11:3; Deut. 14:6].

11b. What is he saying (about the latter)? That (the animal) which receives fodder knows who feeds it, and while it relies on him, it seems content [cf. 10:3, 10c]. He spoke fittingly in view [§5:2:3] of the commandment. 11c. What, then, is he saying? Associate with those who fear the Lord [§5:5:6], with those who meditate [§5:2:17] in their heart on the subtleties of the matter,

---

[b] So HSL (see 10:9); but G has "concerning gnosis" (cf. 1:5; 13:7). It is also possible (perhaps even preferable, since Pseudo-Barnabas tends to comment *after* quotations) to read this as a conclusion to 10:10—"Now your understanding is complete . . ." (so GL, which begin 10:11 with "But"), or to punctuate and render it "You are having it fully! 11. And concerning food, Moses . . ." (see HS).

---

in Ps. 1:1. The *ethical* approach of 10:10, however, was not dominant; instead, later interpretations tend to apply these three parts of the quotation to three groups of people classified according to beliefs—for example, Gentiles, Jews, heretics (Clement [in part], Irenaeus; cf. R. Loewe, *TU* 63 [1957], 492 ff.). Similarly, the symbolism of "split-hoof" and "cud-chewing" animals (10:11) also had become doctrinally oriented already by the time of Irenaeus and Clement, so that the true Christians are those who do both, while Jews only "ruminate" (study scripture) and heretics only "part the hoof" (acknowledge Father and Son)—since Gentiles do neither, they are totally "unclean." In these matters again (cf. 2:4–3:6; 9:4b–6), Barnabas stands closer to Hellenistic Judaism and the Two Ways approach than to the developing Christian interest in doctrinal distinctions.

with those who proclaim the Lord's righteous ordinances [§5:5:2] and keep them, with those who realize that study is a joyful occupation, and who "ruminate" [§5:2:16] on the Lord's word [§5:8]. 11d. And what does the "split-hooved" mean? That the righteous man both walks in this world and anticipates the holy aeon [§5:3].

11e. See [§5:2:3] how appropriately Moses legislated! 12. But how could they perceive or understand [§5:2:18, 23] these things? [See 9:4b.] But since we rightly understand [§5:2:18] the commandments [§5:5:4], we are speaking as the Lord desired. 12b. This is why he circumcised our ears and hearts [9:1, 4a], so that we might understand [§5:2:23] these things.

V. BAPTISM AND THE CROSS
FORESHADOWED (11:1–12:11)

Transition to the new section (11:1a)

11 But let us investigate [§5:2:13] whether the Lord was concerned to reveal beforehand [§5:2:25] concerning the water and concerning the cross.

Concerning the water (11:1b–5)

1b. First, concerning the water, it is written with reference to Israel how they never will accept the baptism which conveys forgiveness of sins [§5:11], but they will build (cisterns) for themselves. 2. For the prophet says:

11:1a. As the respective openings words show, Barnabas **11–16** deals topically with four main themes: the Water and the Cross (**11:1**), the Two People (13:1), the Sabbath (15:1), and the Temple (16:1, 6). The only major digression occurs at the end of the present section, where the allusion to Joshua's acts (see 12:2) stimulates comparison with the later "Joshua"–Jesus (12:8–11).

11:1b–5. This passage depicts the plight of rebellious "Israel" in contrast to God's true people (§5:6, 11) by means of two fairly lengthy composite quotations. There is good reason to believe that Pseudo-Barnabas had little to do with synthesizing these passages from "the prophet." Justin, apparently without depending on Barna-

Be astounded, Heaven, and shudder greatly at this, Earth,
For this people has committed two wicked acts—
They have forsaken me, the living fount [see 1:3] of water,[c]
And they have dug out for themselves a pit of death [d] [Jer.
    2:12–13].

3. Has my holy mount Sinai become an arid rock?
    For you shall be as the fledglings of a bird,
        fluttering about when they are taken from the nest [e] [Isa.
        16:1b–2].

4. And again the prophet says:
    I will go before you, and I will level mountains
        and shatter gates of brass and break iron bars,
    And I will give you treasures—dark, hidden, unseen—
        that they might know [§5:2:4] that I am the Lord God
        [Isa. 45:2–3a].

5. And you will dwell in an elevated cave made from solid rock,
        and [f] its water supply is dependable.
    You will see a king in his glory,
        and your soul will meditate [§5:2:17] on the fear of the Lord
        [§5:5:6; Isa. 33:16–18].

---

[c] So H (see G, "living fount"); but L has "fount of the water of life,"
while S has "fount of life." LXX MSS show similar variety.

[d] So HS; but G(L) reads "broken cisterns" (= LXX), and L continues as
in LXX, "which cannot hold water."

[e] So HS (i.e., as young birds learning to fly?); but G has "when their nest
is stolen."

[f] So HSL; but G strangely reads, "Then what does he say in the Son" (cf.
var. to 9:2), apparently taking the following words to refer directly to
baptism—"his water is sure/faithful." This has led some editors to begin
verse 5 with this clause.

---

bas, also cites Jer. 2:13 plus Isa. 16:1 (plus Jer. 3:8) as a single
quotation (*Dial.* 114:5; see *JBL* 79 [1960], 346 ff.). Furthermore, the
reason why the quotations are given at all is their supposed connection
with the theme "water" (11:1b). But there is nothing in Isa. 45:2–3a
which relates to that theme—11:4–5 would be rather irrelevant were
it not for the allusion to a well-watered rock fortress, which contrasts
with the "desert rock" and "pit of death" in 11:2–3. Pseudo-Barnabas,
then, apparently accepted this material from his tradition in approximately the form preserved for us. On the connection between baptism
and forgiveness of sins (11:1b), cf. Mark 1:3 (Luke 3:3); Acts 2:38,
etc.; Hermas, Mand. 4:3; Justin, *Apol.* 61:10; 66:1; Theophilus, *Ad
Autol.* 2:16, etc.

Concerning water and wood together (11:6–11)

6. And again he says in another prophet:
And he who does these things will be like the tree planted by
    springs of waters,
    which produces its fruit at the proper time,
    and which has leaves that will not wither;
And everything he does will prosper.
7. The impious are not like this—not in the least.
But rather, they are like the dust which the wind drives from
    the face of the earth.
For this reason, the impious will not appear for judgment
    [see 10:5],
    nor sinners in the council of the righteous.
For the Lord knows the Way of the Righteous,
    and the Way of the Impious will perish [Ps. 1:3–6].
8. Perceive [§5:2:1] how he referred to the water and the cross
together.

8b. For this is what he is saying: "Blessed" [Ps. 1:1] are those
who, having placed their hope in the cross [12:3], descend into
the water. 8c. For the reward, he says, comes "at the proper time"

11:6–11. There is reason to believe that Pseudo-Barnabas is following a well-known traditional exegesis of Psalm 1 in 11:8. Note that a
knowledge of the entire Psalm (not just vss. 3–6) is presupposed in
the word "blessed" in 11:8b (Ps. 1:1), and perhaps by the fact that
the idea of meditating also occurs in Ps. 1:2b, which may have provided the link between 11:5 and 11:6. Furthermore, Clement shows
a wide influence of this Psalm in his thought—including its link with
Two Ways symbolism (Paed. 3:[12]:87—see §2), and the idea that
the "impious" have already been judged (Str. 2:[15]:68—cf. Barn.
10:5, 10; John 3:18; Cyprian, Testimonies 3:31). Possibly the material
from Ps. 1:1 in Barn. 10:10 comes from the same background. In
11:9–10, another quotation dealing with water and trees is given,
although the interpretation has been allowed to separate the first line
from the remainder (Clement, Str. 3:[12]:86, also quotes the first
line and its interpretation, without mentioning Barnabas). The source
is unknown, but it has its closest affinities with Ezekiel (20:6, 15 [cf.
2 Baruch 61:7]; 47:1–12) and thus may come from a Pseudo-Ezekiel
apocalyptic writing about the eschatological "Eden" (?).
In relationship to the rest of the epistle, this material is most similar

[11:6]—then, he says, I will repay. 8d. But as for the present, what does he say? "The leaves will not wither" [11:6]. He is saying this, that every word [§5:8] which flows forth from you—through your mouth [see 16:9]—in faith and love [§5:5:1, 5], will be a means of conversion and hope *g* to many [§5:5:1].

9. And again, another prophet says:

And the Land of Jacob was praised more than any land— he is saying this, he glorifies *h* the vessel of his spirit [§5:2:20]. 10. Then what does he say?

And there was a river flowing from the right side,
    and beautiful trees came up out of it.
And whoever eats of them will live forever.

11. He is saying this, that we go down into the water full of sins and vileness, and we come up bearing fruit in our heart, having in the spirit [§5:2:20] fear [§5:5:6] and hope in Jesus [§5:5:1]. 11b. "And whoever eats from these will live forever" [11:10]. He is saying this: Whoever, he says, hears [§5:2:2] these things which are spoken [see §5:8] and believes [§5:5:1] will live forever [cf. 6:3a].

g So HSG; but L has "of hope and resurrection," which in some ways fits the context better (see §5:3).

h So HS* (see Cl. A.); but GS2(?) have "he will glorify," apparently with reference to Jesus' resurrection.

---

to 6:8–19 and 16:6–10, which deal with the eschatological new creation and which also employ running, symbolic interpretation of key quotations. The symbolism of **11:8–11** seems to be as follows (cf. Odes Sol. 11): basically, the "tree" (**11:6**) is the cross and the "waters" are baptism; but the tree also is the believer (so **11:10–11a**; cf. 1 Clem. 23:4 = 2 Clem. 11:3–4) who is rooted in baptism and who now produces the "fruit" of fear and hope (**11:11a**) and will ultimately receive the "reward" (**11:8c**) of salvation (§5:4)—or more specifically, of resurrection (? cf. 1 Clem. 24:2); the "leaves" (**11:8d**, cf. **11:11b**) are the words of believers (§5:8—cf. the Rabbinical interpretation in b. *Sukka* 21b, where the "leaf" is the casual conversation of scholars; cf. also Odes Sol. 12:2); the "praised land" (**11:9**) is probably the new creation in which the Lord dwells (see 6:13–16; 16:8–10; cf. 21:8?), although it could also be argued that Jesus, come in the flesh, is in view (cf. 6:9a; 7:3c); eating (**11:11b**) is hearing and believing (cf. 10:11).

Concerning the cross (12:1–7)

12 Similarly, he explains again concerning the cross in another prophet who says:

And when will these things come to pass, says the Lord? [i]

When a tree falls down and rises up, and when blood drips from a tree.

1b. Again, you have (information) concerning the cross and the one who was destined to be crucified [cf. 12:2a, 7d].

2. And again he says in the (book of) Moses, when Israel was under attack from foreigners—and so that he might remind those who were being attacked that they had been given over to death because of their sins [see 12:5b]—the spirit [§5:10] says to Moses, in his heart, that he should make a type [§5:2:24] of the cross and of him who was destined to suffer [6:7; 12:1b]. 2b. If they do not, he is saying, place their hope on him [§5:5:1], they will be under attack forever. 2c. Thus Moses piled one shield upon another in the midst of the battle, and as he stood elevated above them all he stretched out his hands. And as long as he did so, Israel again prevailed; but whenever he let (his hands) drop, they were again being killed [Exod. 17:8–15]. 3. Why? So that they might know [§5:2:4] that they could not be saved unless they hope on him [12:2b, 7b; §5:5:1].

[i] Or possibly, ". . . pass? The Lord says, When . . ." (see L).

12:1–7. The apocalyptic quotation in **12:1a** is repeated verbatim in Pseudo-Gregory of Nyssa, *Testimonies* 7, and similar ideas are not infrequent in late Jewish and early Christian literature—see 4 Ezra 4:33; 5:5; Slavonic "Ladder of Jacob" 7 (M. R. James, *Lost Apocrypha of the Old Testament* [London, 1920], 101); Pseudo-Jerome, *Commentary in Mark* 15:33 (cf. Orac. Sib. 3:683, 804). The nearest Old Testament parallels seem to be Job 14:7 ff. and Hab. 2:11, but they are not very close. The quotation probably dealt with signs of the end times in its original setting (a lost Jewish apocalypse?), but it is doubtful that Pseudo-Barnabas was aware of its original setting—it is an isolated proof-text to him. For a detailed discussion, see J. Daniélou, *Recherches de science religieuse* 50 (1962), 389 ff.

Almost all of the remaining materials in chapter **12** demonstrably were topics of discussion in late Judaism; and among Christian authors they grew in popularity and application. Barnabas is very restrained, relatively speaking, in his "Christianized" presentation of these mate-

4. And again, in another prophet he says:
> The whole day I have stretched out my hands to a people
> who are disobedient and who oppose my Righteous Way
> [Isa. 65:2; see Rom. 10:21].

5. Again, Moses makes a type [§5:2:24] of Jesus—(signifying) that it was necessary for him to suffer [5:13a; 7:5] and that he whom they supposed had perished [see 7:9b] would bestow life [7:2; 12:7b]—in the standard *j* (set up) when Israel was smitten (by a plague). 5b. For the Lord made every serpent to bite them, and they were dying, so that he might demonstrate to them that it was because of their transgression—since transgression took root in Eve because of the serpent [Gen. 3:1 ff.]—that they will be given over to mortal affliction [12:2a].

6. Furthermore, it is this same Moses who commanded,
> You shall have neither a cast-metal nor a carved image to
> your God [see Lev. 26:1; Deut. 27:15]—

he it is who makes (such an image) in order to provide a type of Jesus [§5:2:7, 24].

6b. Moses, then, makes a bronze serpent and sets it up in a prominent place and calls the people together by means of a

---

j Literally "by a sign," but the Greek allows the meaning "standard" and this is the word used in LXX Num. 21:8 f., apparently in that sense. It could also mean "by a miracle."

---

rials—the "cross" is the supposed catchword here, but actually, Pseudo-Barnabas is more interested in the suffering and saving represented by the cross (12:2, 5; cf. chs. 5–8) than in mechanical typological equations such as came to be popular. Nor has Barnabas derived most of these materials directly from the Old Testament (compare 12:5–7 with Justin, *Apol.* 60); rather, they resemble the expanded Pentateuchal paraphrases (full of "targumic" details) which we have already met in 4:7 f. = 14:2 f.; 6:8 ff.; chs. 7–8, 10 (see also ch. 13).

The Israel vs. Amalek story (see also 12:10), with Moses lifting his arms for victory (12:2–3), and the "serpent in the wilderness" episode (12:5–7; cf. Wisd. Sol. 16:5 ff.; John 3:14) also are juxtaposed in Rabbinic sources (Mishna *Rosh ha-Shana* 3–8; *Mekilta:* Amalek 1) to show that dependence on God, not some kind of magic (note the similarity to Barnabas' emphasis on "hope"), brings victory and healing. Similarly, Justin (*Dial.* 90 f., 111 f.) and Tertullian (*Adv. Judaeos* 10 = *Adv. Marcion.* 3:18) both employ this "tradition block" material, apparently without depending on Barnabas (see L. Wallach, *Review of Religion* 8 [1943/44], 131 ff.; T. W. Manson, *JTS* 46 [1945],

proclamation. 7. Therefore, when they came together they begged
Moses to offer a prayer on their behalf, that they might be healed.
7b. But Moses said to them:
> Whenever, he says, anyone is bitten, let him come to the serpent
> which is erected on the wooden pole. And let him hope, believ-
> ing [§5:5:1] that this dead object is able to bestow life [12:5a],
> and he will be healed immediately [12:3].

7c. And they did so [Num. 21:6–9].

7d. Again, you have also in these things the glory of Jesus [cf.
12:1b]—for all things take place in him and for his sake [k] [cf.
Rom. 11:36].

Whose Son is "Jesus"? (12:8–11) [§5:6–7]

8. Again, what does Moses say to "Jesus" son of Naue, when he
had given this name to him [Num. 13:8, 16] who was a prophet
[Sirach 46:1; cf. Deut. 18:15] so that all the people might hearken

[k] This entire benediction is lacking here in L, but occurs (with slight
variation) in the conclusion to L at 17:2.

---

129 ff.). Furthermore, Philo discusses both stories (but not together),
and in treating the latter, he introduces the contrast between "Moses'
serpent" and "Eve's serpent" (12:5b; see *Leg. Alleg.* 2:71–81; *Agric.*
94–98). Also one of the Jewish disputants in Justin's *Dialogue* (94:4)
complains that his teachers have failed to answer satisfactorily the
problem of why Moses forbade making images and then made one
himself (see 12:6a). One of the few Pentateuchal narratives "over-
looked" by Josephus in his *Antiquities* is the "brazen serpent" episode
which, along with the "golden calf" story (Exod. 32, also "over-
looked"), must have proved very embarrassing to Hellenistic Judaism.
All this evidence indicates that Pseudo-Barnabas once again is working
from a strongly Jewish background, and that his type of Christianity
felt it could provide the answers to problems which had long been discussed in Judaism. In 12:4 the tradition is supplemented with an obvious parallel from Isa. 65:2; it is not clear whether Pseudo-Barnabas or
his predecessors are responsible for this (cf. Odes Sol. 27 = 42:1–3).

12:8–11. Although this section is tangential, it is not unrelated to
the "cross" typology of 12:1–7. It was "Jesus" (= the Hebrew "Joshua")
who led the army against the Amalekites in the scene depicted in 12:2,
and it was after that battle that the mysterious (apocalyptic) "book"
(12:9) was mentioned (Exod. 17:9–14). Perhaps these facts help us

[§5:2:2] to him alone? 8b. For the Father [§5:9] is making all things clear [§5:2:25] concerning his Son "Jesus." 9. Thus Moses says to "Jesus" son of Naue, to whom he had given this name when he sent him to spy out the land:

> Take a book in your hands and write what the Lord says, that "Jesus" *l* the Son of God will cut off the entire house of Amalek by its roots at the end of days [see Exod. 17:14].

10. Again, notice [§5:2:10] "Jesus"—not the son of a man *m* but the Son of God, and manifested in flesh by a type [§5:2:25, 24].

10b. Since, then, they were going to say that Messiah is David's Son, David himself—fearing and perceiving [§5:2:23] the error of the sinners [8:1]—prophesies:

> The Lord said to my Lord, "Sit at my right hand until I make your enemies a footstool for your feet" [Ps. 110:1].

l So L; but HSG lack "Jesus."

m So HSG; but L has "son of Naue," which is contextually and historically correct, but misses the (possible) theological play on the title "Son of man."

---

to understand more clearly what Pseudo-Barnabas had in mind in 12:2—the lesson related as much (or more) to the symbolism of "Jesus" vs. "Amalek" as to that of the "cross"! Both for Jewish and Christian interpreters, "Amalek" signified that which is opposed to God and to his people. The Rabbinic sources tell how God would ultimately blot out "Amalek" from this world and the next by the hand of "Messiah son of Ephraim" (a "Joshua" type?; cf. Num. 13:8; 4 Ezra 7:28 f.) who dies after the victory is won (see G. H. Dix, *JTS* 27 [1926], 130 ff.; C. C. Torrey, *JBL* 66 [1947], 253 ff.). Similarly, Justin (with whom the Joshua/Jesus parallelism reaches its apex) argues that on the cross, Jesus defeated the evil powers ("Amalek") with a "hidden hand" (cf. LXX Exod. 17:16), and would return in open victory in the last times (*Dial.* 49:7 f., etc.; cf. Barn. 12:9). This contrast between the human leader of old, who received the special name "Jesus" (12:8a, 9a—an extremely popular theme in the Christian apologetic, and not unknown in Hellenistic Judaism; cf. Sirach 46:1; Philo, *Mut. Nom.* 121 f.), and the eschatological victor, called "Son of God" (12:9), leads to a discussion of—and a rejection of—the (Jewish) Messianic title "Son of David" (12:10b–11; cf. Mark 12:36 parr. [Koester, 145 f.]; Acts 2:35; Heb. 1:13, etc.). There is a very interesting parallel in the Pseudo-Clementine *Hom.* 18:13, where the passage "no one knows the Father" (Matt. 11:27 par.) is applied to "all the Jews, who suppose that David is Messiah's father and that Messiah is his son, and who do not recognize God's Son, . . . since they

11. And again, Isaiah says as follows:

The Lord said to my Messiah, the Lord,[n] whose right hand I held, that nations would become obedient to him, and "I will demolish the strength of kings" [Isa. 45:1].

11b. Notice [§5:2:10] how David says he is "Lord," and does not say "Son." [o]

VI. THE COVENANT AND ITS RECIPIENTS
(13:1–14:9)

Transition to the new section (13:1)

13 But let us see [§5:2:10] if this people is the heir [13:6; 14:4 f.] or the former people, and if the covenant is for us or for them [4:6b].

[n] So GS²L; but HS* lack "Messiah" and read "my Lord," in agreement with the previous quotation. "Lord" (*kyriō*) here is a widely attested Greek corruption of "Cyrus" (*kyrō*).

[o] So HS* (see L); but GS² have "and Son of God"!

---

all say 'David' instead of 'God' "—cf. Clement's "quotation" from Jesus, "there are many who say 'Son of David have mercy on me,' but few recognize [gnostically?] the Son of God" (*Str.* 6:[15]:132:4). Although the exact opponents envisioned in *Barn.* 12:10 f. are not obvious (Pharisaic Jews? Ebionites?) the polemic overtones of this section are clear.

The "proof" from Isa. 45:1 (**12:11a**), which is really incidental to the argument, probably is included because this passage traditionally was linked to Ps. 110:1 (**12:10b**). Such linkage could hardly have been avoided in the developing tradition since the passages are so similar—in later Christian literature they are regularly found together (see *JBL* 79 [1960], 341 f.). On the "human son" vs. "Son of God" allusion in **12:10a**, cf. Odes Sol. 36:3 and Victorinus of Pettau, *Commentary in Revelation* to 1:13. The "fleshly type" in **12:10a** probably refers back to Joshua, although Jesus' coming in humility is not completely excluded (see 5:1 ff.).

13:1–14:1a. The "two people" theme was well known in Philonic Judaism. In fact, Philo twice discusses Gen. 25:21 ff. and Gen. 48:9 ff. in the same context (*Leg. Alleg.* 3:87–93; *Sobriet.* 26–29), and on numerous other occasions refers to one or the other of these texts. He

The "Two People" (13:2–14:1a) [§5:6]

2. Therefore, hear [§5:2:2] what the scripture says concerning "the people":

And Isaac was making entreaty for Rebecca his wife, because she was barren. And she became pregnant.[p] Then Rebecca also went to inquire of the Lord, and the Lord said to her [see Gen. 25:21 f.]:

Two nations are in your womb, and two peoples in your belly.
And one of the people will dominate the other,
    and the greater will be subject to the lesser [Gen. 25:23].

[p] So SG; but H reads "and she did not conceive" (despite Gen. 25:21b). L lacks these words.

---

also enumerates the senses in which Abraham is "father of many nations" (see 13:7b) and paraphrases God's words to Abraham in Gen. 17:4 as: "Do not seek [the covenant] in writing, for I myself am, in the highest sense, the genuine covenant" (*Quest. in Gen.* 3:42; *Mut. Nom.* 57 ff.). This is especially interesting in view of Barnabas' implication that in some sense Jesus *is* the Christian's covenant (see 14:4b–5, 7; cf. 4:8; 6:14b; 16:8–9). Philo's interpretation of the "two people" imagery characteristically centers in the distinction between the virtuous man who rules himself by reason-mind-knowledge, and the more earthly type who is ruled by passion. Thus for Philo, Isaac = gladness, Rebecca = patience, the unborn twins = good and evil, or master and slave, and so on. Unfortunately, Pseudo-Barnabas feels no need to interpret the Isaac-Rebecca imagery in 13:3 (cf. 4:6a), but later Christian authors tend to identify them with Christ and Church, or God and Holy Spirit, respectively. At least Barnabas is not ambiguous as to the respective identities of the "two people." Notice the "targumic" nature of Barnabas' Pentateuchal materials here (see also ch. 12). On the text of the "Oracle of Rebecca" in 13:2b, which agrees with a quotation in Irenaeus against LXX, see *JTS* 13 (1962), 318 ff.

Probably the Abraham material in 13:7 comes from a larger traditional discussion dealing with God's covenant with Abraham and its relationship to circumcision. In Romans 4, Paul also reflects such a discussion, but emphasizes the aspect of circumcision (cf. Barn. 9:6 f.). On the other hand, Barn. 13:7 betrays the fact that circumcision was important in the source from which the material comes (13:7b, "uncircumcised"), but does not use the material for that reason. The agreement between 13:7b and Rom. 4:11 on the non-Old Testament wording, "who believe although uncircumcised," is hardly proof that Pseudo-Barnabas used Paul, but rather, it emphasizes the traditional background of this "quotation."

3. You ought to perceive [§5:2:1] who Isaac (represents) and who Rebecca, and with reference to whom he had pointed out [§5:2:7] that "this people" is "greater" than "that."

4. And in another prophecy Jacob says it even more clearly [§5:2:25] to his son Joseph, when he says:

Behold, the Lord has not (yet) deprived me of your presence. Bring your sons to me, so that I might bless them [Gen. 48:11, 9b].

5. And he brought Ephraim and Manasse near, intending that Manasse [q] should receive the blessing since he was older—thus Joseph brought (the latter) to his father Jacob's right hand [Gen. 48:13]. 5b. But Jacob saw, in the spirit, a type [§5:2:20, 24] of "the people" which was to come afterward. 5c. And what does it say?

And Jacob crossed his hands and placed his right hand on the head of Ephraim,[q] the second and younger (son), and blessed him [Gen. 48:14–15a]. And Joseph said to Jacob: "You should transpose your right hand to Manasse's [q] head, for he is my first-born son." And Jacob said to Joseph: "I know, child, I know, [§5:2:10] but the greater will be subject to the lesser" [see 13:2b].

And thus (Ephraim) received the blessing [Gen. 48:18–20]. 6. Take note [§5:2:3] on which of them he placed (his right hand)— this "people" is to be first, and heir of the covenant! [13:1.]

7. Was, then, this situation also in view in the case of Abraham? [r] We are receiving the perfection of our gnosis! [1:5; §5:1–2.] 7b. What, then, does he say to Abraham when for his belief alone he was established in righteousness? [see Gen. 15:6.]

Behold, I have established you, Abraham, as the father of nations which believe in God while uncircumcised [see Gen. 17:4–5; Rom. 4:11].

14   Indeed, it was! [r]

---

[q] Strangely, throughout this context S depicts Ephraim as the older, Manasse as the younger!

[r] The construction here is difficult. In view of the close parallelism between 14:1b and 13:1, and the tendency of Pseudo-Barnabas to comment at the close of a section, we have taken the affirmative particle in 14:1a (which is lacking in HL) as the conclusion to 13:7, and thus have begun the paragraph with a question. It could also be rendered "If, then, ("the people") also was mentioned in the case of Abraham, we have received. . . ."

The Covenant given and received (14:1b–9) [§5:6]

1b. But let us see [§5:2:10, 13] if he has given the covenant which he promised the fathers [5:7] he would give to "the people." 1c. He has given it, but they were not worthy to receive it because of their sins [14:5]. 2. *For* the prophet *says:*

And Moses was fasting on Mount Sinai, when he was to receive *the* Lord's *covenant* with the people, *for forty days and forty nights. And* Moses *received* from the *Lord* the two *tablets inscribed by the finger of the Lord's hand,* in the spirit [§5:2:20]. And when Moses received (them), he brought (them) down to give to the people. 3. And the *Lord* said to Moses:

Moses, Moses, descend immediately, because your people which *you led out from the land of Egypt has sinned.*

And Moses understood [§5:2:23], for they had again made molten images for themselves, *and he hurled the tablets from* (his) *hands, and* the tablets of the Lord's covenant were shattered [see 4:7–8].[8]

4. Moses, then, received (it), but they did not prove worthy.

4b. And how did we receive it? Learn! [§5:2:15.] Moses received it in the capacity of servant [see Exod. 14:31; Heb. 3:5];

[8] The italics indicate Greek wording identical to 4:7–8.

14:1b–9. For the most part, chapter **14** focuses on materials and themes which we have already encountered—see esp. 4:7–8 (the giving and losing of the covenant); 5:1, 7, 11 (why Jesus came—§5:7); and 6:8–19 (the "good land" to be inherited—§5:6). The quotations in **14:7–9** present a special problem. They are related to the context and to one another in that they fill out the picture of Jesus' role as "liberator" who brings "light" to dark places (**14:5b;** cf. the Two Ways imagery!). Nevertheless, it is tempting to think that there may have been some early displacement (or secondary expansion) here, since the conclusionlike cry of **14:7b** is somewhat unnatural where it now stands, and the reference to liberation in **14:8** would be more congenial to the context of **14:5b–6** (plus 7b). Perhaps family G is correct in including "14:8" after **14:5a,** but that does not solve all the difficulties either. Despite the extreme popularity of these three quotations in early Christian literature, nothing can be said with confidence about whence Barnabas derived them—from an anthology of "Messianic" texts, or from Isaiah itself?

but the Lord himself gave it to us, to a "people" of inheritance, by submitting for us [5:1]. 5. And he was made manifest [§5:2:25] so that they might fill up the measure of their sins [5:11], and we might receive it through Jesus, who inherits the Lord's covenant *— 5b. he was prepared for this reason, that by appearing himself and liberating from darkness our hearts which had already been paid over to death and given over to the lawlessness of error [16:7b], he might establish a covenant in us by a word [§5:8]. 6. For it is written how the Father [§5:9] commanded him to prepare a holy people for himself [5:7] when he had liberated us from the darkness. 7. Therefore the prophet says:

I, the Lord your God, have called you in righteousness,
    and I will grasp your hand and empower you;
And I have given you as a covenant to people, as a light for the
        nations,
    to open the eyes of the blind,
    and to release from their bonds those who have been shackled,
    and to lead out from their prison house those sitting in dark-
        ness [Isa. 42:6–7].

7b. Know *u* [§5:2:4], then, whence we were liberated! 8. Again the prophet says: *t*
Behold, I have placed you as a light for the nations,
that you might beam salvation to the end of the earth.
Thus says the Lord God who liberated you [Isa. 49:6–7].

9. Again the prophet says:
    The Lord's spirit [§5:2:20] is on me,
    wherefore he anointed me to announce benefaction to the
        oppressed, *v*
he sent me to heal those who are broken hearted,
    to proclaim pardon to the captives and restoration of sight
        to the blind,
    to announce the acceptable year of the Lord, and the day
        of recompense [see 21:1],
        to comfort all those who are in mourning [Isa. 61:1–2]. *t*

---

t G places 14:8 after 14:5a, while HS²L have it at 14:8 and S* includes it after 14:9.

u So GL (cf. 16:2c); but HS read "we know."

v So G; but S has "to announce (news) to the poor" (see LXX) and L has "to announce (news) to men." H lacks several words here.

VII. CONCERNING THE SABBATH (15:1-9)

15 And furthermore, concerning the sabbath. It is written in the "Ten Words" by which (the Lord) spoke to Moses face to face [see Exod. 33:11; Deut. 5:4; 34:10] on Mount Sinai:

> And you shall keep the Lord's sabbath holy [see Exod. 20:8; Deut. 5:12; Jer. 17:22]
>
> with clean hands and a clean heart [see Ps. 24:4; 51:10].

2. And elsewhere he says:

> If my sons guard the sabbath [see Exod. 31:16],
>
> then I will bestow my mercy on them [see Isa. 56:1-8].

3. He mentions "the sabbath" at the beginning of creation:

> And God made the works of his hands in six days,
>
> and he finished on the seventh day.
>
> And he rested on it, and kept it holy [see Gen. 2:2-3].

15:1-9. The three "sabbath" quotations in **15:1-3** provide the basis for the eschatological instruction in **15:4-7**. With the exception of **15:3**, which reasonably resembles Gen. 2:2-3, the "quotations" are not found as such in extant forms of the Old Testament, although its wording is reflected—despite the quite concrete formula in **15:1** (see §4:1). The first two texts are concerned with how to keep the sabbath (**15:1**) and the results of such action (**15:2**)—a theme to which the discussion returns in **15:6-7**. Although the third quotation (**15:3**) is not devoid of these concerns, and clearly plays a role in the teaching of **15:6-7**, it also opens up another avenue of investigation—the eschatological symbolism of the "sabbath" day itself (**15:4-5**). The concluding paragraph in **15:8-9** builds from this symbolism and introduces the contrast between Jewish cultic sabbath observance and the Christian Sunday celebration.

Unless the text of **15:3-4** is itself corrupt, and there is little reason to think it is, Barnabas' tradition has used two alternative forms of the Gen. 2:2 material: "he finished on the *seventh* day" (**15:3**) is the reading of the traditional Hebrew Old Testament (= Vulgate, etc.), while the "Samaritan Pentateuch," Syriac, and LXX (Old Latin, Philo) have "he finished on the *sixth* day" (cf. Exod. 20:11; 31:17). Now the interpretation in **15:4ac** requires the latter sense—the eschatological rest is ushered in *after* the judgment, and so on (**15:5**), has taken place. But **15:8b** seems to require the former sense—during the "sabbath rest" the creation of the new world takes place. In fact, Philo argues similarly that God's "six days" of creation concern mortal things, but on the seventh day "he begins the configuration of other things more divine" such as paradise, the "heavenly man," and so on (*Leg. Alleg.* 1:5 f.). Could it be that Pseudo-Barnabas or his tradition

4. Pay attention [§5:2:21], children [§4:3], to what he says: "He finished in six days." He is saying this, that in six thousand years the Lord will finish everything. For with him the "day" signifies a thousand years.[w] 4b. And he bears me witness (on this point) saying:

Behold, a day of the Lord [x] shall be as a thousand years [cf. Ps. 90:4].

4c. Therefore, children, "in six days"—in six thousand years—"everything" will be "finished."

5. "And he rested on the seventh day" [15:3b]. He is saying this: When his Son [§5:7] comes he will put an end to the time of the Lawless One,[y] and judge the impious [cf. 10:5; 11:7], and change the sun [5:10] and moon and stars [§5:3]—then he will truly rest "on the seventh day."

   [w] S[2] mg. uniquely adds: "For David bears me witness, saying that . . ." and cites Ps. 90:4 verbatim as in LXX.

   [x] So HS; but G(L) has "today will be a day as a thousand years."

   [y] Or, "of lawlessness" (see 4:1b, 9b; 5:3). This is the reading of L; but G has "cut short his time" (see 4:3b), and HS have "bring time to an end."

---

has intentionally left this matter ambiguous? Or that two traditional interpretations of Gen. 2:2–3 have here been mixed with little attempt to harmonize them?

Ideas about the millennial epochs, and so forth (15:4–5), are so frequent in Jewish and early Christian literature that Pseudo-Barnabas cannot be considered an innovator here. This is also true for the "quotation" in 15:4b, which occurs in almost the same form in numerous Rabbinic and early Christian (Justin, Irenaeus, Hippolytus) sources, and even in the Muslim Qur'an (22:47). The idea antedates the book of Jubilees (second century B.C.?), where it is used (4:29 ff.) to explain how Adam could both live to be nine hundred and thirty years old (Gen. 5:5) and die in the "day" he ate of the forbidden fruit (Gen. 2:17; see also Justin, *Dial.* 81:3). The fact that Pseudo-Barnabas uses a tradition that speaks of the eschatological consummation coming "in six thousand years" in no way detracts from the air of eschatological immediacy which permeates the epistle (§5:3; despite Grant, 114). The intentions of his source traditions are not always comprehended by Pseudo-Barnabas (see §4:4). In fact, it might be considered strange if Pseudo-Barnabas or his tradition interpreted the "six thousand years" *literally!* For him, *whenever* the end comes, *that is when* the period is completed—not vice versa. It is unfortunate that Pseudo-Barnabas is rather vague about what will happen during the eschatological "sabbath rest." Apparently it is ushered in *after* the judgment *during* the "seventh millennium" (cf. Irenaeus, *Adv. haer.* 5:28:3 [Gk]; cf. Rev. 20; Justin, *Dial.* 81:4). Barnabas, however,

6. Furthermore he says: "Keep it holy with clean hands and a clean heart" [15:1b]. 6b. If, then, anyone at present is able, by being clean in heart,[z] to keep holy the day which God hallowed, we have been deceived in everything! [Cf. 9:4b; 16:1.] 7. But if he keeps it holy [a] at that time by truly resting [15:5b], when we ourselves are able (to do so) since we have been made righteous [cf. 4:10] and have received the promise [6:19]—when lawlessness is no more and all things have been made new by the Lord [6:13; 15:5]—at that time we will be able to keep it holy, when we ourselves first have been made holy!

8. Further, he says to them [see 2:5b]:

> I cannot bear your new moon celebrations and sabbaths [Isa. 1:13].

8b. See [§5:2:10] how he is saying that it is not your present sabbaths that are acceptable to me, but that (sabbath) which I have made, in which, when I have rested everything, I will make

---

[z] So HS*; but GS²L have "except he (who) is clean in heart," suggesting that it is possible even "now" truly to keep the sabbath holy, or perhaps making an exception in the case of Jesus?

[a] The text is hopelessly corrupt here. H has "But if *we* will keep it holy . . ."; S* probably read "But if not, *we* will keep it holy . . ."; S²⁽?⁾ possibly understood it as "See [§5:2:10], therefore, *we* . . ."; G has "But if not, *he* keeps it holy . . ."; and L has "Seeing, therefore, that *he kept* it holy. . . ." If "he" is accepted (as above), it could refer to the "anyone" of 15:6b, but more probably refers to the Lord—because he will rest then, we will also.

---

probably saw the "rest" period as just that—an interim between the old and new worlds (**15:8b**; see 2 Enoch 33:2; cf. 4 Ezra 7:30, where the judgment follows the "rest"). The "eighth day" symbolism for the new world (**15:8b**) is also found in 2 Enoch 33, Clement (*Str.* 6:[16]:141), and Orac. Sib. 7:140.

The rather incidental allusion to Sunday as a special Christian day (**15:9**)—not a day of rest or idleness, as the cultic Jewish Sabbath was observed (cf. 4:13; **15:6b**), but a day of life and joy—is one of the earliest clear allusions to this practice (see Ign. Magn. 9:1 [?]; Did. 14:1 [?]; Justin, *Apol.* 67). The tone of the passage suggests that Pseudo-Barnabas rejected "the present sabbaths" as having any special significance, although Eastern Christianity tended to observe both Sabbath and Sunday into the fourth century (and later); see *Andrews University Seminary Studies* 3 (1965), 18 ff. The idea that Jesus' resurrection and ascension both took place on a Sunday (the *same* Sunday?) resembles G.Peter 13:56 (cf. Luke 24:50 f.), although early Christian opinions varied greatly on these matters (e.g., Acts 1:3 ff.; see Koester, 146 ff.).

the beginning of an eighth day—that is, the beginning of another
world [see 6:13; 16:6c]. 9. Wherefore also we observe the eighth
day [§5:11] as a time of rejoicing, for on it Jesus both arose from
the dead and, when he had appeared [see §5:2:25], ascended into
the heavens.

VIII. CONCERNING THE TEMPLE (16:1–10)

The old, physical Temple (16:1–5)

16 And finally, concerning the Temple. I will show you how
those wretched men, when they went astray [§5:6], placed their
hope [§5:5:1] on the building and not on their God who created
them [§5:9]—as though *b* God has a house! 2. For, roughly speaking, they consecrated him by means of the Temple, as the pagans
do! 2b. But how does the Lord speak when he sets it aside? [2:6;
9:4b.] Learn! [§5:2:15.]

Who measured the heaven with a span, or the earth with a hand?
Was it not I, says the Lord? [Isa. 40:12.]

b Or perhaps, "(and) that God has a house" (see 16:6–10); G has "But
that. . . ." Less likely, but not impossible, would be "as if it were God's house"
or "as long as God's house stood."

16:1–5. In his attitude toward the cultic Temple, Pseudo-Barnabas
once again mirrors views that had long been current in the (Hellenistic) Jewish world, as well as in non-Jewish Hellenism—God does not
need a "house" any more than he "needs" sacrifice (2:4–3:6) or requires other cultic acts (9:4b ff.; 10:2; 15:8). Philo had argued similarly—God's "Temple" is the universe, although he also eulogizes the
unique Jerusalem Temple (*Quest. in Ex.* 2:83 ff., *Spec. leg.* 1:66,
etc.)—and he knows of Jews who were less cultically minded than he
(*Migr. Abr.* 92). The Jewish "Sibyl" also plays on this theme (*Orac.
Sib.* 4:8; 4:24 ff.), which is taken up with a vengeance in "Stephen's
Speech" in Acts 7 (cf. §6:8), and is often repeated in later Christian
literature (see esp. Clement, *Str.* 5:[11]:74 ff.). The Isaiah texts of
16:2b were extremely popular "proofs" in this connection (cf. 1 Kings
8:27), despite other Old Testament passages that tend to give the
Temple special honor (e.g., Isa. 60:7; Jer. 7:11; see Mark 11:17,
parr.).

The apocalyptic quotations in **16:3, 5b** can no longer be identified.
The first echoes ideas such as 1 Esdras 6:15–19 (see Tob. 14:4–6; Isa.
49:17) projected eschatologically. The second has vague similarities

The heaven is my throne, and the earth is the stool for my feet.
What sort of house will you erect for me,
   or what place for me to rest? [Isa. 66:1; see Acts 7:49.]
2c. You knew *c* that their hope [16:1] was vain!
   3. Furthermore, he says again:
      Behold, those who tore down this Temple will themselves
      build it.
4. It is happening.*d* For because of their fighting it was torn down
by the enemies. And now the very *e* servants of the enemies will
themselves rebuild it.
   5. Again, it was made clear [§5:2:25] that the city and the
Temple and the people of Israel were destined to be abandoned.
5b. For the scripture says [cf. 5:12b]:
   And it shall be at the end of days that the Lord will abandon the
   sheep of the pasture, and the sheepfold, and their watchtower
   to destruction!
5c. And it happened just as the Lord announced!

The new, spiritual Temple (16:6–10) [§5:6]

   6. But let us inquire [§5:2:13] whether there is a Temple of
God? There is, where he himself says he makes and prepares (it)!
6b. For it is written:

   c So HS; but G(L) has "Know" (see §5:2:4; 14:7b).
   d So G (L prefixes "and"); but HS lack this affirmation.
   e So HGL; but S has "they and the servants" (see §6:4).

---

to the symbolism in 1 Enoch 89:50–73. Although the discussion in
16:3–5 presupposes the destruction of the Temple in A.D. 70, and its
current state of ruin, little more can be inferred from it concerning
the exact date when Pseudo-Barnabas wrote (see §6:4).

   16:6–10. The teaching about the eschatological, spiritual Temple is
presented in the form of a *midrash* on another unidentified apocalyptic
text. There are several passages in Jewish literature which speak of the
apparently physical (re)building of the Temple in the last days: e.g.,
1 Enoch 91:13 (after the seventh week!), Tob. 14:5b (built "gloriously"; cf. T. Benj. 9:2); Orac. Sib. 5:415 ff. (cf. Ezek. 40 ff.). The
reference to the "hebdomad," or symbolic "week," in **16:6b** suggests
that this quotation may be related to the timetable speculations of
15:4–8. Whatever its origins, Pseudo-Barnabas does not interpret it as
referring to an actual future building, but to the "new creation," the
"holy people" who are now being perfected as God's Temple (§5:6)—

And it shall come to pass when the "hebdomad" is finished, God's Temple will be built gloriously in the Lord's Name.
7. Thus I find [§5:2:12] that there is a Temple.

7b. How, then, will it "be built in the Lord's Name"? Learn! [§5:2:15.] Before we believed [§5:5:1] in God the dwelling place of our heart was corrupt and infirm—truly a Temple built by human hands [see 2:6, Acts 7:48]. For it was full of idolatry, and was a house of demons, through doing whatever things were contrary to God. 8. But "it will be built in the Lord's Name"—pay attention [f]—so that the Temple of the Lord may be "built gloriously." 8b. How? Learn! [§5:2:15.] When we receive the forgiveness of sins and place our hope [§5:5:1] on the Name,[g] we become new, created again from the beginning [§5:6]. Wherefore God truly dwells in our "dwelling place"—in us [6:15]. 9. In what way? The word [§5:8] of his faith, the invitation of his promise, the wisdom [§5:2:22] of his righteous ordinances [§5:5:2], the commandments [§5:5:4] of his teaching [18:1a]; himself prophesying in us, himself dwelling in us—by opening for us the door of

[f] So, possibly, G Cl.A. (L)—or perhaps, ". . . Name. Pay attention, in order that. . . ." HS require the latter construction and include a conjunctive particle: "But pay attention," or perhaps (ethically), "But walk circumspectly" (see §5:2:21).

[g] So HS*Cl.A. (G part); but S²L (G part) add "of the Lord" (see §5:7).

in this, Barn. 16:7–10 strongly shares the approach of 6:8–19 (cf. 14:5 f.; Ign. Eph. 15:3).

Pseudo-Barnabas becomes so enwrapped in the gnosis of this passage that grammatical relations are abandoned in 16:9, and 16:10 is a syntactical nightmare. Nevertheless, the blurred picture that emerges provides an excellent key to appreciating the "mystical" approach which controls Pseudo-Barnabas' presentation here: Jesus, the "Lord's Name" (§5:7), cleans out our "heart" to make it his habitation (cf. T. Dan 5:1b; T. Gad 5:4; T. Joseph 10:3; Eph. 2:22, etc.), thus recreating us and speaking out through us (the mouth, the word, is the true Temple's "door"—see Odes Sol. 12:3; 42:6; Ign. Rom. 8:2) to others who need salvation. This Temple is "glorious"—it is incorruptible and pneumatic. It produces an amazing message (gnostic?) controlled by the indwelling Lord, not by the apparent speaker—16:10a could mean that the speaker (who trusts the Lord, not himself, for salvation) is amazed at his own words, or perhaps that the listener is amazed at the one who proclaims the unexpected "words" to him (cf. 19:9b). On the general outline of 16:6 ff., see G. Schille, ZNW 49 (1958), 31 ff.

the Temple, which is the mouth, and giving us repentance, he leads those who had been in bondage to death [14:5] into the incorruptible Temple. 10. For he who longs to be saved [§5:4] looks not to the (external) man, but to him who dwells in him and speaks in him, and he is amazed at the fact that he never either had heard him speak such words [§5:8] from his mouth nor had himself ever desired to hear (them)! 10b. This is a pneumatic [§5:2:20] Temple built for the Lord!

CONCLUSION (17:1–2)

17 To the best of my ability, and in simplicity, (I have tried) to make (these things) clear [§5:2:8] to you—I hope that I have not neglected anything (vital).[h] 2. For if I keep writing to you concerning things present or [i] to come [1:5; 5:3], you would never comprehend [§5:2:18] because they are contained in parables [§5:2:19]. 2b. So much, on the one hand, for these matters.[j]

[h] So HS*L (literally "my soul hopes..."); but a longer form of this material is contained in GS[2]: "My (mind and, S[2]) soul hopes, in accord with my desire, that I have not neglected anything of the (present, G [transposed from 17:2a]) things which are necessary to you for salvation" (cf. 1 Clem. 45:1; Did. 16:2a; Heb. 6:9).

[i] So HSL; but G lacks "present or" (see note h above).

[j] L concludes at this point (lacking the Two Ways): "Again you have (understanding) concerning the majesty of Christi [! §5:7], how all things take place in him and through him [12:7b]—to whom be honor, power, glory, now and forever. HERE ENDS THE EPISTLE OF BARNABAS."

17:1–2. The Greek of **17:1** is condensed and cryptic (cf. 1:2–5), and strongly resembles the opening section of Irenaeus' *Apostolic Preaching*: "... according to our power we will not fail to speak with you a little by writing, and to show forth in brief the preaching of the truth.... We send you, as it were, a more essential reminder [?], that by little you may attain much, learning in short space ... and receiving in brief the demonstration of the things of God. So shall it be fruitful to your own salvation...." It may be that literary convention has played a role here (see to 1:5, and §1:2, n.2). Pseudo-Barnabas' expressed excuse for not writing more (**17:2a**) sounds especially strained, since he already has covered various "present and future" matters (see 4:3 ff.; 6:8 ff.; 15:3 ff.; 16:6 ff.) which seem to us to have been rather mysterious, if not in "parables" (cf. Justin, cited in Irenaeus, *Adv. haer.* 5:26:2). The concluding words in **17:2b** set the stage for 18:1a, which speaks, "on the other hand," of another gnosis.

THE TWO WAYS

(Barn. 18:1–21:9; Did. 1:1–6:2)

INTRODUCTION (Barn. 18:1–2; Did.[a] 1:1a–1b)

Barn.				Did.
1a	**18**	But let us move on to another gnosis [§5:2:6] and teaching		
1b		*There are two ways*	**1** *There are two ways* [b]—	1a
		of teaching and authority: that of light and that of darkness.	one of life, and one of death.[c]	
1c		*And there is a great difference between the two ways.*	*And there is a great difference between the two ways.*	1b

[a] The title of the Didache in MS H (see Georg, §7:4) is "Teaching of the Twelve Apostles: Teaching of the Lord Through the Twelve Apostles to the Nations."

[b] Dctr adds "in the world" (cf. Qumran *Manual* 4:2).

[c] Dctr reads "of life and of death, *of light and of darkness*. In these there *are stationed* two *angels;* one of righteousness, the other of iniquity" (cf. Barn., Qumran *Manual*).

Barn. 18:1–2; Did. 1:1–1b. Barn. 18:1a introduces the Two Ways section as a separate tradition from what has preceded—it is not exegetical but ethical gnosis (§5:1–2); not mysterious "teaching" which must be uncovered (as in 9:9) but direct commandments from the Lord (see 16:9). The ensuing description (**18:1b–2**) is vividly eschatological (see §2:2–4, §5:3) by comparison with **Did. 1:1a–b.** The

Barn.

1d For over one are ap-
pointed light-
bearing angels
of God,
but over the other,
angels of Satan
[§5:3].

2 And the former is Lord
from everlast-
ing to everlast-
ing,
but the latter is ruler
of the present
time of lawless-
ness.

Did.

Didache quite briefly states that there is a sharp contrast between the ways, but does not attempt any general description beyond the identification with "life" and "death." That this life/death imagery was already commonplace is clear from such passages as Deut. 30:15 (Jer. 21:8); Sirach 15:17 (Matt. 7:13 f.); Orac. Sib. 8:399 f., Ign. Magn. 5:1 (cf. Barn. 19:2c; 20:1b). **Barn. 18:1b,** on the other hand, prefers the light/darkness symbolism which also was widely popular, especially in apocalyptically oriented literature (see Prov. 4:18 f.; T. Levi 19:1; Qumran *Manual* 3:13–4:26; 2 Enoch 30:15; Col. 1:12 f.; Ps-Clem. *Hom.* 20:2). The Doctrina incorporates both the life/death and the light/darkness contrasts (cf. Irenaeus, *Ap. Preach.* 1b), and adds (in connection with the angels) a third traditional set, righteousness/iniquity (cf. Barn. 1:4; 4:10; 5:4; Hermas, Mand. 6:2:1 ff.). Other characterizations of the Two Ways include truth/error (Qumran *Manual* 3:18 ff.; T. Judah 20:1; see T. Benj. 6:1; Odes Sol. 38; Aristides, *Apol.* 15 [Gk.]; Justin, *Dial.* 35:2), good/evil (Deut. 30:15; T. Asher 1:5; see Sirach 17:7), law of the Lord/works of Belial (T. Levi 19:1; cf. Ps-Clem. *Hom.* 20:2); straight/crooked (Hermas, Mand. 6:1:2 ff.; see Matt. 7:13 f.; Barn. 20:1a), right hand/left hand (Lactantius, *Epitome* 59).

The similarities between **Barn. 18:1b–2** and the Qumran *Manual's* Two Ways are striking. Both traditions visualize the present time as an era in which "authority" or "dominion" has been granted to the rulers of each of the paths, darkness as well as light. Both speak in terms of angelic agents, although at this point the Doctrina with its *two* angels (= Hermas) is closer to the *Manual* with its "angel of darkness" (cf.

T. Joseph 20:2; Barn. 4:10a; 20:1) vs. "angel of truth"—it should be noted here, however, that the *Manual* prefers the imagery of *spirits* to that of angels (cf. T. Judah 20:1; T. Dan 6:1–7). The "dominion" of the agents of darkness is temporary, and will be brought to an end "in the appointed time of judgment." For the *Manual,* the spirits of light and darkness alike are creations of God and both are present in every person's heart—the goal is to maintain as great an imbalance in favor of truth as possible (cf. the "two inclinations" in Jewish, esp. Rabbinic, thought). Barnabas nowhere deals with these details, although the creator God alone is pictured as eternal and ultimately sovereign (see §5:9), and the recipients are warned that they are continually in danger of the adversary gaining the upper hand (see §5:3). For **Barn. 18:2,** the *Manual* provides an interesting parallel: "One of the spirits God loves for all the ages of eternity, and with all its deeds he is pleased forever; as for the other, he abhors its company, and all its ways he hates forever." In terms of the broader theology of Barnabas, additional similarities emerge, such as the ultimate goal of knowledge and wisdom for those who are upright and blameless, and the new creation which apparently follows the present time of testing. The *Manual* tradition, however, leaves more of an impression of divine determinism than is found in Barnabas (cf. Sirach 15:11–20; Pss. Sol. 9:7–9).

The implications of the above analysis for determining precisely what material derives from the "common source" and what has been contributed by the developing traditions are at best ambiguous. It cannot be denied that the Two Ways pattern was employed in strongly eschatological settings at an early date (*Manual;* 2 Enoch; Testaments), but it is also clear that it had a strictly ethical, noneschatological application in some traditions (Proverbs, Sirach; see also Hermas). The most likely solution seems to be that the source was at least mildly eschatological in orientation (thus Barn. 4:9b = Did. 16:2b; see §2:3, 7), and that the Barnabas tradition has characteristically heightened the eschatology, while the Doctrina-Didache tradition gradually eliminated it (see §2:4–6). Notice that the Doctrina preserves the terminology of light/darkness and angels, but cannot really be called eschatological in emphasis (cf. also Dctr 6:2!). The same can also be said of Hermas' Two Ways presentation.

I. THE WAY OF LIGHT/LIFE

(Barn. 19:1–12; Did. 1:1c–4:14)

Barn.		Did.
1a	**19** *Therefore, the Way of Light is this—*	On the one hand, *then,* 1c *the Way of Life is this:*
1b	if anyone who desires to traverse the way to the appointed place is diligent in his works.	
1c	Therefore, the gnosis [§5:1–2] which is granted to us to walk in it is of this sort [see 9:8b]:	[cf. 1:3a]

Barn. 19:1–2a; Did. 1:1c–3a. The word "diligent" in **Barn. 19:1b** refers not only to the idea that salvation is a quest that requires concentrated attention and righteous works (see §5:4), but also to the eschatolagical *urgency* of the situation—temporal as well as moral. It could as well be translated ". . . hastens to perform his works," just as the author has *hastened* to send the epistle (1:5; 4:9; 21:9a) because the times are short (see §5:3). The use of concrete spatial imagery for ultimate salvation ("the appointed place," cf. Acts 1:25; 1 Clem. 5:4–7; 44:5; Ign. Magn. 5:1; Polyc. Phil. 9:2) is reminiscent of such eschatological concepts as the "good land" or the "new world" (see §5:3, 6). It may be that **Barn. 19:1c** and **Did. 1:3a** represent the same passage of the common source. In any case, Barnabas depicts ethical gnosis as synonymous with "the way of Light," a conjunction of ideas which is also approximated in the Testaments (see T. Levi 4:3; 18:3, 9; T. Gad 5:7; T. Benj. 11:2).

Barn. 19:2a = Did. 1:2a leave little doubt that the initial item in the original "Way of Light/Life" spoke of love for the creator (cf. Justin, *Apol.* 15:6b). But it is not so clear what followed. The twofold commandment of **Did. 1:2a–b** could have been derived from a Jewish manual independently from the Synoptic tradition (Mark 12:28 and parr.)—the Testaments attest a similar juxtaposition of the love commandments (T. Isachar 5:2; 7:6; T. Dan 5:3; cf. T. Benj. 3:3; *Pirke Abot* 6:1), and there is no reason to assume that the Synoptic tradition (or Jesus) was the first to unite Deut. 6:5 with Lev. 19:18b.

Barn.		Did.
	First,	2a
2a	*You shall love* him *who made you;* fear him who formed you; [k] glorify him who redeemed you from death.	*you shall love* the God *who made you.*[d]
	[see 19:5b]	
	Second, your neighbor as yourself [Lev. 19:18b].	2b
	And whatever you do not want done to you, do not do to anyone else.	2c
[cf. 19:1c↑]	Now this is the teaching of these words:	3a

[k] G lacks this phrase (see §5:5:6).

[d] ApCo, Shenuti, and Syntagma-Fides lack "who made you" and supplement the text with additional reflections from Deut. 6:5 (Mark 12:30 f., etc.). CO does similarly, but retains "who made you" and also includes the final phrase of Barn. 19:2a.

Furthermore, it is evident from the New Testament alone that Lev. 19:18b was widely used in Judaism as a capsule form of Torah-Law (Rom. 13:9; Gal. 5:14; Jas. 2:8)—Rabbi Akiba (*ca.* A.D. 130) called it "the greatest principle in Torah" (*Sifra, ad loc.;* cf. Hillel in *Pirke Abot* 1:12). The "negative golden rule" of **Did. 1:2c** (cf. Matt. 7:12 = Luke 6:31) also was a popular summary of Torah in Judaism (see Tob. 4:15; Hillel in b. *Shabb* 31a), and had wide vogue in early Christianity (Acts 15:20, 29 [D text], Didascalia 1, etc.)—it is also attributed to ancient non-Jewish/Christian figures such as Confucius. It has left no clear trace in Barnabas.

Somewhat more suspicious, however, is the *numbering* of the love commands in **Did. 1:2a–b,** which parallels Mark 12:29–31 almost exactly. Whatever the explanation may be for the Doctrina and its allies here, it is almost certain that the final editor of Didache both knew the Synoptic tradition in some form (§9:4) and had to struggle with the presence of these numbers, "First ... second ... ," as he expanded his Two Ways material. Whether he interpreted **Did. 1:2** as a

The "interpolation" (Did. 1:3b–2:1) [§8:2]

3b. Bless those who curse you [Luke 6:28a; Matt. 5:44 var.]
and pray for your enemies
but fast for those who persecute you [Luke 6:27, 28b;
Matt. 5:44];

---

single, "first" commandment with multiple parts (cf. Mark 12:33), or
saw 1:3–6 as the "teaching" for only 1:2c is not clear; but for some
reason 2:1–4:14 became "the second commandment of the teaching" (!). The resulting sequence of "First . . . second . . . second" created further problems in the continuing Didache tradition—ApCo
drops the "second" from 1:2b, while P.Ox makes some adjustment at
Did. 1:4 (P.Ox is not preserved for 1:2). A similar ambiguity occurs
in 5:1, "first of all."

Barn. 19:2a shows no awareness of these problems, but presents a
simple tristich (see §2:6) concerning one's attitude to the creator
(see §5:9; esp. Barn. 2:10*) who delivers men from death (see
14:5–8, "from darkness"!). A strikingly similar approach is found in
Sirach 7:29 ff., "with your whole soul, reverence the Lord . . . , with all
your might love him who made you . . . , fear the Lord and glorify the
priests . . ." (cf. Hermas, Mand. 1: "Believe that the God who created
everything is one . . . and fear him").

Did. 1:3b–2:1. Most of the material in 1:3b–4 is closely related to
teachings attributed to Jesus in the Synoptic tradition—specifically,
Luke 6:27–35 (which also includes the "golden rule"; cf. Did. 1:2c)
and Matt. 5:39–48. But the precise nature of the relationship is difficult to determine. The Didache sometimes parallels the wording of
Matthew, sometimes that of Luke, sometimes has elements of both
intertwined—and sometimes includes non-Synoptic material! Probably
the Didache is not directly dependent on the written Gospels as we
know them, but either uses a "harmony" tradition which developed
from them or, more likely, used the kind of material which they fixed
in writing but which continued to circulate (in various forms) after
they were written (so Koester).

Some of the non-Synoptic wording deserves notice: (1) the admonition to "pray for your enemies" (1:3b) is in the P.Ox 1224 fragments
of an unknown Gospel, and was also known to Justin (Apol. 15:9;
Dial. 133:6b) as words of Jesus. Thus we are dealing here, at least
in part, with traditional gospel material that is not now found in our
Gospels. The reference to fasting in 1:3b (cf. 8:1) is more difficult to
explain, but may be related to the practice attested in later Eastern
church manuals of fasting for the Jews at Passover/Easter time (ApCo
5:14:20; 5:19:2 ff. = Didascalia Syr. 21). (2) There is an exact parallel to the final words of 1:3c in Didasc. 1 (lacking in ApCo 1:2):

3c. For wherein do you excel if you love those who love you?
[Luke 6:32a]

don't the Gentiles also do likewise? [Luke 6:33b; Matt.
5:46b, 47b]

But you should love those who hate you [Luke 6:27; see Matt.
5:44],

and you will not have an enemy.[e]

---

[e] Or, "and have no enemy" (?)—cf. 1 Pet. 2:15; 3:13. P.Ox adds "Hear
what you must do to save your spirit: First of all..." (cf. 5:1!).

"... in the Gospel it says, 'Love those that hate you, and pray for those
that curse you, and you will have no enemy.'" Again, this may be a
traditional saying of Jesus—it is certainly not clear that Didascalia depends on the Didache here (see also 2 Clem. 13:4; Justin, *loc. cit.*).
(3) The final phrase of 1:4b interrupts the pattern of 1:4 and may be
a late gloss. It resembles the repeated phrase in 1:5, "he is blameless."
The attribution of spiritual/moral "perfection" became common in
Eastern Christianity. (4) The final words of 1:4e (another gloss?) are
obscure (see Georg!). Similar material is found in Syntagma with the
meaning, do not demand interest on what is borrowed! For the older
tradition, however, this probably is to be taken in the context of non-
retaliation (do not take him to court—cf. 1 Cor. 6:1 ff.; Didasc. 11
[ApCo 2:46]), or of resignation (you are helpless to resist), or of
unselfish almsgiving (perfection requires total sharing; cf. 1:5a; 4:8).

The Synoptic parallels to 1:5 are limited to the beginning and end,
while most of the intervening material is closely paralleled by Hermas,
Mand. 2:4–6 (italics indicate exact Greek wording common to the
Didache): "Do what is good, and from that which God has given you
from your labors [cf. Barn. 19:10d], give single-mindedly to all who
are in need, not being in doubt as to whom you should or should not
give [cf. Did. 4:4 = Barn. 19:5a]. *Give to all, for* God *desires that all
be in receipt of his* benefits. Thus those who receive shall render account to God as to *why* they *received and with what results.* For those
who *receive* while in affliction will not be punished, but those who
receive hypocritically will pay a *penalty.* Thus *the one who gives is
blameless....*" Jewish literature abounds with similar interests—see
Deut. 15:7 ff.; Prov. 3:27 f.; Sirach 4:1 ff.; 7:32 f.; Tob. 4:7—and early
Christian tradition often credited Jesus with words on this subject
which are not in our Gospels (e.g., Acts 20:35). Thus the reference to
"the command" can be variously interpreted—even the Hermas context
speaks of a "command" (to be single-minded). The motive for giving
in 1:5a is found in the Doctrina at the close of the Two Ways giving
section at Did. 4:4–8; perhaps the Two Ways source (which also
seems to have been known to Hermas in some form) at one time contained 1:5a—note that manuscripts S²G of Barn. 19:11a also cite part
of this material. The evidence points in the direction of a common

4. Abstain from fleshly and bodily *f* desires.

4b. If someone hits you on your right cheek,
   turn the other to him also [Matt. 5:39b; see Luke 6:29a]
   and you will be perfect [see §7:5; Matt. 5:48; 19:21].

4c. If someone compels you to go one mile, go with him for two
   [Matt. 5:41].

4d. If someone takes your coat, give him your shirt too [Luke
   6:29b; see Matt. 5:40].

4e. If someone takes from you what is yours [Matt. 5:42b; Luke
   6:30b]
   don't demand its return [Luke 6:30b]
   for you cannot *g* [cf. Matt. 5:39a].

5. Give to all who ask you, and don't ask for it back [Luke 6:30;
   see Matt. 5:42];
   for the Father wishes that all men should receive from his
   own gifts.

5b. Blessed is he who gives according to the command,
   for he is blameless.

5c. Woe to him who receives;
   for if someone who is in need receives, he is blameless,
   but he who is not in need will be called to account
   as to why he received and with what results, and when
   he has been imprisoned, he will be interrogated concerning
   his actions, and he will not be released from there until he
   repays the last penny [cf. Matt. 5:25 f.; 18:34; Luke
   12:58 f.].

6. But it has also been said concerning this matter:
   Let your alms sweat in your hands
   until you know to what end you are giving.

2 And the second [see 1:2] commandment of the teaching is:

---

f So H (Georg?). P.Ox lacks "and bodily" (see 1 Pet. 2:11); ApCo reads "and worldly" (see Tit. 2:12). Cf. 4 Macc. 1:32: "some desires are of the mind, others of the body."

g ApCo lacks this phrase (see §7:5); Georg has "and neither can you do this because of the faith" and lacks 1:5–6.

---

tradition about giving behind Didache and Hermas—the former placed it in a Synoptic framework while the latter adapted it to his "commandment" about single-mindedness. Apparently another form of this

Barn.		Did.
2b	Be upright in heart [see Ps. 36:10] and rich in spirit [cf. Matt. 5:3!].	
2c	Do not associate with those who are proceeding [1] in the way of death.	

[1] H reads "who are acting wickedly."

---

tradition has survived in Didascalia 17 = ApCo 4:3—in fact, ApCo even attributed it to "the Lord" (Jesus): "Blessed is he who gives rather than he who receives [cf. Acts 20:35; Didasc. has ". . . who is able to help himself . . ."] . . . , woe to those who have and receive in hypocrisy, or who are able to help themselves and wish to receive from others. For each will render account to the Lord God in the day of judgment." Or again, in a fragment from Clement of Alexandria: "Give alms, but with discernment and to those who are worthy, so that we might find recompense from the Most High [see Sirach 12:2]. But woe to those who have and who receive in hypocrisy, or who are able to help themselves and wish to receive from others. For he who has and receives through hypocrisy or laziness will be sentenced."

Did. 1:6 appends a supporting quotation from an unknown source (unless it is a rather free, variant rendering based on Sirach 12:1–7). Notice that here some kind of responsibility on the part of the *giver* is implied. In 1:5 it was the *recipient* who was accountable (every recipient according to Hermas, only the pretenders in the Didache).

Barn. 19:2b–4b; Did. 2:2–7. Barnabas contains a few phrases not paralleled in the Didache which merit special comment. The concern about one's companions in 19:2c is typical of the Barnabean tradition (cf. 10:3–11), but neither is it foreign to the Two Ways as such (see Did. 3:9b; 5:2c = Barn. 19:6b; 20:2c). The "way of death" (not darkness) allusion, taken in connection with 20:1b (cf. 19:2a!), shows that Barnabas is conscious of (but does not prefer) the life/death Two Ways imagery (see Did. 1:1). There is nothing particularly Barnabean about the non-Didachean phrases in 19:3a (cf. Shenuti, "but always be humble"!) and 19:3c (cf. Dctr to 3:9a). These words, along with the entire context, are strongly Jewish in flavor as the following passage from *Pirke Abot* 5:22 (cf. 6:5–6) illustrates: "A good eye and a humble spirit and a lowly soul characterize the disciples of our father Abraham; an evil eye and a haughty spirit and a proud soul characterize the disciples of Balaam the wicked one."

Barn.		Did.
2d	Hate everything that is not pleasing to God.	[= 4:12b]
2e	Hate all hypocrisy.	[= 4:12a]
2f	Do not forsake the Lord's commandments.	[= 4:13a]
3a	Do not exalt yourself, but always be humble-minded.	[= 3:9a]
3b	Do not allow yourself to become arrogant.[m]	[= 3:9a]
3c	Do not take glory on yourself.	
3d	Do not plot wickedly against your neighbor.	[= 2:6b]
		Do not murder [e] [Exod. 20:15(13)]. 2a
4a	Do not be sexually promiscuous.	[see below]
	Do not commit adultery.	Do not commit adultery [Exod. 20:13(14)].
	Do not be sexually perverted.	Do not be sexually perverted.
	[see above]	Do not be sexually promiscuous [Deut. 23:17 f.].

[m] So H, but SG place this item after 19:3d.

[e] See note e on p. 144.

Barn. 19:4a deals only with sexual misconduct (as in 10:6–8), while **Did. 2:2a–3d** groups together a number of succinctly stated vices (some of which are paralleled later in Barnabas; cf. also Did. 5:1 = Barn. 20:1) resembling the "second tablet" of the decalogue. Some items are difficult to translate with precision: e.g., the reference to sexual perversion in **Barn. 19:4a = Did. 2:2a** literally reads "do not be a corrupter of children/boys" and has specific reference to homosexual misconduct in which young men are adapted for the female sexual role, thus "corrupting" their natural sexual functions and often leading to castration or (it was believed) to impotence. The term was extended to include sodomy/homosexuality in general (so ApCo in-

Barn.   *Did.*

4b   Let not the word of God   [cf. 2:5b]
[§5:8] depart from
you with any sort
of impurity
[see 19:8c].[n]

Do not steal [e] [Exod.
20:14(15)].
Do not practice magic
[see Deut. 18:10 f.].
Do not engage in sorceries
[see Deut. 18:10 f.].

[n] S[2] mg. adds "Do not plot wick-   [e] The order differs in Dctr (cf.
edly" (= 19:3d).   5:1!): adultery, murder, false testimony (2:3b), etc.; stealing is not
mentioned in Dctr.

---

terprets it here)—see T. Levi 17:11; Justin, *Dial.* 95:1; Tatian, *Discourse* 8:1; Clement, *Paed.* 3:(12):89 (as part of the decalogue). Philo, *Spec. leg.* 3:37 ff. and *Migr. Abr.* 135 f., discusses this practice at length (cf. 2 Enoch 10:4[A]; Rom. 1:27; Hippolytus, *Refutation* 9:15; Barn. 10:6). A related phrase occurs in **Did. 2:2b** = Barn. 19:5c where the reference to *abortion* (so Dctr) literally reads "murder a child by destruction/corruption" (apparently before birth since infanticide is next mentioned, cf. Diognetus 5:6), which might also apply to primitive birth control (esp. onanism [Gen. 38:9]). The word that is traditionally rendered "fornication" appears in **Barn. 19:4a** = **Did. 2:2a** as *sexual promiscuity* since the meaning of the Greek is quite broad and usually includes such relationships as prostitution and adultery (see Did. 3:3). On magic and sorceries (or "making potions" [**Did. 2:2a**]), see Did. 3:4; Gal. 5:20; Rev. 9:21, etc. The problem of *oath breaking* (**2:3a**) was solved in some traditions by prohibiting oaths (Matt. 5:34; Jas. 5:12). On *bearing a grudge* (**2:3d**), see also Lev. 19:18a; 1 Clem. 2:5; 62:2; Barn. 2:8*.

Did. 2:4–7 adds a few stylistically more complex prohibitions. The "deathtrap" imagery in **2:4b** is widely attested (e.g., Ps. 18:5; Prov. 14:27; Tob. 14:10) and is used in connection with false speech in Prov. 21:6 (cf. Sirach 51:2; Jas. 3:5 ff.). Early Christian literature abounds with admonitions to "practice what you preach" (**2:5**)—e.g., 1 Clem. 38:2; Ign. Eph. 15:1; 2 Clem. 4:1 ff. (see Matt. 7:21), etc. Several of the items included in **2:6a** are found in the vice list in 1 Clem. 35:5. It is not clear precisely how the Didachist would have related **2:7** to 1:2b (cf. Barn. 19:5b)—was positive "love" reserved for those *within* the community (= neighbor, brother)?

Barn.		Did.
[= 19:5c]	*Do not murder a child by abortion, nor* kill it at birth.	2b
[= 19:6a]	Do not desire *your neighbor's things* [Exod. 20:17].	2c
	Do not be an oath breaker [see LXX Zech. 5:3b].	3a
	Do not give false testimony [Exod. 20:16].	3b
	Do not speak evilly [see LXX Prov. 20:13(16)].	3c
[= 19:4f]	*Do not ¹ bear a grudge* [see Prov. 12:28; Zech. 7:10].	3d
[= 19:7a]	*Do not be double-minded ⁹ nor double-tongued,*	4
[see 19:7a, 8b]	*for the double-tongue is a snare of death:*	
[cf. 19:4b↑]	Let your word be neither empty nor false	5
	but fulfilled in practice.ʰ	
[see 19:6b]	Be *not greedy,* nor a swindler, nor a hypocrite,	6a
	nor spiteful, nor conceited.ⁱ	
[= 19:3d↑]	*Do not plot wickedly against your neighbor.*	6b
	Do not hate any man,	7
	but reprove some—and pray for them—	
[see 19:5b]	and some *love more than yourself.ʲ*	

¹ ApCo and CO read "nor."

⁹ Dctr adds "in giving advice."

ʰ This phrase is lacking in Dctr, ApCo, CO, and is probably a late gloss (cf. 1:4b, e).

ⁱ Dctr adds "nor quarrelsome [see 3:2] nor bad-mannered."

ʲ Acute textual problems beset this verse. For P.Ox, as above, only two groups of men seem to be in view (?). H could be taken as listing three groups—"reprove some, pray for others, and some love. . . ." Dctr lacks the material between "man" and "some love" (cf. Shenuti). ApCo and Syntagma-Fides paraphrase freely. CO seems to refer to three groups: "some reprove, have mercy on others—and pray for them—and some love. . . ." Georg solves the problem by rendering the final phrase "but you shall love all these in the Lord. . . ." (Cf. Jude 22 f.)

The "fences" tradition (Did. 3:1–6)

3   My child,[k] flee from every evil thing [l]
    and from everything that is like it:
2. Be not prone to anger,
        for the path of anger leads to murder;
    neither be excitable nor quarrelsome [m] nor hot-tempered,
        for from all these are born murders.[n]

[k] Georg adds "I say to you on behalf of the Lord." Cf. T. Benj. 7:1 (etc.)
for the use of "I say to you" in similar contexts. The witnesses vary greatly
on the use of "my child" in this section (see §7:5; cf. §2:5:3).
[l] P.Ox has "every evil act" but the other witnesses could be interpreted to
refer to "every evil person . . . like him" (esp. Dctr).
[m] Dctr lacks "nor quarrelsome"—see its variant at 2:6!
[n] Dctr reads "fits of anger" (!) and lacks any equivalent to 3:3.

Did. 3:1–6 clearly is a unity both with reference to style (five
commands with two subdivisions each) and to content. It has sometimes been dubbed "The Fences" because it aims at making it more
difficult for certain forbidden acts to occur (murder, adultery, idolatry,
theft, calumny) by prohibiting attitudes or actions which foster them.
A similar approach to law (especially cultic law) is basic to Rabbinic
Judaism—see Pirke Abot 1:1, ". . . make a fence around Torah." The
style may be described as catechetical, using a personal approach (cf.
§4:3; Did. 4:1) and a set pattern that facilitates memorization (cf.
Barn. 10:3–5, 6–8 for similar patterns). Barnabas shows no clear
knowledge of this material, and it is only in Did. 5:1 that there seems
to be any significant relationship between 3:1–6 and the Two Ways
ethic of the Didache (see R. H. Connolly, JTS 33 [1932], 241 f.).
Thus this section probably was added to the Didache branch of the
Two Ways soon after the Barnabas form had separated from the common stock, and it came to influence the list of vices in 5:1 (see §2:4–5;
§8:4–5).

The precise background of 3:1–6 is not clear, but the best parallels
come from the Testaments: see T. Judah 14:1, "My children, do not
become intoxicated with wine, for wine turns the mind from the truth
and introduces lustful passion and its path leads the eyes to error"; or
19:1, "My children, love of money leads along the path to idolatry. . . ."
3:1 (cf. Barn. 4:1) is very similar to T. Benj. 7:1 ("my children, I
say to you, flee the evil of Beliar . . .") and T. Dan 6:8 ("keep yourselves, my children, from every evil work"). Notice the general syno-
nymity of "promiscuity" (see 2:2a) and "adultery" in 3:3. The vocabulary of magical practices in 3:4 (cf. 2:2a; 5:1) is difficult to translate
with precision. It prohibits augury (literally, interpreting behavior of
birds), use of incantations, astrology, and magical purification rites
(for healing purposes?; see W. L. Knox, JTS 40 [1939], 146 ff.)—cf.
Lev. 19:26, 31; Deut. 18:10 ff.; Orac. Sib. 3:218 ff. The first part of

3. My child, be not lustful,
    for the path of lust leads to sexual promiscuity;
  neither be obscene in speech nor have roving eyes,
    for from all of these are born adulteries.
4. My child, be not a diviner of omens
    since its path leads to idolatry;
  neither be an enchanter, nor astrologer, nor magician—
    nor even wish to see or to hear *o* such things—
    for from all these is born idolatry.*p*
5. My child, be not a liar,
    since the path of lying leads to theft;
  neither be fond of money, nor vainglorious,
    for from these all are born thefts.
6. My child, be not one who complains,
    since its path leads to blasphemy;
  neither be stubborn nor evil-minded,
    for from all these are born blasphemies.

o So Georg, Dctr, CO: H lacks "or to hear."

p Dctr has an abridged and reworked form of 3:4: "Do not be an astrologer nor a magician, which things lead to manifold superstition, nor desire to see or to hear such things."

Barn.		Did.
4c	Do not show *partiality in reproving* any-one for *transgressions.*	[= 4:3c]
4d	Be *meek,*	But be *meek,* 7 since "the meek will inherit the earth." *q*
		q Dctr has "the holy land" (!), while CO reads "the kingdom of the heavens/God." See Ps. 37:11; Matt. 5:5.

3:5 is cited by Clement (*Str.* 1:[20]:100) without precise indication of its source ("scripture")—he may have known the tradition from which the Didache drew **3:1-6.** Outside of **3:6,** "blasphemy" (i.e., abusive speech, which ultimately slanders God) is not mentioned by the Didache (or Barnabas) despite its presence in other early vice lists such as Mark 7:21 f. (= Matt. 15:19) and Hermas, Mand. 8:3. The word is also rare in the LXX and absent from the Testaments. But similar ideas occur in Did. 2:3c, 5 and Barn. 19:4b, e; 20:2h.

	Barn.	*Did.*	
		Be patient and merciful and without guile	8
	be *quiet,* be *one who fears the words which you have heard.*	and *quiet* and good and always *fearing the words which you have heard.*[r]	
4e	Do not take the Lord's name in vain.[o]		
4f	*Do not bear a grudge* against your brother.	[= 2:3d↑]	
5a	Do *not be undecided as to whether or not a thing shall come to pass.*	[= 4:4]	
5b	*Love* your neighbor *more than yourself.*[p]	[see 1:2b; 2:7↑]	
5c	*Do not murder a child by abortion, nor,* again, destroy that which is born.	[= 2:2b↑]	
5d	Do not remove *your control from your son or your daughter, but from youth up, teach the fear of* the Lord.	[= 4:9]	
6a	Be not desirous of *the things of your neighbor.*[q]	[= 2:2c↑]	

[o] H includes this decaloguelike commandment here (see Exod. 20:7 = Deut. 5:11; Lev. 19:12), but SG place it after 19:5a.

[p] S* wrote "more than your enemy" (!) but immediately corrected it. S^2 later changed it to "as yourself" (see Did. 1:2b, etc.).

[q] H lacks 19:6a entirely.

[r] A great deal of confusion exists among the witnesses here, probably because of the similarity to Isa. 66:2b. Thus ApCo and CO lack "always," while ApCo (see Shenuti, Syntagma-Fides) reads "words of God." Dctr has "Be patient and by your industry be good and fearing all the words which you have heard."

Barn.	*Did.*

6b Be *not greedy,*
    [= 19:3a–b↑]

 [= 2:6a↑]

Exalt not yourself,[8] *nor* **9a**
allow your soul to
become arrogant.

    neither be yoked
    from *your* soul
    with the haughty;
    but associate with the
    righteous and lowly.

Let not **9b**
your soul be yoked
with the haughty,
but associate with the
righteous and lowly.

6c *Whatever befalls you,*
    receive these ex-
    periences as good,
    knowing that nothing
    happens without
    God.[r]

Whatever befalls you, **9c**
receive these experi-
ences as good,
knowing that nothing
happens without *God.*

7a *Be not double-minded*
    nor double-
    tongued [8]
    for the double tongue
    is a snare of death.[t]

 [= 2:4↑]

7b Be subject *to those over*
    you as though to
    God,
    in reverence and fear.

 [= 4:11]

7c Do *not* give an *angry*
    command to your
    slave or maid-
    servant, who trust
    in the same God,[u]
    lest they fear not the
    God who is over
    you both;

 [= 4:10a]

---

[r] Did. and Barn. use different words for "without," and Barn. G lacks "knowing . . . God."

[8] So HG (= Did.), but S has "talkative" (cf. 19:8b).

[t] Only G preserves this clause here (cf. 19:8b) as in Did.

[u] G reads "who have the same hope" (see §5:5:1).

[8] Dctr adds "nor glorify yourself before men" (cf. Barn. 19:3c).

Barn.   *Did.*

	Because he came *not to call men according to status,* *but to call those in whom he prepared the spirit* [§5:10].	[= 4:10b]
8a	*Share all things with your* neighbor *and do not claim that anything is exclusively yours;* *For if you are sharers in that which is* imperishable, *how much more so in what is* perishable.	[= 4:8]
8b	Be not overtalkative, for the mouth is *death's snare* [cf. 19:7a↑].	[cf. 2:4↑]
8c	To the extent of your ability, be pure for your soul's sake [see 19:4b↑].	[cf. 6:2]
9a	*Do not be one who stretches out his hands to receive but who holds them back when it comes to giving.*	[= 4:5; see Sir. 4:31; Deut. 15:7 f.]
9b	Love as the apple of your eye all who proclaim the Lord's *word to you.*	**4** My child [cf. 3:1–6] 1a him who proclaims *to you the word* of God, *remember*
10a	*Remember* the day of judgment *night and day* [§2:3; §5:3],	*day and night,* and honor him as the Lord.

Barn.		Did.
	For wherever the king-ship is proclaimed, the Lord is there.	1b
10b	and *pursue* (the quest) *each day* *v* [§5:4]	
	And *seek out daily* *t* the company of the saints so that you might find refreshment in their words [see 16:2a; §2:3, 7].	2
10c	either by the word,*w* by toiling and trav-eling in order to ad-monish and by taking pains to save a soul by the word [§5:8], [= 19:12a]	
	Do not cause divisions, but make peace between disputants.	3a
[= 19:11d]	*Judge justly.*u	3b
[= 19:4c↑]	*Do not show partiality in reproving trans-gressions.*v	3c
[= 19:5a↑]	*Do not be of two minds* *w* *whether or not some-thing should be.*	4
[= 19:9a↑]	*Do not be one who stretches out his hands to receive, but holds them back when it comes to giving.*	5

v G and S² mg. add "the company of the saints," thus modifying the meaning of what precedes to agree with Did.

w S² mg. adds "and work and labor."

t Dctr lacks "daily," but cf. its con-clusion at 6:1!

u Dctr adds "knowing that you will be judged."

v Dctr has "Do not oppress any-one in his misfortune" [?].

w ApCo and CO (partly) add "in your prayer."

Barn.

Did.

	If you have acquired something *through the work of your hands,*
10d	or *by your hands,* by working to provide *a ransom for your sins.*
	give it as *a ransom for your sins.*
11a	*Do not hesitate to give nor grumble when you give,*[x] *for you know who is the good paymaster of the reward.*
	Do not hesitate to give nor grumble when you give, for you know who is the good paymaster of the reward.

6

7

Do not turn away from 8
the needy man,[x]
but *share everything
with your* brother,
*and do not claim that
anything is exclu-
sively your own;*
For *if you are sharers in
the* immortal,
how much more in the
mortal things? [y]

[= 19:8a↑]

---

[x] G and S² add "Give to all who ask you" (= Did. 1:5a).

[x] So Dctr (see Sir. 4:5a). The Greek texts could be rendered "Do not turn the needy away." One MS of CO ends here, after adding "for you will receive the worthy reward from the God who loves men, to whom be the glory forever, Amen" (cf. Dctr's ending at 6:1).

[y] Dctr reads "for if we are sharers in mortal things, how much more ought we henceforth to be, having made such a start [?]. For the Lord wishes to give to everyone from his gifts" (= Did. 1:5a!). The reason for this strange text is not immediately apparent. At this point, some MSS of CO introduce material from Barn.

Barn.   *Did.*

[= 19:5d↑]   Do not relax *control over*   9
                                your son or daughter,
                                but from youth on-
                                ward, teach them *the*
                                fear of God.*z*

[= 19:7c↑]   *Do not give a command*   10a
                                in your anger to
                                your slave or maid-
                                servant, who trust in
                                the same God,
                                lest they fear not the
                                God who is over you
                                both;

[= 19:7c↑]   For he comes *not to call*   10b
                                men according to
                                worldly prestige,
                                but those on whom
                                he prepared the
                                *spirit.*a*

[= 19:7b↑]   And you slaves, be sub-   11
                                ject *to* your *masters*
                                as if to God, in
                                respect and fear.

[= 19:2e↑]   *Hate all hypocrisy*   12
[= 19:2d↑]   and *everything that* is
                                not *pleasing to the*
                                Lord.

21:2–4, plus a phrase from Did.
4:13, to end the Two Ways section.
Nor does Shenuti preserve parallel
material to 4:9–14b.

z So H, ApCo (= Barn. S): but
Georg, Dctr, CO (1 MS) have "the
Lord" (= Barn. HG). One MS of
CO continues with phrases from
Did. 4:14a, 13a, 14b, 12, 13b, 14c
to conclude the Two Ways section.

a Dctr has ". . . in whom he found
the spirit." On this phrase see
§5:2:20; §9:10 (ApCo lacks 4:10b).

Barn.		Did.
	[= 19:2f↑]	
	Forsake not the Lord's commands,[b]	13a
11b	*Guard what you received, neither adding nor subtracting anything.*	*but guard what you received— neither adding* [c] *nor subtracting anything.*	13b
11c	Hate evil completely.	[cf. 4:12a↑]	
11d	*Judge justly.*	[= 4:3b↑]	
12a	*Do not cause divisions, but make peace with disputants* by bringing them together.	[= 4:3a↑]	
12b	*Make confession* for your sins.	In church,[d] *confess* your transgressions,	14a

[b] Dctr lacks this exhortation (cf. some MSS of CO).

[c] Dctr adds "things contrary to it" (cf. 5:1a and ApCo).

[d] So H (Georg); but ApCo and CO (1 MS) lack "in church," while Dctr lacks all of 4:14a (including the "and" of 4:14b).

Barn. 19:4c–12; Did. 3:7–4:14. Items that are unique to Barnabas in the remainder of the "Way of Light" include: **19:4e,** which may be a late addition to the Barnabas Two Ways (note the textual problem); **19:8b** seems to be a doublet of **19:7a** (= Did.); the exhortation in **19:8c** is reminiscent of Did. 6:2 and has an ascetic tone to it, although elsewhere Barnabas does not seem to be overly inclined to asceticism (cf. 4:10b); the phrase "apple of your eye" in **19:9b** (also in CO) is quite Semitic and biblical (see Deut. 32:10; Ps. 17:8; Prov. 7:2, etc.)—cf. G. Thom. 25: "Jesus said, Love your brother as your soul, guard him as the apple of your eye"; the summary statement in **19:11c** may be a doublet of Barn. 4:10a and echoes Prov. 8:13 (cf. Qumran *Manual* 4:1, God "hates forever" all the ways of the spirit of darkness).

The unique elements in the Didache are less frequent. In **3:7,** the scriptural allusion is probably an expansion of the older tradition; expansion may also be present in **3:8** with its piling up of virtues. **Did. 4:1–2** is consistent with other emphases in both Didache and

Barn.		Did.
12c	*Do not go to prayer with an evil conscience.*	
	and *do not go to prayer with an evil conscience.*	14b
12d	*This is the Way of Light.*[y]	
	This is the Way of Life.	14c

[y] S[2] mg. G include 19:12d, but S*H lack it.

Barnabas—e.g., on frequent fellowship, see §2:3, 7; on reverence for God's servants, see Did. 12:1; 15:2; and on the spokesman of God's word, see Barn. 16:8 ff., etc. The exact meaning of **Did. 4:1b** is problematic, but it at least identifies the Lord's presence with the preaching of "the things of the Lord." In **4:14a**, it may be that the Didache tradition has reworked an original reference to "gathering together" (see **Barn. 19:12a**, *synagagōn*) into a precise reference to "church" (the former "synagogue"?).

With respect to the materials shared by Barnabas and Didache here, the latter presents them in a more organized fashion. **Did. 3:7–9** treats personal attitudes and conduct; **4:1–2** duties toward other Christians in general; **4:3** Christian judging; **4:4–8** obligations toward the needy (**4:4** probably means do not hesitate to give alms or doubt that all men are worthy in God's sight—see Georg and Did. 1:5); **4:9–11** family and household duties; **4:12–13** summary exhortation; **4:14** purity of life (?). There are numerous instructive parallels to these various commandments of the "Way of Light/Life," but the reader must be referred to the larger commentaries for assistance in such matters.

II. THE WAY OF DARKNESS/DEATH

(Barn. 20:1–2; Did. 5:1–2)

Barn.				*Did.*
1a	**20**	*But the Way* of the Black One *is* crooked *and full of cursing.*	**5** *But the Way* of Death is this: *e* First of all,*ƒ* it *is* wicked *and full of cursing—*	1a
1b		For it is entirely a way *ᶻ* of eternal death with punishment, in which lie the things which destroy men's souls—		1b

---

ᶻ So Syr, cf. H ("for it is entirely [*holos*] of eternal death"): SG have "for it is a way [*hodos*] of eternal death."

e Dctr has "is contrary to this" (cf. 4:13b!).

ƒ Dctr lacks "of all" (cf. 1:2a).

Barn. 20:1–2; Did. 5:1–2. In both Barnabas and the Didache the "Way of Darkness/Death" consists of three sections: the introduction, followed by a list of vices, and finally characteristic acts of those who walk in this path. The Barnabas form of the introduction (**20:1a–b**) is characteristically eschatological (see §5:3), with its reference to Satan, the Black One (see 4:10a), and to "eternal death with punishment" (cf. 10:5—Barnabas nowhere gives the details about the "punishment" of the wicked). Barnabas does not repeat the phrase "Way of Darkness" (18:1b) here, and again shows knowledge of the "death" imagery (see 19:2a). On the symbolism of the "crooked" path, see LXX Prov. 21:8; 22:5, 14, etc. **Did. 5:1a** is consistent in using "way of death" (see 1:1a). Strangely, the "first" of **Did. 5:1b** (see 1:2a) is not followed up by a "second" (at **5:2a?**; see 1:2b; 2:1). On the relationship between such vices and cursing (**Barn. 20:1a = Did. 5:1b**), see esp. Deut. 27:15 ff.; 28:15 ff. (with the punishment spelled out!).

Numerous problems arise when the lists of vices in **Barn. 20:1c** and **Did. 5:1c–d** are compared. Barnabas gives the shorter version, and in one way or another the Didache tradition includes all of the items of Barnabas except "transgression" (see Barn. 12:5). Several items in **Barn. 20:1c** have already been mentioned in the "Way of Life"—arrogance

Barn.			*Did.*
1c	*idolatry, arrogance, pride* in power, *hypocrisy, duplicity, adultery, murder,* robbery, *conceit,* transgression, *guile, malice, stubbornness, sorcery, magic, greediness.*	*murderers,*[g] *adulteries,* lusts, sexual promiscuities, thefts, *idolatries, magic* arts, *sorceries, robberies,* false testimonies, *hypocrisies, duplicities,*[h] *guile, conceit, malice, stubbornness, greediness,* foul speech, jealousy, *arrogance, pride,* boastfulness.	1c
			1d

[g] Both the order and content of this vice list varies considerably in Dctr (cf. 2:2 f.)—adulteries, murders, false testimonies, fornications, evil desires (= duplicities? lusts?), magic arts, wicked deceptions (= sorceries), thefts, vain superstitions (= idolatries; see 3:4), robberies, affectations (= lusts?), haughtiness (= conceit?), malice, capriciousness (= stubbornness?), greediness, foul speech, jealously, audacity (= arrogance), elevated pride, vanity (= boastfulness). There does not seem to be any equivalent for "guile," and it is not clear if or where "lusts," "hypocrisies," and "duplicities" are represented.

[h] So ApCo (cf. Dctr); H (Georg?) has "duplicity" (singular).

(19:3b), pride (19:3a), hypocrisy (19:2e), adultery (19:4a), greed (19:6b). Of special interest is the presence of idolatry at the head of the list. Elsewhere Barnabas shows concern for this sin (4:8; 9:6; 16:7; cf. 12:6; 14:3), thus its precedence may be related to the attitude reflected in certain other Jewish vice lists which see idolatry as the primal sin—for example, the Decalogue; Wisd. Sol. 14:12 ff., 27;

Barn.			Did.	
1d	*Without fear* of God,*ᵃ*		*Without fear,ⁱ*	2a
2a	*persecutors of the good;*		*persecutors of the good;*	
2b	*Hating truth, loving a lie;*		*Hating truth, loving a lie;*	2b
2c	*Not knowing the reward of righteous-ness,*		*Not knowing the reward of righteousness;*	2c
	not associating with what is good;		*Not associating with what is good,*	2d

ᵃ So HGS², but S* lacks the words "of God" (see Did. 5:2a).

ⁱ So ApCo (see Barn. 20:1d in MS S*); cf. Ps-Clem. *Hom.* 1:18. Dctr* had "not fearing," and a later hand added "God." H (Georg?) lack these words.

T. Levi 17:11; 2 Enoch 34:1 (cf. such Christian lists as Rom. 1:23; Justin, *Dial.* 95:1; Theophilus, *Ad Autol.* 2:34 f.).

Apparently the vice list in the Didache has been reorganized and expanded significantly as that tradition developed. Possibly Did. 3:1–6 has influenced the inclusion of such items as "foul speech" (**5:1d;** see 3:3b) and "jealousy" (see 3:2b, "excitable"—from the same root). The presence of "lusts, promiscuities, thefts ..., false witnessings" (**5:1c**) is explainable on the basis of the Decalogue (the first three also are found in 3:1–6, and they are paralleled in 2:2 f.). "Boastfulness" frequently occurs in contemporary vice lists (1 Clem. 35:5, Hermas, Mand. 6:2:5, etc.). The order of vices differs significantly in the Doctrina, and the same phenomenon in 2:2 f. shows that it is not accidental. For the Doctrina, adultery-murder-false testimony take precedence. It is possible that the Doctrina order has been changed in the Didache under the influence of Matt. 15:19 (or a closely related source). Notice also that the change from plural to singular between **5:1c** and **5:1d** is paralleled in Mark 7:21 f. (but not Matt. 15:19), and roughly at the same point ("guile").

It is not entirely clear where the simple vice list ends and the grammatically more complex list of acts begins. Because the normal structure in the latter is simple parallelism (see §2:6 on style), we have linked **Barn. 20:1d** with **20:2a** as most probably representing the intention of the common source (cf. Dctr). But "without fear (of God)" may have been considered the concluding (summary) vice—it represents a frequent emphasis in Barnabas (see §5:5:6) which is not absent from the Didache (4:9). Some of the material in **Barn. 20:2 = Did. 5:2** has already been mentioned under the "Way of Life/Light"

Barn.		*Did.*
2d	Not *judging justly,* not guarding the rights of the widow and orphan;	nor [j] *judging justly;*
2e	*Being alert not with respect to* the fear of God [§5:5:6], *but* to *that which is wicked— from whom courtesy and patience are far off* and distant;	*Being alert not with respect to* what is good, *but* to *that which is wicked— from whom courtesy and patience are far off;* [k]	2e
2f	*Loving what is worthless, pursuing reward;*	*Loving what is worthless,* [l] *pursuing reward;*	2f
2g	*Not showing mercy toward the poor, not laboring on behalf of the downtrodden;*	*Not showing mercy toward the poor, not laboring on behalf of the downtrodden;*	2g
2h	Reckless with slanderous speech, *not knowing him who made them;*	*Not knowing him who made them;*	2h

[j] So H (Georg?) ApCo, but Dctr has "not" (= Barn.).

[k] Dctr reads: "from whom gentleness is far off and pride is near."

[l] Dctr lacks this item.

—e.g., judging justly (19:11d = 4:3b), infanticide and abortion (? 19: 5c = 2:2b). In **20:2d**, Barnabas retains a typically Jewish ethical emphasis that is lacking in the Didache—cf. Isa. 1:17; Jas. 1:27; Polycarp Phil. 6:1, etc. The opposite of **20:2f**, "loving what is vain," is reflected in Barn. 4:10a, which is also strongly oriented to the "Two Ways" scheme (see §2:3, 7). Barn. **20:2h** parallels in thought the idea of "blasphemy" (Did. 3:6).

Barn.		Did.	
2i	*Murderers of children, corrupters of God's creation;*	*Murderers of children, corrupters of God's creation;* [m]	2i
2j	*Turning away from the needy, afflicting the oppressed;*	*Turning away from the needy,* [n] *afflicting the oppressed;*	2j
2k	*Advocates of the rich, lawless judges of the poor—*	*Advocates of the rich, lawless judges of the poor—*	2k
2l	*sinful through and through!* [cf. 21:9b]	*sinful through and through!*	2l
		May you be delivered, children, from all these. [o]	2m

[m] Dctr reads: "destroyers of their children, abortionists" (see 2:2b).

[n] For 5:2j–l, Dctr has: "Turning themselves from good works, oppressing the afflicted, avoiding the appeals of the just."

[o] Dctr has: "Abstain, (my) child, from . . ."

CONCLUSION TO THE TWO WAYS OF THE DIDACHE (Did. 6:1–2)

6 Beware lest anyone cause you to wander from this way of teaching,[p] since such a one teaches without regard to God. 2. For if you can bear the whole yoke of the Lord, you will be perfect; but if you cannot, do what you can [cf. Barn. 19:8c].

[p] Dctr concludes here with these words: ". . . from this teaching, otherwise you will be taught apart from the (true) instruction. If you do these things daily [see 4:2] with deliberation, you will be near to the living God. But if you fail to do them, you will be far from truth. Store up all these things in your soul, and you will not be beguiled from your hope [see §5:5:1], but through these holy contests you will persevere to gain a crown. Through the Lord Jesus Christ, who reigns and rules with God the Father and the Holy Spirit for ever and ever. Amen."

Did. 6:1–2. The conclusion in the Didache (cf. also 11:1–2 and §2:3, 7) shows little relationship to Barnabas 21. **Did. 6:1b** (cf. Barn.

CONCLUSION TO THE TWO WAYS
OF BARNABAS (Barn. 21:1–9)

21 Therefore it is fitting that when one has learned the ordinances of the Lord [§5:5:2]—as many as have been written—
he walks in them.

1b. For he who does these things will be glorified in God's
kingdom;
he who chooses those will perish with his works [§5:3].

1c. For this reason there is resurrection,
for this reason there is recompense [see 5:7].

2. I urge *b* those who are in a high position—if you accept any
of my well-intentioned advice [§4:3]—to make sure that there are
among you those to whom you may do that which is good *c*
[§5:11]. Do not fail in this. 3. The day is near in which all things
will perish together with the Wicked One [§5:3]. The Lord is
near, and his reward [see 11:8].

b The material in 21:2–4(6, 8) is reflected in some MSS of CO as
follows: "We urge you, brethren, while there is yet time and there are among
you those for whom you may work, do not fail in any respect if you have the
power [cf. 21:8]. For the Day of the Lord is near in which everything will
perish with the Wicked One. For the Lord is coming and his reward is
with him. Be lawgivers among yourselves, be good advisers taught by God"
(then 19:11b = Did. 4:13b).
c G (= CO) lacks "that which is good" (cf. 20:2e [Did. 5:2e]).

5:4b) can be contrasted with Barn. 21:6a, "be God-taught," and with
the title of the Didache, "Teaching of the Lord." The present form
of **Did. 6:2** is linked to 6:3 by its atmosphere of concession, which is
also evident elsewhere in the Didache (see §8:3; cf. Hermas, Mand.
12:3:4 f.!). But the *style* of 6:3 links it with 7:1 (9:1; 10:8; 11:3)
not with **6:2**. It would seem that something like **6:2** was found in the
common source, and has also left its influence on Barn. 19:8c (cf.
Did. 1:4b, 5b–c; 16:2b; Qumran *Manual* 4; on the "Lord's yoke," see
Barn. 2:6; Matt. 11:29 f.; Acts 15:10; Justin, *Dial.* 53:1).

Barn. 21:1–9 forms a comprehensive conclusion to both the Two
Ways section and to the entire tractate. Its emphasis on striving for
the eschatological salvation which is near at hand is characteristic of
the epistle (§5:3–4). The conclusion to the Doctrina faintly preserves
similar material (see also Hermas, Mand. 6:2:10!), and resembles the
Qumran *Manual* in using the imagery of "truth" and the ultimate

4. Once more and again I urge you; be good lawgivers among
yourselves, persevere as faithful advisers to each other, remove
all hypocrisy [20:1c] from among you. 5. And the God who has
dominion over the whole universe [§5:9] will give you Wisdom,
Insight, Understanding, Gnosis of his ordinances, Endurance
[= 2:3].

6. Be taught by God [see 21:1a], seeking out what the Lord
seeks from you; and so act that you may find (what you seek) *d*
in the day of judgment [§5:3–4]. 7. And if there is any remem-
brance of what is good, remember me as you meditate [§5:2:17]
on these things, so that my earnest longing and my sleeplessness
might lead to some good result [§4:3].

8. I urge you, begging your favor, while the "good vessel" is
still with you do not fail in any respect, but continually seek out
these things and fulfill every commandment [§5:5:4]—for they are
worthy. 9. Wherefore, I hastened all the more to write whatever
I could [see 1:5; 17:1].*e* 9b. May you be saved, children of love
and peace [cf. Did. 5:2m; §4:3]. 9c. The Lord of glory and of all
grace be with your spirit.*f*

---

d So H (Cl. A. lacks "and so act"); but S has "that you may be found,"
and G has "that you may be saved" (cf. 19:10a-b!).

e GS² add "so that you might rejoice" (cf. 1:8; §5:5:6).

f G adds "Amen," after which some of its MSS read: "The epistle of the
apostle Barnabas, traveling companion of the holy apostle Paul." S has simply
"Epistle of Barnabas," while H has no subscription.

"crown." The "good vessel" of 21:8 apparently signifies the physical
body which the spirit indwells (cf. 7:3; 11:9)—probably Pseudo-
Barnabas means that the recipients should act while *they* have the
chance (in this life; cf. 4:9b = Did. 16:2b?), although he might be
referring to *his own* presence in this life. The chapter reads as though
it had been expanded in various stages, possibly by uniting an older
conclusion to chapters 1–17 (21:2–5?) with the Two Ways conclusion. Note that 21:9 parallels the final phrase of Did. 5:2, that 21:5
sounds very much like part of a benediction, and that 21:4a and
21:6a form a rough doublet. In fact, CO's version of 21:2 ff. resolves
much of this awkwardness—does it reflect an older form?

THE DIDACHE 6:3–16:8

I. INSTRUCTION AND RECEPTION OF CATECHUMENS (6:3–11:2)

[Continuation of the Two Ways Catechism (Did. 1:1–6:2)]

Concerning food (6:3) [§8:5:2]

3. Now concerning food, observe the traditions as best you can [§8:3]. But be sure to refrain completely from meat which has been sanctified before idols, for it represents the worship of dead gods.

Concerning baptism, fasting, and prayer (7:1–8:3) [§8:4; §8:5:2; §9:2]

7 Now concerning baptism [cf. 6:3]. Baptize as follows, when you have rehearsed the aforesaid teaching [see 11:1]: Baptize in the name of the Father and of the Son and of the Holy Spirit

---

6:3. In terms of content, this verse is unique in the Didache, although it is stylistically parallel to 7:1; 9:1; 11:3 ("Now concerning ... do thus ...."; cf. 10:1, 8; 15:4). Probably it represents a larger, older source which listed the various relevant food laws which Christianity had adopted from the Jewish "Noachic Laws" for sympathetic Gentiles (see Acts 15:20, 29; 21:25). When these specifics were omitted, possibly under the pressure of growing Christian "liberalism" (see Rom. 14; 1 Cor. 8; 1 Tim. 4:3 ff.; Barn. 10; Diognetus 4:1), the "thus do" section of the teaching was softened to "bear what you can." But the Didache tradition drew the line at meat that had been slaughtered in pagan temples—in agreement with much of early Christianity (e.g., Acts 15:20; Rev. 2:14, 20; Justin, *Dial.* 35:1–2; Ps-Clem. *Hom.* 7:4, 8; etc.; contrast 1 Cor. 8:4; 10:25!).

7:1–8:3. On the probable development of this section around the basic theme of baptism, see §8:4–5. The "hypocrites" tradition originally may have referred to Pharisaic practices (cf. Matt. 23:13), although the Didachist might mean simply practicing Jews (after A.D.

[§9:8–10], in running water. 2. But if you do not have running water, use whatever is available. And if you cannot do it in cold water, use warm [§10:4]. 3. But if you have neither, pour water on the head three times—in the name of Father, Son, and Holy Spirit [§8:3]. 4. And prior to baptism, both he who is baptizing and he who is being baptized should fast, along with any others who can. And be sure that the one who is to be baptized fasts for one or two days beforehand.

70, Pharisaic Judaism became dominant). If the communities which later used the Didache (e.g., ApCo) are indicative of the earlier practices, the Christianity represented here held baptism once each year, at Passover/Easter time. The Two Ways tradition provided the material for prebaptismal instruction (Did. 7:1; 11:1 f.; see Athanasius in §10:2; contrast Matt. 28:19 f.?), and after baptism the catechumens were anointed with oil (see to 10:8) and allowed to partake of their first Eucharist (see to 9:1 ff.). According to 7:2–3, immersion in a river or a spring (cold, flowing water) was preferred practice, but still water (pools, cisterns, fonts) could be used if necessary (cf. Tert., Bapt. 4). As a last resort, affusion was permissible—this is probably the earliest reference to that practice in Christianity (cf. Tert., Poen. 6; Bapt. 12; Acts of Thaddeus 4). The threefold formula was employed (so Matt. 28:19; Justin, Apol. 61:3; Tert., Adv. Prax. 26; Acts of Peter with Simon 5, etc.; cf. 1 Cor. 6:11) rather than the also popular baptism "in the name of Jesus" (see 9:5; Eusebius' text of Matt. 28:19; Acts 2:38; 8:16; 10:48; 19:5; Acts of Paul and Thecla 34, etc.)—this does not, however, necessarily imply a conscious, full-blown "trinitarian" theology as it was later defined. Liturgy may provide the materials for theologizing as well as vice versa!

The connection between fasting and baptism is widely attested in early Christianity (Justin, Apol. 61:2; Tert., Bapt. 19–20; Ps-Clem. Rec. 7:37; Hippolytus, Ap. Trad. 20:7; Passion of Paul 19; etc. (see Grant, 175). It is interesting that ApCo seems to understand Did. 8:1 as referring directly to fasts in passion week (thus including the prebaptismal fast). But the contrast with (Pharisaic) Jewish fasts on Monday and Thursday (see b.Shabb. 24a; Taʿanit 2:4–7; cf. Luke 18:12) indicates a weekly, not an annual, practice. In view of the predilection of the Jubilees-Qumran Calendar for Wednesday-Friday-Sunday special days (see J. van Goudoever, Biblical Calendars [Leiden, 1961]), it would be interesting to know if and when that kind of Judaism practiced weekly fasts. In any event, the Wednesday and Friday fasts were widely observed in early Christianity (e.g., Tert., Ieiun. 2; Clement, Str. 7:[12]:75:2), although there also was reaction to this sort of ritualism (see Barn. 3:1–5; Hermas, Sim. 5:1; Diognetus 4:1).

Prayer three times each day (8:3) is an old Jewish practice (Ps.

8 But do not let your fasts fall on the same days as "the hypocrites" [see Matt. 6:16 ff.], who fast on Monday and Thursday. Rather, you should fast on Wednesday and Friday.

2. Nor should you pray as "the hypocrites" do [see Matt. 6:5 ff.], but pray as the Lord commanded in his gospel [§9:4], thus:

> Our Father who is in heaven, may your name be revered.
> May your kingdom come, may your will be done on earth as it is done in heaven.
> Let us partake today of our heavenly fare [cf. 10:3],
> And forgive what we owe accordingly as we forgive those who are in debt to us.
> And do not bring us into testing, but rescue us from evil [cf. 10:5].
> For power and glory are yours forever [Matt. 6:9 ff.].

3. Thrice daily you should pray in that manner.

Concerning the giving of thanks—in connection with the Eucharist (9:1–10:8) [§8:4–5; §9:2]

9 Now concerning the giving of thanks [cf. 6:3]. Give thanks in the following manner. 2. First, concerning the cup:

> We thank you, our Father [§9:9], for the holy vine of David your servant,
> > which you have made known to us [§9:7] through Jesus your Servant [§9:8].
> Glory to you forever!

55:17; Dan. 6:10, 13; Qumran *Manual* 10:1–3) which was adapted in many Christian communities (e.g., Tert., *Ieiun.* 10; Clement, *Str.* 7:[7]:40:3), although it is not clear whether the Didache had the third-, sixth-, ninth-hour prayers in mind (as Tertullian and Clement of Alexandria), or dawn-noon-dusk (cf. Jewish practices). The form of the Lord's Prayer in **8:2** varies only insignificantly from Matt. 6:9 ff., and uses a doxology (lacking reference to "the kingdom," cf. 9:2, 3, 4; 10:2, 4, 5) which seems to have been known in Egypt (see the Coptic versions of Matt. 6:13) and Syria (§10:6).

9:1–10:8. Ever since the initial publication of the Didache, the prayers of chapters **9–10** have occasioned much discussion. At first glance they seem to represent a "Eucharist" liturgy—the (weekly)

3. And concerning the broken loaf:
> We thank you, our Father, for the life and knowledge [§9:7]
>> which you have made known to us through Jesus your
>> Servant.
>> Glory to you forever!

4. Just as this loaf previously was scattered on the mountains
[§10:4], and when it was gathered together it became a
unity,
> So may your Church be gathered together from the ends of
> the earth into your kingdom.
> For glory and power are yours forever, through Jesus Christ!
> [§9:8.]

5. But let no one eat or drink from your Eucharist except those
who are baptized [7:1–4] in the Lord's Name [§9:8]. For the
Lord also has spoken concerning this:
> Do not give what is holy to dogs [Matt. 7:6].

10 And after you have been filled, give thanks as follows:
2. We thank you, Holy Father, for your holy Name [§9:8]
> which you have made to dwell in our hearts;
> and for the knowledge [§9:7] and faith and immortality
>> which you have made known to us through Jesus your
>> Servant.
>> Glory to you forever!

---

ritual celebration of the "sacrament" of the Lord's Supper (see Ign.
Philad. 4; Justin, *Apol.* 66:1, 67:5). But the mere occurrence of the
noun *eucharistia* (9:1, 5) and related verbal forms (9:1, 2, 3; 10:1, 2,
3, 4, 8) must not be given too much weight, since these words originally indicated prayer and "giving thanks" in general (see Rom. 14:6;
1 Cor. 14:17; 1 Tim. 4:3; Rev. 4:9, etc.). Furthermore, the fact that
a meal is in view in **10:1** (cf. Luke 22:20; 1 Cor. 11:25) and that 14:1
refers to a rite which more closely resembles the liturgical Eucharist
as it came to be held (separately from any meal, as an "offering"), led
many commentators to suggest that **Did.** 9–10 refers to early Christian
"Love Feasts" (the "Agape" meal—cf. Jude 12) which were patterned
after formal Jewish "fellowship" meals and which sometimes seem to
have been held in association with the ritual Eucharist and also baptism (see Ign. Smyrn. 8:2). The background and early development
of these practices are discussed in detail by G. Dix, *The Shape of the
Liturgy* (Glasgow, 1945), ch. 4, who sees in **Did.** 9–10 a Love Feast
(pp. 90–95). The absence of any reference to Jesus' body or blood,

3. You, Almighty Master [§9:9], created everything for your
   Name's sake;
   you have given food and drink to men ^q for their pleasure,
      so that they might give you thanks.^q
   And to us you have graciously given spiritual food and
      drink [see 8:2],
   and life eternal through Jesus ^r your Servant.

^q The Cop fragment begins here, reading ". . . to the sons of man" and
lacking "so that they might give you thanks."
   ^r So Cop (see Georg); but H lacks "Jesus."

---

or to "remembering" him (cf. **10:5**) adds further support to the Love
Feast hypothesis, although the rather technical use of *eucharistia* in
9:5 causes some hesitation. The freedom granted to the "prophets"
in **10:7** (cf. **11:9**) could fit either case, as could the unusual order of
cup-loaf in **9:2 f.** (see Luke 22:17, 19 f.; 1 Cor. 10:16).

But the problems and possible solutions extend beyond these alternatives. How are we to account for the "ointment" prayer in some
traditions at **10:8**? If it was *artificially* constructed in imitation of
Did. 9:2, 3; 10:2, what was the interpolater's motive? He must have
envisioned some connection between the ceremony of **Did. 9–10** and
the "ointment." And if **10:8** reflects an actual prayer used in the
Didachist's Christianity, the same questions must be answered: what
was its connection with the other prayers? They all *obviously* have
similar origins! In a quite different vein, even if we grant an original
Love Feast setting for the prayers (which seems probable), must we
assume that the compiler of our form of the Didache tradition was
conscious of this background? We must ask further concerning the use
of these prayers in *his* experience, and *his* reasons (if any) for placing
them in their present context in the Didache.

An important clue to solving such questions might be uncovered if
the significance of the "ointment" or "perfume" (fragrant oil) of **10:8**
were known. It is not impossible that this too is a vestige from Christian Love Feasts, since the Jewish fellowship meal ritual included a
blessing on aromatic spices ("ointment"?) which usually were burned
(see Dix, *Liturgy*, 425 f.). But ointment/oil was used in many connections in early Christianity: for anointing the sick (Jas. 5:14) and
the dead (Mark 16:1, etc.), anointing catechumens in preparation for
baptism (esp. to exorcise evil spirits), mixing with the baptismal
waters to symbolize the Holy Spirit's presence, and so on. And in at
least two special rites, well known in Eastern Christianity, ointment
is closely connected with the Eucharistic bread and cup: (1) at the
ordination of bishops (Hippolytus, *Ap. Trad.* 4 [Ethiopic]); and (2)
at the baptism-confirmation-communion service at Easter time (see to

4. Most of all, we thank you because you are mighty.[s]
   Glory to you forever! [t]
5. Lord, remember your Church—
   rescue it from all evil [see 8:2] and perfect it [§9:5] in
      your love—
         and gather it, the sanctified one,[u] from the four winds
            into your kingdom which you have prepared for it.
   For power and glory are yours forever! [t]

[s] Georg adds "and good" (cf. ApCo, "faithful and true").
[t] Cop adds "Amen" in 10:4, 5, 6a.
[u] Cop lacks "the sanctified one" (cf. ApCo).

7:1, 4) when catechumens became full members of the community
(Hippolytus, *Ap. Trad.* 20–23, etc.).

This annual Baptism-Eucharist service seems to provide the most
satisfactory setting for **Did. 9–10**—indeed, for Did. 1–10 (see §8:4–5).
The climax of this service was the special Eucharistic meal that immediately followed the anointing and baptism of the catechumen, and
from which all nonbaptized persons were excluded (**9:5**; cf. Ethiopic
Ap. Trad. 40 [see §7:6]). Such an approach to Did. 9–10 does not solve
all the problems—we should expect **10:8** to precede the meal, and
10:7 is best explained as a vestige from the older Love Feast setting
—but there seldom is a tidy answer to the enigmas of evolved literature!

The symbolism intended in the phrase "David's vine" (**9:2**) is not
entirely clear—the best possibilities seem to be the Messianic hope (see
Isa. 11:1; 2 Baruch 36–40; John 15:1 ff.; Rev. 22:16) or the new
Israel concept (see Ps. 80:8 ff.; Isa. 5:1 ff.; Jer. 2:21; Hos. 10:1; 4
Ezra 5:23; 9:21 f., etc.). The image in **9:4** seems to be that as the
grain from which the loaf was made had come from widely scattered
origins, so ultimately the widely dispersed Church would be unified.
The prayer of **10:2–5** echoes certain phrases of the "Lord's Prayer"
(see 8:2)—the "holy Name," spiritual sustenance, rescue from evil, the
doxology—which also are common in Jewish table prayers. In **10:4–6**
it is possible that antiphonal prayer is represented, with the leader
saying one line and the congregation saying the next, or perhaps inter-
jecting an "Amen" (see esp. Cop; cf. Justin, *Apol.* 67:5). The phrases
in **10:6c, d** are especially similar to Rev. 22:11, 20 (see 1 Cor. 16:22).
The concession to "prophets" in **10:7** allows them to pray for a longer
time, or more frequently—or perhaps to hold Eucharist as often as they
like—in comparison to other leaders (see §9:3). The symbolism of the
"ointment" (cf. Exod. 30:25; Isa. 25:7 LXX) in **10:8** is not obvious—
perhaps the fellowship of believers is intended (see Ps. 133:2), or the
presence of God's Spirit, or immortality (see ApCo; Did. **10:2**; Ign.
Eph. 17:1).

6. Let grace come,*v* and this world pass away [§9:5].*t*
   Hosanna to the God *w* of David [§9:9].
   If anyone is holy, let him come;
      if anyone is not, let him repent [see 15:3].
   Marana Tha (Our Lord, Come). Amen.
7. But permit the prophets [11:3–12] to give thanks as they see
   fit [§8:3].
   8. And concerning the ointment,*x* give thanks as follows:
      We thank you, (our) Father, for the fragrant ointment
         which you have made known to us through Jesus your
         Servant.
      Glory to you forever! Amen.

The approved teacher (11:1–2) [§8:4–5]

11   Thus, whoever comes and teaches you all the aforesaid
things [see 7:1], receive him. 2. And if the teacher [§9:3; §4:3]
himself turns aside and teaches another *didache* which under-
mines the aforesaid, do not listen to him [cf. 11:12]. But if his
teaching fosters righteousness and knowledge [§9:7] of the Lord,
receive him as the Lord [cf. 4:1a; 11:4; Matt. 10:40; John 13:20].

   v Cop has "May the Lord come" (see ApCo, which places "Marana Tha"
[10:6d] here; cf. Rev. 22:20).
   w So H (Georg?). Cop has "house of David" (cf. Origen to Matt. 21:9,
15), and ApCo "son of David" (Matt. 21:9, 15). Possibly Did. 10:6b
originally read "to David's Lord" (see Ps. 110:1), which easily could give
rise to the three preserved readings. A similar textual problem is found in
Acts 7:46, "house/God/[Lord?] of Jacob."
   x The prayer for the "ointment" (perfume) is found in slightly divergent
forms in Cop and ApCo, but it is lacking in H and Georg (see §8:2). Its
style parallels (imitates?) 9:2, 3; 10:2.

   11:1–2. Whatever its background (see §8:4–5), the present position of **11:1–2** provides an excellent transition to the section which
follows by introducing the theme of how to tell a true from a false
Christian minister. In general, these verses resemble Gal. 1:6–9 and
2 John 9–10; it is possible that **11:2a** was originally autobiographical—
"even if I, your teacher, turn. . . ."

II. INTRACOMMUNITY RELATIONSHIPS
(11:3–15:4)

Concerning apostles and prophets (11:3–12) [§9:3]

3. Now [y] concerning the apostles and prophets. Act in accordance with the precept of the gospel [§9:4]. 4. Every apostle who comes to you should [z] be received as the Lord [see 11:2; 12:1]. 5. But he [z] should not remain more than one day, and if there is some necessity a second as well; but if he should remain for three,[a] he is a false prophet [cf. 11:6, 9–10]. 6. And when the apostle departs, he should receive nothing but bread until he finds his next lodging. But if he requests money, he is a false prophet.[a]

7. And you must neither make trial of nor pass judgment on any prophet who speaks forth in the spirit. For every (other) sin will be forgiven, but this sin will not be forgiven [see Matt. 12:31]. 8. And not everyone who speaks forth in the spirit is a prophet, but only if he has the kind of behavior which the Lord approves. From his behavior, then, will the false prophet and the true prophet be known. 9. And every prophet who, in the

[y] For all practical purposes, ApCo lacks 11:3–12 (see §7:5).

[z] Eth (cf. Cop) lacks "should. . . . But he," possibly correctly in the light of the parallelism between 11:4–5 and 11:6.

[a] Eth makes three days the maximum approved period (see 12:2), "and if he stays longer, he is a false prophet," and lacks 11:6.

11:3–12. The rubric of introduction in 11:3 parallels exactly 7:1; 9:1 (see 6:3). Some of the material in the section on "apostles" is paralleled in 12:1–2. The use of "apostle" to indicate itinerant missionaries is not unknown in the New Testament (see Rom. 16:7[?]; 1 Cor. 12:28 f.; Phil. 2:25[?]; Acts 14:14, etc.), although from early times the title came to be reserved for "the Twelve" and Paul (see Grant, 160 ff.; note also the title of the Didache). Similarly, "prophets" appear in the New Testament (1 Cor. 12:28 f.; 14:1; Acts 13:1, etc.; cf. Eph. 2:20; 4:11), and are treated with special care since their conduct "in the spirit" [§9:10] is noticeably different from normal activity (see Acts 11:27 f.; 21:10 f.). But just as there are false spirits (see to Barn. 18:1) there can be false prophets (Matt. 24:24, etc.), and some criterion for judging was needed in the community. Whereas 1 John 4:1 ff. advocates a doctrinal test, **Did.** 11:7 f. speaks of a testing of

spirit,[b] orders a table to be spread shall not eat therefrom; but
if he does, he is a false prophet [11:5–6]. 10. And every prophet
who teaches the truth, but does not do the things he teaches, is
a false prophet [11:5–6]. 11. And every prophet who has met
the test [cf. 12:1]—who is genuine—and [c] who performs a worldly
mystery of the church but does not teach others to do what he is
doing,[c] he shall not be judged by you. For he has his judgment
with God—for the ancient prophets also did similarly. 12. And
whoever says in the spirit, "Give me money," or anything else,
do not listen to him [cf. 11:2]. But if he says that it should be
given for others who are in need, let no one judge him.[d]

Hospitality toward traveling Christians (12:1–5)

12 But let everyone who comes to you in the Lord's Name
[§9:8] be received, and then when you have examined him [cf.
11:11] you will know—for you have insight—the nature of the
situation.[e] If, on the one hand, he is simply passing through, help

---

[b] Cop lacks "in the spirit."

[c] So H (Georg): Cop has something like ". . . and witnesses (?) to a
worldly tradition in the church," while Eth reads "who acts in the assembly
of men and acts unlawfully."

[d] Georg adds, "for what he has done will be judged by the Lord God"
(see 11:11).

[e] Literally "you will know . . . right and left" or perhaps "you have insight
(as to) right and left." On this peculiar idiom ("true and false"?), see Jonah
4:11; Acts of John 114 (and similar Gnostic usage).

---

conduct—with the divine dictates, or perhaps the life of the Lord
(11:8b is ambiguous) as the standard. But even to this rule there can
be an exception (11:11), if an acknowledged genuine prophet performs some personal action which otherwise would be suspect (is Hos.
1–3 in mind here? and the practice of "spiritual marriage" in early
Christianity?). Implicitly at least, the "apostles" are identified with
the "prophets" through the unexpected use of "false prophet" (not
"false apostle"; 2 Cor. 11:13; cf. Rev. 2:2) in 11:5–6; note that
neither should derive profit from their ministries (11:6, 12) or give the
impression of being a "free loader" (11:5, 9). Did. 13:1–2 returns to
the theme of support for such ministers. It is not clear to what gospel
"dogma" reference is being made in 11:3—possibly (with 13:1–2) to
Matt. 10:10b, but Matt. 10:40 might be a better candidate (see 11:4).

12:1–5. This section on traveling Christians interrupts the treatment
of prophets (see §8:4–5) and especially resembles 11:4–6. The com-

him *ᶠ* as much as you can. 2. But he must not remain with you except for two or three days if some necessity arises [cf. 11:5]. 3. On the other hand, if he wants to settle among you [cf. 13:1] and knows a trade, let him work and eat.*ᵍ* 4. But if he does not know a trade, use your own judgment to determine how he should live with you as a Christian without being idle. 5. But if he does not wish to cooperate, he is a Christ-peddler [§10:6]. Beware of such!

Material support for God's ministers (13:1–7) [§8:4–5]

13 And every true prophet [11:3] who wishes to settle among you [cf. 12:3] deserves his food. 2. Similarly, a true teacher [11:1–2] also deserves, like the laborer, his food [cf. Matt. 10:10b]. 3. Take, therefore, every first fruit—of the produce of wine press and threshing floor, and of cattle and sheep—and give it to the prophets. For they are your high priests. 4. But if you have no prophet, give to the poor. 5. If you make a batch of dough [§10:6], take the "first fruit" and give it in accord with the commandment [§9:4]. 6. Similarly with a jug of wine or of oil,*ʰ* take the "first fruit" and give to the prophets. 7. And so with money, and clothing, and every possession—take whatever "first fruit" seems appropriate to you and give it in accord with the commandment [13:5].

ᶠ Cop abruptly ends here, leaving the remainder of the column blank!
ᵍ Georg adds "with you in all unity and peace."
ʰ Eth (see ApCo) adds "or of honey."

---

munity is obligated to show hospitality to the visitor who claims to be a Christian (12:1, 4) until they have been able to evaluate his claim—presumably by observing his conduct and perhaps by other means. If he passes the test, they should aid him as best they can for as many as three days (12:2). Thereafter he should either leave or settle down to work (12:2–3)—Christians are not to be idle, not to live off other men's labors, for in that case they are "Christ-peddlers," or perhaps better, "Christ-parasites" (cf. 2 Thess. 3:10).

13:1–7. We now return to the theme of "prophets," but, like the Christian of 12:3, these are prophets who wish to settle. If ch. 12 had not provided such a neat transition, we might have expected this material to follow 11:12 (see §8:4–5). The additional note on "teach-

The community "sacrifice" (14:1-3)

14 And when you gather together [§9:2] each Lord's Day, break bread and give thanks [9:1 ff.]. But first confess your transgressions so that your "sacrifice" may be pure [see 4:14]. 2. And let no one who has a quarrel with his friend join you until they are reconciled, lest your "sacrifice" be profaned [see Matt. 5:23 f.]. 3. For this is what the Lord was referring to:

In every place and at all times offer a pure sacrifice to me [Mal. 1:11]. For I am a great King, says the Lord, and my name is marvelous among the nations [Mal. 1:14b].

---

ers" in **13:2** is rather strained and superfluous to the remainder of the chapter, but it does prepare us for **15:1-2**.

The "first fruit" section in **13:3-7** sounds like an adapted Jewish *halakic* tradition based on passages such as Exod. 22:29 f.; Num. 18:12-30; Deut. 18:1-5 (cf. Neh. 10:35 ff.; Ezek. 44:30). The ancient high priests are replaced by the prophets (do the teachers equal the Levites of old?; cf. 1 Clem. 40:5), and provision for the needy is retained (**13:4**, cf. Deut. 26:12). Apparently fixed clergy (**15:1-2**) had not yet replaced the itinerant ministers when this material was incorporated into the developing Didache tradition. The allusions to "the commandment" (**13:5, 7**) are obscure. Perhaps the Old Testament laws mentioned above are in view, or some saying attributed to Jesus (see Matt. 10:10b, or Irenaeus, *Adv. haer.* 4:17:5—"[the Lord] counseled his disciples to offer first fruits to God . . ."!), although in the latter case we might expect reference to the "gospel" (see **8:2; 11:3; 15:3 f.**). The inclusion of personal possessions in **13:7** may be based on the "offering" extracted from the Egyptians by the Exodus Israelites (see Exod. 3:22; 12:35; cf. Acts 20:33). The allowance that, within the general obligation to give, the giver has some freedom to determine his exact contribution (**13:7**; cf. **6:2 f.**!) is similar to Justin's claim in *Apology* 67:6 (cf. Acts 5:4).

14:1-3. The connection between **Did. 14** and its surroundings is not entirely clear, but probably it continues the idea of "first fruit" offerings in **13:3-7** by referring to the Christian "sacrifice" now offered (cf. 1 Clem. 40-41). The description of early Christian worship here is frustratingly vague. More detailed pictures are found in (1) the letter of Pliny to Trajan (see Grant, 88 f.), where a typical Christian service includes predawn meetings on a predetermined day, a hymn, a moral pledge, and later an "ordinary and harmless" meal; and in Justin, *Apology* 65-67: Christians meet on Sunday, greet each other with a kiss, read scriptures, have prayer and Eucharist conducted by "foremost brethren" with deacons serving absent members, contribu-

Respect for indigenous leaders (15:1-2)

15 Appoint for yourselves, then, bishops and deacons who are worthy of the Lord [cf. 13:1-2]—men who are unassuming and not greedy, who are honest [cf. 1 Tim. 3:2-13; Tit. 1:5-9] and have been proved [cf. 11:11; 12:1]. For they also are performing for you the task of the prophets [11:3] and teachers [11:1]. 2. Therefore, do not hold them in contempt, for they are honorable men among you [cf. 13:3b], along with the prophets and teachers.

---

tions for the needy are received, and so forth. Probably the "Lord's (Day) of the Lord," as **14:1** literally reads (cf. Rev. 1:10), refers to regular Sunday meetings (see Barn. 15:8 f.; §2:3), although C. W. Dugmore has argued that only Easter is meant (*Supplement to Novum Testamentum,* vol. 6 [1962], 282 ff.). The breaking of bread (**14:1**) has usually been interpreted as a Eucharistic service (so Georg), but the passage is by no means unambiguous and a regular community meal could be in view (see to chs. 9–10; cf. Acts 20:7 and Pliny's description). Nor should we jump to the conclusion that "sacrifice" in **14:1-2** necessarily indicates the Eucharistic "sacrament"—prayers and praise often were called "sacrifices" in this period, both in Judaism and in Christianity (see Barn. 2:10; Justin, *Dial.* 117:2b, etc.). Mal. 1:11 f. (**14:3**) was widely used in the early Church (in various forms) to "prove" God's acceptance of Christian prayers and/or Eucharistic observances throughout the world, and to attack Jewish cultic ritual (cf. Barn. 2–3).

15:1-2. This is one of the most recently composed sections of the Didache (see §8:3–5), reflecting the transition from dependence on itinerant ministers, some of whom have settled (13:1–2), to indigenous leaders (see §9:3). Notice that there is no indication here of a single bishop leader (cf. Ign. Trall. 2–3, etc.), but of appointing (or choosing, electing; cf. Acts 14:23; 2 Cor. 8:19; later it can mean "ordaining"; §10:6) a group of "overseers" (elders, who probably led community worship) and of deacons (with more menial functions, such as distribution of food, alms, etc.)—cf. Phil. 1:1; 1 Clem. 42:4 f.; Hermas, Vis. 3:5:1, and so forth. The translation "hold in contempt" (or "upbraid") in **15:2** may be too strong—"disregard" or "ignore" also are possible.

Community discipline and conduct (15:3–4) [§9:2:10]

3. And reprove one another [see 2:7], not irately but peaceably [see 4:3a], as you have it in the gospel [§9:4]. And let no one speak to any person who has wronged another,[i] nor let him hear what is said among you until he repents [cf. 10:6]. 4. But perform your prayers [cf. 14:1?] and your acts of charity [see 1:5 f.; 4:5–8; 13:5] and all your actions as you have it in the gospel of the Lord [§9:4].

III. ESCHATOLOGICAL ADMONITION
(16:1–8) [§2:7; §8:5:4]

16 Watch over your life [see 1:1]—do not let your lamps be extinguished, nor your waist be ungirded [cf. Luke 12:35]. But be ready, for you do not know when our Lord is coming [see Matt. 24:42, 44; Mark 13:35; Luke 12:40]. 2. And be gathered together frequently, seeking out the things which are necessary

[i] So H (Georg?), but a minor change in the Greeek would permit the reading "his friend/companion" (cf. 14:2).

15:3–4. This very general treatment of intracommunity relationships twice appeals to "the gospel" teachings, but does not cite any passages (cf. 8:2; 11:3). The best parallels to **15:3** are Matt. 5:22–26; 18:15–17, 21 f. (cf. Sirach 10:6 f.), and to **15:4**, Matt. 6:1–18. Probably "the gospel" here does not consciously refer to a written document accessible to all, but to the teachings of Jesus (like 1:3b–4; 8:2) which were regularly repeated in community gatherings. The Greek in **15:3b** is cryptic and could mean "nor let him be heard among you." A similar passage about "heterodox" Christians in Ign. Smyrn. 7:2 has "and say nothing, either privately or publicly, about them." Probably **15:3b** advocates giving an errant brother "the silent treatment" both privately and publicly. It is not clear whether this exclusion from public teaching/preaching also involves exclusion from meals, Eucharist, and so on.

16:1–8. Certain aspects of this apocalyptic "appendix" have been discussed in §2:3, 7. In general, it is closely related to the "synoptic apocalypse" in Mark 13; Matt. 24–25; Luke 21—see also 1 Thess. 4:13–5:11; 2 Thess. 2:1–12; 1 Cor. 15:23–28; Jude; 2 Pet. 2–3; Rev. 3–22. Furthermore, the Ethiopic Apocalypse of Peter (M. R. James, 511) opens with a strikingly parallel passage, including references to

for your souls [see §2:3]. For the whole time of your faith will
be of no use to you unless you are perfected in the last time
[= Barn. 4:9b; §2:3].

3. For in the last days, false prophets and corrupters will
abound [Matt. 24:11], and they will turn the "sheep" into
"wolves" and love will be changed to hate [Matt. 24:12]. 4. For
as lawlessness increases, men will hate one another [cf. 2:7],
and persecute and betray [Matt. 24:10], and then the world-
deceiver will appear as a son of God and will do signs and
wonders [Mark 13:22 par.], and the earth will be given into his
hands and he will commit such abominations as have never
been done before [see Dan. 12:1; Mark 13:19 par.]. 5. Then the
creation of men will come to the fire which tests and many will
fail and will perish. But those who endure in their faith will be
saved [Mark 13:13 par.] by him who was accursed.[j]

6. And then the signs of the truth will appear: first the sign
spread out in heaven [Matt. 24:30], then the sign of a sound of

---

[j] H can mean this (cf. Barn. 7:9; Gal. 3:13), or "by the curse itself," or
"by that which is cursed" (the earth?; see Gen. 3:17); Georg, however, has
something like "from this frightful curse" (i.e., the fiery test, or destruction).
Audet takes the phrase to mean "from the grave itself" (cf. Rev. 21:4; 22:3).

---

the sign-working "deceiver" (see 16:4), the cross preceding the Lord
as he comes (also in the Epistle of the Apostles 16 [or 27; James,
490]; cf. 16:6, the "sign spread out in heaven"!), the regal procession
and judgment (16:8). On the imagery of that which is commendable
being "corrupted" to its opposite (16:3), cf. 2 Baruch 48:35, "honor
will be turned to shame, and strength humiliated to contempt, . . . and
beauty will become ugliness." The "Antichrist" figure in 16:4 is frequent in apocalyptic literature, Jewish and Christian—see Dan. 7:25;
11:36 ff.; 2 Thess. 2:8; 1 John 2:18; Rev. 13, and so on. The testing
by fire in 16:5 (cf. Zech. 13:9; 1 Pet. 1:7; Rev. 16:8 f.) does not represent the final world conflagration envisioned in some sources (as
2 Pet. 3:10, 12—with a Stoic background), but the climactic crisis for
mankind before the triumphal return of "the Lord" (apparently Jesus
—see §9:8). Perhaps the allusion to the fiery destruction of the lawless
men in Qumran *Hymns* 6:17 ff. reflects a similar concept (cf. Rev.
20:15). In fact, it may be that 16:5 is intended as a reference to
judgment taking place *before* the Lord's return (but then, what does
"the world" mean in 16:8a?), and that the Didache should end as in
MS H, without further reference to judgment. The resurrection
of 16:6–7, in any case, is only for "the saints," as a reward for endurance and a sign of triumph.

a trumpet [Matt. 24:31; 1 Thess. 4:16], and thirdly, the resurrection of the dead [1 Cor. 15:52]—7. yet not of all (the dead), but as it was said:

The Lord will come and all his saints with him [Zech. 14:5b]. 8. Then the world will see the Lord coming on the clouds of heaven[k] with power and dominion [Mark 13:26 parr.] to repay each man according to his work [Ps. 62:12; Matt. 16:27], with justice, before all men and angels. Amen.

[k] MS H concludes here (with the remainder of the page left blank), but both Georg and ApCo lack the words "of heaven" and continue with a reference to the final judgment. The above translation follows Georg's ending. ApCo has "... with angels of his power, upon a kingly throne [Matt. 25:31], to judge the world-deceiving devil [16:4] and to repay each person according to his work. Then the wicked will depart to eternal punishment, but the righteous will enter life eternal [Matt. 25:46], inheriting the things 'which eye saw not ... [cites 1 Cor. 2:9],' and they will rejoice in the kingdom of God which is in Christ Jesus [see Matt. 25:34]."

INDEXES

I. QUOTATIONS AND SCRIPTURAL PARALLELS
in Barnabas 1:1–17:2 [cf. §4:1]

1. Relatively verbatim quotations of (Greek) Scripture

Passage	Barnabas	Introductory Formula
Gen. 1:26a	5:5	... he who is Lord of the whole world, to whom God said at the foundation of the world
1:26	6:12a	For the scripture is speaking about us, when he says to the Son
1:28	6:12b	... the Lord said
1:28	6:18a	But as it was already said above
2:2–3	15:3	He mentions "the sabbath" at the beginning of creation
25:23	13:2	Hear what the scripture says ... and the Lord said to her [Rebecca]
Deut. 10:16	9:5b (Gk)	And what is he saying?
Ps. 1:1	10:10	And David also ... says
1:3–6	11:6–7	And again he says in another prophet
18:44a	9:1a	The Lord says in the prophet
22:22	6:16b	He says
42:2b (?)	6:16a	For the Lord says again
51:17	2:10 (L)	For to us he speaks thus (for Gk, see below, unidentified Hymnic materials)

179

Passage	Barnabas	Introductory Formula
90:4	15:4b (S²ᵐᵍ)	For David bears me witness, saying that
110:1	12:10b	David himself . . . prophesies
118:22	6:4a	And again the prophet says
118:24a	6:4b	And again he says
Prov. 1:17	5:4	But the scripture says
Isa. 1:2a	9:3a	And again he says
1:10 (see 28:14)		
1:11–13(14)	2:5	For he made it clear to us through all the prophets . . . as he says in one place
1:13	15:8a	Further, he says to them
3:9b–10a	6:7b	For the prophet says concerning Israel
5:21	4:11	For the scripture says
16:1b–2	11:3	(follows Jer. 2:12–13 in composite quote)
28:14 (or 1:10)	9:3b	And again he says
28:16a	6:2b	And again . . . the prophet says of him
33:13	9:1c	And again he says (composite quote followed by ?; cf. Deut. 10:16; Jer. 4:4)
33:16–18	11:5	(follows Isa. 45:2–3a in composite quote)
40:3 (?)	9:3c	And again he says
40:12	16:2b	But how does the Lord speak . . . ? (composite quote followed by Isa. 66:1)
42:6–7	14:7a	Therefore the prophet says
45:1	12:11	And again, Isaiah says as follows
45:2–3a	11:4	And again the prophet says (composite quote followed by Isa. 33:16–18)

Passage	Barnabas	Introductory Formula
49:6–7	14:8	Again the prophet says
50:6a, 7b	5:14	And again he says
50:7b (?)	6:3c (Gk)	For he says
50:8b–9 (?)	6:1–2a	... what does he say?
53:5, 7b	5:2	For it is written concerning him—partly with reference to Israel and partly to us— and it says thus
53:5b	5:12a (L)	And Isaiah says
58:4b–5	3:1–2	Therefore he speaks again ... to them
58:6–10a	3:3–5	But to us he says
61:1–2	14:9	Again the prophet says
65:2	12:4	And again, in another prophet he says
66:1	16:2b	(follows Isa. 40:12 in composite quote)
Jer. 2:12–13	11:2	For the prophet says (composite quote followed by Isa. 16:1b–2)
4:3–4	9:5	And he says to them
7:22–23	2:7–8	And again he says to them (composite quote followed by Zech. 7:9 f./8:16 f.)
9:26 (?)	9:5c	And again he says
Zech. 7:9–10 / 8:16–17 } (?)	2:8	(follows Jer. 7:22 f. in composite quote)
13:7 (?)	5:12b	For God says that the afflicting of his flesh came from them (cf. Lat: And another prophet [after citation of Isa. 53:5b; see above])
Matt. 22:14 (?)	4:14b	(see below, unidentified Apocalyptic materials)

2. Quotations not clearly traceable to any known text-forms of Jewish Scripture [cf. §4:2]

(1) Apocalyptic materials (see commentary for scriptural parallels)

Passage	Barnabas	Introductory Formula
	4:4	And the prophet speaks thus
	4:5	Similarly, Daniel says concerning the same one
	4:14b	... as it is written (see Matt. 22:14)
	5:12b	(see above to Zech. 13:7)
	6:9	And what does "gnosis" say?
	6:13b	And the Lord says
	6:14b	As he says again in another prophet
	11:9a, 10	And again, another prophet says ... Then what does he say?
	12:1a	Similarly ... in another prophet who says
	12:9	Thus Moses says to Jesus son of Naue
	15:4b	He bears me witness, saying
	16:3	Furthermore, he says again
	16:5b	For the scripture says
	16:6c	For it is written

(2) Hymnic materials

	2:10a	To us, then, he speaks thus
	5:13b	For one who prophesies concerning him says
	6:6	What, then, does the prophet say again?

(3) Legal/Cultic (halakic) materials

	7:3b	Hear how the priests of the Temple made even this clear when the commandment was written

Passage	Barnabas	Introductory Formula
	7:4	What, then, does he say in the prophet?
	7:6	Pay attention to what he commanded
	7:7a	... he says ...
	7:8a	Pay attention to how the type of Jesus is made clear
	10:1	Now when Moses said
	10:2a	Further, he says to them in Deuteronomy
	10:11a	Moses says again
	12:6a	It is this same Moses who commanded
	15:1	It is written in the "Ten Words" (or, "Decalogue") by which (the Lord) spoke to Moses face to face on Mount Sinai
	15:2	And elsewhere he says

(4) Narrative (haggadic) materials

Passage	Barnabas	Introductory Formula
	4:7	For the scripture says
	4:8	For the Lord speaks thus
	6:8	What does the other prophet, Moses, say to them?
	6:10a	What, then, does he say
	6:13c	... the prophet proclaimed
	9:8a	For it says
	12:7b	But Moses said to them
	13:2	Hear what the scripture says
	13:4–5	And in another prophecy, Jacob says it even more clearly ... when he says
	13:7	What, then, does he say to Abraham ... ?
	14:2	For the prophet says
	14:3(?)	And the Lord said to Moses

(5) Miscellaneous unidentified materials

Passage	Barnabas	Introductory Formula
	6:3a	Then what does he say?
	6:10c	For the prophet says
	9:1c	And again he says
	9:2	And again he says

(6) Words attributed to Jesus or his opponents

	7:5	(no formula; Jesus speaking)
	7:9b	and they will say
	7:11b	... he says ...

3. Strong allusions to scriptural incidents and/or phraseology (it is not always clear whence Barnabas derived such materials)

Gen.	3:1–6, 13	12:5b	
	14:14	9:8a	
	15:6	13:7b	
	17:4–5	13:7b	
	17:11	9:6	
	17:23	9:8a	
	22:9	7:3c	
	25:21–22	13:2	
	48:9–20	13:4–5	
Exod.	17:8–15	12:2	[with formula]
	17:14	12:9	
	20:8	15:1	
	31:16	15:2	
	33:1, 3 (etc.)	6:8 (etc.)	
Lev.	11:3	10:11a	
	11:5	10:6a	
	11:7–15	10:1, 3–5	
	11:29	10:8a	
	16:1–28	7:4–11	
	23:29	7:3b	
	26:1	12:6a	
Num.	13:8, 16	12:8a	
	19:1–10	8:1–6	
	21:6–9	12:5, 6b–7	

II. QUOTATIONS AND SCRIPTURAL PARALLELS
in the Two Ways Material
(Barnabas 18:1–21:9; Didache 1:1–6:2)

1. Explicit quotation

(unknown source;   Did. 1:6 But it has also been said con-
cf. Sir. 12:1–7)   cerning this matter

2. Strong verbal parallels

(only a selection of the most obvious parallels is provided here;
see the commentary for numerous others)

Exod. 20:7	Barn. 19:4e		
20:13–15	Barn. 19:4a	=	Did. 2:2a
20:16			Did. 2:3b
20:17	Barn. 19:6a	=	Did. 2:2c

Passage	Barnabas	Didache
Lev. 19:18b	Barn. 19:5b	Did. 1:2b
Deut. 6:5	Barn. 19:2a =	Did. 1:2a
Ps. 37:11a		Did. 3:7
Sir. 4:5a		Did. 4:8a
4:31	Barn. 19:9a =	Did. 4:5
Matt. 5:5		Did. 3:7
5:25–26 par.		Did. 1:5c
5:38–48		Did. 1:3b–5a
7:12 par.		Did. 1:2c
Mark 12:30–31 parr.		Did. 1:2a–b
Luke 6:27–35		Did. 1:3b–5a
John 6:45a	Barn. 21:6a	
Eph. 6:5	Barn. 19:7b =	Did. 4:11
Phil. 4:5b	Barn. 21:3b	
Heb. 13:7	Barn. 19:9b =	Did. 4:1a
1 Pet. 2:11b		Did. 1:4a

III. QUOTATIONS AND SCRIPTURAL PARALLELS
in Didache 6:3–16:8

1. Explicit quotations

Passage	Didache	Introductory Formula
Zech. 14:5b	16:7	As it was said
Mal. 1:11, 14b	14:3	For this is what the Lord was referring to
Matt. 6:9–13	8:2	Pray as the Lord commanded in his gospel, thus
7:6	9:5b	For the Lord also has spoken concerning this

2. Strong verbal parallels

(for other parallels, see the commentary)

	Passage	Didache
Matt.	5:23–24	14:2
	6:5	8:2
	10:10b	13:1–2
	16:27	16:8
	24:10–12	16:3–4
	24:30–31	16:6, 8
	28:19	7:1, 3
Mark	3:28–29 parr.	11:7
	13:13 par.	16:5b
	13:19 par.	16:4
	13:22 par.	16:4
	13:26 parr.	16:8
	13:35 parr.	16:1
Luke	12:35	16:1
1 Thess.	4:16	16:6
1 Tim.	3:2–13	15:1
Tit.	1:5–9	15:1